I DARE TO SAY

I DARE TO SAY

AFRICAN WOMEN SHARE THEIR STORIES OF HOPE AND SURVIVAL

HILDA TWONGYEIRWE, EDITOR

FEMRITE, THE UGANDA WOMEN
WRITERS ASSOCIATION

Lawrence Hill Books
Chicago

Library of Congress Cataloging-in-Publication Data
I dare to say : African women share their stories of hope and survival / edited by
Hilda Twongyeirwe.
      p. cm.
Includes index.
ISBN 978-1-56976-842-6 (pbk.)
1. Women—Africa—Social conditions. I. Twongyeirwe, Hilda.
HQ1787.I5 2012
305.42096--dc23

                              2011035625

Cover design: Debbie Berne Design
Cover photograph: David Sacks/Stone+/Getty Images
Interior design: Sarah Olson

The essays in *I Dare to Say* first appeared in *Beyond the Dance* (2009), *Farming Ashes*
(2009), *I Dare to Say* (2007), and *Tears of Hope* (2003), copyright © FEMRITE, the
Uganda Women Writers Association, Kampala, Uganda. Editorial changes have
been made throughout. "The Cut" copyright © 2006 by Maryam Sheikh Abdi.

To the unsung heroines of Africa

Then the women stood up
They were no longer silent
They stood
Ready to proceed
Ready . . .
Like a river
Breaking banks sometimes
Breaking and breaking
In the course that must be taken.

—Hilda Twongyeirwe, "Breaking Banks"

Contents

◎◎

I

Tears of Hope: Surviving Abuse and Reclaiming Our Own and Our Children's Lives

II

I Dare to Say: Facing HIV/AIDS with Courage

III
Farming Ashes: Tales of Agony and Resilience

IV
Beyond the Dance: The Torture and
Trauma of Female Genital Mutilation

ACKNOWLEDGMENTS

◎◎

FEMRITE is indebted to the following institutions, which supported the publication of the testimonials contained herein: Africalia; Artaction, currently known as Freedom to Create; the Austrian Development Cooperation; and the African Women Development Fund. FEMRITE recognizes the major contributions of its anthology editors: Violet Barungi, Susan Kiguli, Hilda Twongyeirwe, and Ayeta Anne Wangusa.

FEMRITE is grateful to Susan Betz, senior editor at Lawrence Hill Books, for nurturing the relationship that has led to the publishing of this anthology, which brings African women's voices together. One of FEMRITE's strategic objectives is to build new reading audiences; Lawrence Hill Books has contributed to this objective by taking these voices to new readers. We also acknowledge the support of Litprom and the German Foreign Office, which supported FEMRITE's participation in the 2010 Frankfurt Book Fair.

The next project for which FEMRITE is seeking funding is the publication of testimonies of women in prison. Currently, there are few stories of experiences of women prisoners. FEMRITE seeks interested partners to record these stories.

FEMRITE is very grateful to all the women who shared their experiences, but, in order to protect their identities, assumed names have been used in this collection.

INTRODUCTION

FEMRITE, the Uganda Women Writers Association, was established in 1995 by a small group of women of which I was very privileged to be a part. The major concern then was the lack of published women writers in Uganda. Honorable Mary Karooro Okurut, the originator of the idea, was at the time a lecturer in the literature department of Makerere University. In her lecturing career, she noted the glaring gender gap that existed on Uganda's literary landscape. The organization started off by creating opportunities for Ugandan women to get published. Indeed, by 2003, more than twenty members of the organization had published novels, short stories, and poetry. Others had published literary articles in the organization's magazine, *New Era*.

As time went on, however, FEMRITE saw that there were other stories that needed to be told, stories that could not be captured effectively in fiction. This need gave birth to FEMRITE's themed testimonies. Other objectives were to make stories of marginalized women heard, to make a contribution to the scanty feminist literature that existed, to disseminate true-life information about women's experiences, to provide material for the lobbying and advocacy of women's issues, and to use storytelling as therapy.

Five books have been published under this project so far: *Beyond the Dance, Farming Ashes, I Dare to Say, Tears of Hope,* and *Today You Will Understand.* For each of them, FEMRITE selected writers from among its members and trained them in interviewing and recording skills. The writers discussed the subjects they were given with knowledgeable activists, who gave them background information on the topics to enable them to build cohesive stories. For each project, FEMRITE had a partner to consult with and sometimes to help in identifying respondents: REACH Kapchorwa during the *Beyond the Dance* project; Gulu Support the Children Organisation (GUSCO) and Integrated Regional Information Networks (IRIN) during the *Farming Ashes* project; the AIDS Support Organisation (TASO) of Uganda during the *I Dare to Say* project; and FIDA Uganda, also known as the Uganda Association of Women Lawyers, during the *Tears of Hope* project.

When scriptwriters are in the field, in order to avoid duplication, they continually update their project coordinator about their stories. The coordinator advises on which areas have not been covered and encourages them to venture beyond the stories on the surface.

Once the testimonies have been gathered, the scriptwriters attend peer-review meetings, where they discuss the stories with the editor of the project. They help each other understand the narratives, identify any gaps that may exist, and provide each other with information. This stage involves a high level of teamwork. Sometimes, after such meetings, some scriptwriters are asked to go back to the field and collect more information or even to abandon the shallow stories they already have and collect better ones. During such interactions, writers hear questions such as "Where is the story here?" or "What is unique about this story?"

After peer assessment, scriptwriters transcribe the material, then submit the stories to the editor. The editor occasionally goes back to the scriptwriters, storytellers, or activists to verify facts. Because FEMRITE is understaffed, additional editors are sourced from among the membership or from outside the organization.

Then, in order to build debate about the issues, FEMRITE organizes book launches and distributes free copies of the publication to the press and to activists.

FEMRITE approached the Austrian Development Corporation for support in 2002; it was a very big breakthrough that resulted in the publication of eight women's testimonies. In these stories, the women tell of the shocking abuse of their rights by those they loved and least suspected could betray them. The collection is titled *Tears of Hope*. The title was inspired by the fact that all the women who contributed stories had shed tears. However, they all had hope that one day all that would change and they would receive whatever was due to them.

The next theme was women and HIV/AIDS. The stories that were recorded describe the untold suffering that women have endured under the scourge. Many mothers and daughters have found their lives in the pages of *I Dare to Say*. The collection is a daring voice that refuses to be silenced. It is a message of the realization that HIV/AIDS does not happen to trees but to people. FEMRITE is indebted to the African Women Development Fund, which funded the project.

The theme of women and war saw the publication of two collections: *Today You Will Understand* and *Farming Ashes*. For about twenty years, there were many print and online newspaper stories telling of the atrocities committed against women and girls in war-torn northern Uganda. FEMRITE deemed it important to go to the affected areas and collect and disseminate their stories as a way of empathizing with them. The testimonies show the unbearable conditions of armed conflict. However, as much as everything is in ashes, the storytellers still manage to carry on with hope for a better life. The two publications were done in partnership with Africalia, the German embassy in Uganda, and IRIN, and they were aimed at making a contribution toward the peace process and negotiations to end the war.

Testimonies of female genital mutilation in the collection titled *Beyond the Dance* were the last to be recorded. FEMRITE gathered these women's voices during the heat of the battle against the practice. The goal was to provide human rights activists with moving firsthand accounts to use in their fight to end the cultural ritual.

Let us reflect on these stories and together work toward creating a world that cherishes and promotes peace and human dignity for all.

1

Tears of Hope

Surviving Abuse and Reclaiming
Our Own and Our Children's Lives

"I salute all the brave women and the countless others who refuse to be defeated despite the severity of abuse they suffer, who continue to work for a better life for their families despite the odds against them emanating from tradition, culture, poverty, ignorance, greed, and gender. They are the unsung heroes on whose backs development is built. May their tears one day be seen by those with the power to make a difference."

—Irene Ovonji-Odida, Uganda Association of Women Lawyers

We all carry two feelings, love and pain, as burdens in our hearts. Sometimes these two feelings make us stronger and wiser. Many times, it is the people we love who cause us pain. Often that spouse whom you married after a romantic courtship or even your kin, who seem not to value the saying "Blood is thicker than water," cause you pain. And more often than not, women carry the biggest burden of pain because they are victims of societal norms defined by patriarchy. Society expects women to bear their pain in silence and lead normal lives. But there are women who have dared to say no to inequality; they carry their stories in their hearts so that they can have the strength to defy injustice.

The true stories in this section reflect the predicament of African rural women, specifically Ugandan rural women, in a male-dominated society. Some of these women have suffered silently while others have spoken out, attempting to rectify wrongs even in the face of seemingly insurmountable legal challenges. They have vowed to die fighting for their rights.

The collection reflects the ironies created by the patriarchy on which most African cultures hinge. For instance, in traditional marriages, women are valued only as part of the labor force, working land controlled by men but receiving none of the profits. However, equilibrium is desta- bilized once women start earning money, thus undermining patriarchal rules. Where Christian marriages are performed, a woman is fairly pro- tected if the man dies and leaves a will. Otherwise, traditional culture is upheld, and a co-wife at times may unfairly benefit from property that the legal wife and husband jointly accumulated.

The stories of these women present the conflict between traditional and modern Africa, where the extended family tends to have control over the well-being of the nuclear family. After a woman marries, be it a traditional, Christian, or Muslim marriage, she ceases to belong to her maiden home. If she seeks refuge there in times of marital strife, she is made to feel like an interloper.

Domestic violence is another recurrent theme. Most girls are not con- sidered part of the clan, because they are expected to marry and join another clan. When family property is distributed, they are naturally left out. In families that allocate property to daughters upon the parents' death, conflicts between them and their brothers usually arise. How- ever, this becomes even more intricate with the backdrop of the AIDS scourge and the refugee situation in Kisoro created by the 1994 Rwanda genocide, which left many women widowed and homeless.

The unfair legal system in Uganda favors male spouses in cases of divorce. Despite ample evidence of adultery, physical torture, neglect, and desertion, a woman often cannot get a divorce if the man is not ready to let her go.

Bride-price is another issue laced throughout these stories of bravery. Most traditional marriages are recognized only when bride-price is paid. It is this symbolic rite of passage—even after marrying, a girl remains a girl until the family has received bride-price from her husband—that often keeps women stuck in abusive marriages.

Women are considered valuable only because they can carry on familial lines and add to the labor force. The patriarchy turns women into their own enemies by forcing them to uphold the negative tenets of power that society accords to men. For instance, when men indulge in adultery, it is tolerated, but when women do it, it is abhorred.

These are stories of women who have become wiser by loving and hurting. They have picked up the broken pieces of their lives and have lain awake at night, thinking and reshaping their destinies. Some have found hope by visiting Legal Aid clinics; others have vowed to move even beyond, wherever a flicker of hope may be.

Here are stories of courage by Ugandan rural women. They will surprise the urban woman who suffers the same fate they do but has responded with silence.

VIOLET BARUNGI AND AYETA ANNE WANGUSA

Where Do I Belong?

Hilda Twongyeirwe

Edisa Zayaga sits uncomfortably next to me on the veranda. Her stare dances between the patterned hills and me. The hazy morning sunshine plays on her dark, glistening forehead. A cloud quickly appears, taking with it the much-needed rays. Edisa's brown eyes dig into mine as if mining something from deep inside. Her full lips are tightly closed in a guarded manner. A strong, cold wind blows, forcing us momentarily to fold our bodies like mats. I fumble with my shawl to keep away the biting cold as Edisa quickly buttons her sweater and pulls her pleated brown skirt to cover her short, sturdy legs. We both look with longing at the patches of sunshine running across the Rugarama hills.

Edisa shoots out her left leg and shakes it for a while. Looking at her clean brown canvas shoes, one can hardly believe that she walked all the way to our meeting place! She lifts her right hand and neatly presses her black, natural hair into position. It is about fifteen inches long. Her nails are clean and trimmed short. Her fingers are small but rough, perhaps from tilling the land and splitting firewood. Her meticulous appearance is enhanced by the two strands of white beads she wears around her long neck. They match the white dotted blouse under her pink sweater.

My eyes shift back to her face. It is marred by premature wrinkles running across her forehead. But something else is striking. There is no sadness in her rumpled face. There is a glow behind her deep eyes. I smile at her. She smiles back, shifting her light body to sit more comfortably. She parts her lips briefly, and our steamy breaths, as if looking for more warmth and sisterhood from each other, mingle and waltz in unison above our heads. She clears her throat and begins to speak.

*M*y mother's daughter, I will tell you my story because we belong together—wherever it is we belong.

My name is Zayaga, in short. In full, it is Zayaga Zaburobutoro Zamaromwonyo Zazagiremigina. I am the last born in a family of nine children. When our father married our mother, he was so proud of her. He did not bargain when her parents asked for the best of his father's cows as bride-price. Our mother was blessed. She told us that it did not take long before she conceived and gave birth to a very beautiful baby girl. However, our father was not very happy with a daughter for a first-born. He called her Bakeitwara, meaning the in-laws took the bride-price for nothing when their daughter could not give him a son at the outset. He did not even buy her meat like other husbands do to congratulate their wives upon successful deliveries. He could not wait to make her pregnant again. His prayer for rapid pregnancies was answered, but not with a boy! Two other daughters followed Bakeitwara, and my father's unhappiness increased.

Then, finally, a boy came. Father smiled all the time. He called his son Kurinamanyire, which means "I wish I had known." Mother said that she did not know what he was regretting. He was more than eager for the next child, who also came quite fast. However, it was a girl. Father called her Kuribakanya, which implied that if he could have many children, there would then be more chances of getting more boys. But my father's prayers went unanswered. Kuribakanya was followed by another girl, whom he called Gakibayo. Gakibayo meant there was still hope for the right child. The numerous girls were not the right children. Mother did not give up either.

A few years passed, and my mother got pregnant again. My father, too, got pregnant with hope. The expectant couple regarded each other silently, never discussing their fears and hopes. Days turned into weeks and weeks into months. Soon, nine months were over, and Mother gave birth to a strong, bouncing baby. It was a beautiful girl. Father, who seemed never to run out of cynical names, called her Zibahurire. This implies that fate listens to people's hopes and fears and provides what is contrary to their prayers.

Indeed, fate did exactly that, and a girl he called Bafwokuheka was born next. Bafwokuheka means that one has no choice but to carry whichever baby it is on one's back. When she grew up, Bafwokuheka hated her name so much that she changed it to Tukamuhabwa, meaning that the child was God given. Bafwokuheka Tukamuhabwa is the girl I come after. Father must have guessed that I was going to be the last born to my mother, for he gave me a name that seemed to carry all his venom. My long name talks about cows. Through my name, my father was lamenting the too many cows that would fill his homestead. The many girls would fetch many cows as bride-price, but there would be no boys to use them to get brides. The cows would exhaust all the grass and salt in the area. They would use up all the space in the home, leaving none for the human beings.

That was his line of thought! In African culture, producing only girls is looked at as a curse, because it implies the end of the family line. And, you see, my mother was a third wife. The first two wives had had only one son each. My father had married my mother so as to have more sons. After Mother, he married once more. His fourth wife produced one boy and very few girls. Father lived unhappily thereafter. But we did not hate him.

When I became of marriageable age, I looked forward to proposals, and they soon fell on me like rain. I was very hardworking. I could tend a garden from sunrise to sunset and do all the housework. When I finally chose the man I would marry, I was very happy that at last I was leaving my father's home to go and join a man who appreciated me as a woman. But I did not know many things to do with men yet. My aunt called me aside and instructed me, "Never open your mouth wide while speaking to your man. When he speaks twice, you speak only once. Never cry in front of him. Never turn your back to him, because someone else might be willing to turn her front to him. Treat him like a baby. He is your firstborn." She told me many other dos and don'ts of marriage. When she had finished, I was not sure I still wanted to go.

She was a clever woman, because after that, she told me the sweet side of it. I thought that if I did not get married, I would never die properly. My husband, in appreciation for her instruction, later gave her a goat.

I got married in 1977. My husband was a very nice man. He was called Davida. But I shouldn't have said his name. It is not right to say your spouse's name—he knows you in the manner in which you came from your mother's womb! There is profound respect, and you don't just go calling out their names. Although we are not together, it does not take away the fact that we shared deep secrets at the time. I still respect him. He called me Muhara, and I called him Owangye.

We loved each other very much. He praised me genuinely and made me feel confident and proud to be a woman. Yes, for the first time, I appreciated womanhood.

In 1978, I became pregnant. My husband and I were very happy. At the same time, I was apprehensive, because I did not know what to expect. At the back of my mind, I knew that the sex of the child I would bear would matter to the community. They would use it to label me a curse or a blessing to my husband's family. My husband looked after me very well, never mentioning his wishes or fears.

You know when you are pregnant; you become crazy about some foods and hate others. He provided whatever I wanted, and I prayed that God should do his will. Sometimes he asked me how my stomach felt. I would teasingly tell him to touch it and find out for himself, but he never did. He just laughed.

Soon it was time to deliver. I wanted to surprise my husband with a baby, so I did not tell him that the labor pains had begun. Quietly I went to the old woman who had been monitoring my pregnancy and told her. As usual, she put warm water in a metallic basin and disappeared behind her kitchen. Within seconds, she was back with some herbs, which she dropped in the water and used to gently massage my stomach. With her fingers, she felt my stomach and told me that the baby was very well positioned and that it was on its way out. I smiled in anticipation.

I had been told that labor was tough but that it was proof of real womanhood. I was, therefore, very scared, but at the same time I was happy that I was about to prove myself a capable woman. I walked back to our house and suggested to my husband that he go and do some work in one of our gardens, which was far from our home. I did not want him to see me whimper in pain. He went to the kitchen, picked a *panga* and a hoe from the corner in which we kept them, and left. I did not mind his departure because the old woman, a traditional birth attendant, was around. She made strong black tea and forced me to take cups and cups of it without sugar.

"Tea leaves are good," she insisted. "They will do the trick."

By evening, however, no trick had been done, and the pain was getting worse. The old woman called a few other women, and each brought different herbs. They all sat there staring at me.

"You'll soon make it," they kept saying. "And when you hold the baby in your arms, you'll forget what you are calling unbearable pain."

The contractions seemed to intensify with each cup of sugarless tea I drank and each herb I took. Pain reached the tip of my small toe and the longest strand of my hair. I looked at the women crowding my little room, telling me to push harder, and I felt like spitting in their faces. Soon it was time for my husband to come home. My plan to present to him a baby that evening had flopped. Somewhere in between contractions, I heard metals striking against each other. I knew it was he, putting the hoe and *panga* back in the corner from which he had picked them that morning. One of the women quickly left the room, and we heard whispers outside. The whispers built up until we could hear what they were saying.

"Why can't you let me see her?" he asked.

"OK. Give me a few minutes, and I will see what I can do."

I could hear him pacing up and down, but he never entered the room where I was.

Helped by traditional birth attendants, many women deliver without any problem in their homes. At that time, it was almost a disgrace for a woman worth the name to go and deliver either in a hospital or at a health center where male nurses and doctors would all be staring at her. And we had been told that there, instead of kneeling down to deliver, women were required to lie on their backs and look at the ceiling!

Therefore, I swore that I would never deliver in the hospital. But my people say that when a person accompanies you at night, you wait and thank him in the morning. After experiencing prolonged, severe contractions, I was begging to be taken to a health center. But there was a problem. There is no health center near our home! The nearest hospital that serves our area is Kabale Hospital, several miles away. And another problem—there is no public transport in our village. And even if there were, the road does not reach my husband's home. It stops some miles away. I therefore had to be carried for more than twenty miles to get medical assistance. But thank God for the teamwork that prevailed in the village. My husband's kinsmen agreed to carry me.

But there was yet another hurdle! The traditional stretcher used to carry patients was too small to carry a pregnant woman. So they had to run from village to village looking for one on which I would fit. By the time they got it, it was late, but my husband insisted that they should start the journey despite this. The moon never showed its face during that extremely dark night.

The journey to the hospital was so long! The men carrying the stretcher fell into real and imaginary ditches along the winding and narrow footpaths. The stretcher mercilessly swung left and right and up and down as if it were carrying a bunch of plantains. Even when we got to the road, I could not tell that we had already left the footpath. The stretcher swung even harder! Meanwhile, the contractions seemed to be enjoying the ride, increasing with each swing, tearing at my insides! I just kept biting my lips and fighting hard to remain calm. But it was all like writing on water.

We reached the hospital in the wee hours of the morning. It was a Thursday I will always remember. That Thursday made a deep mark on my life. And it was an incredibly cold morning.

As soon as we got there, some doctors examined me, and, through my tear-filled eyes, I saw their faces fall.

"What is it?" I asked them weakly.

"It is the baby," one of them volunteered.

"What about the baby?"

"It is dead."

My head went blank for a while. Then I recalled that at around 10:00 PM that night, the baby had stopped kicking and behaving the way it had been all along. I suspected it had died then.

I stayed two more days in the hospital before my stillborn child could come out. It was a very trying time, the longest I have ever waited in my life. Time seemed to stand still. I wished there was a way of pulling the baby out, but the doctors said it had to come out on its own. All the nine months of pregnancy, all the days in labor had just gone down the drain.

As if I had not gone through enough already, as soon as my baby—the dead baby—came out, I bled like a cow whose head has just been chopped off. I became so weak that everybody waited for me to breathe my last. Doctors crowded around my bed, and I closed my eyes in pain as one after the other drove their fat hands through the fresh wounds of my womanhood, trying to detect what was wrong. My heart was threatening to give way from the shame of all these people staring down at me. Not even my husband had ever looked at me there. At some point, my limbs felt so weak that I failed to spread my legs wide.

The doctors did their dreaded but necessary best, and eventually the bleeding stopped. The four days' rigorous contractions, the severe bleeding, and the loss of my baby all left me limp. My previous thoughts no longer mattered; whether it had been a boy or a girl no longer mattered. What mattered now was getting well. Indeed, it did not take very long before I got better.

One morning, one of the doctors who had been tending to me came to my bed.

"How do you feel now?" he asked me.

"Better. Much better," I told him.

"You are a very strong woman. But your case was very severe. We hope all will be well because . . ." Without completing the sentence, he pulled at an instrument he wore around his neck, looked away, and wished me well. For a few seconds, I wondered what he was concerned about. I was getting well, and he should have been happy for me. I dismissed his worries and hugged the fact that I was feeling much better.

A few days later, my husband took me back home. I promised myself that the next time around, I would not hesitate to go to the hospital. I had graduated from a timid girl to a mature woman. I had to forget the grueling past and look forward to the future—a bright future, I hoped, with experience as the best teacher.

But something else had gone wrong. I did not know where the problem was! My mother's daughter, I had gone through so much pain, lost my firstborn, and lost more than half of my blood. Shouldn't that have been enough?

A few days after I reached home, I began leaking. I had a mild but constant flow of urine. At first I kept quiet, thinking it would soon cease on its own like menstrual blood. At every opportunity, I would check myself to see whether I was dry, only to be prompted to cushion myself more. An hour rolled into a day, and the day rolled into a week. I had to be very careful to keep my secret. You can imagine the tension we suffer during three or four days of menstruation. The week turned into a month! Oh, it was terrible! I had to tell someone. For days, I debated over whom to tell.

Then I decided that it had to be my husband. But how would he react to the news? I was not sure. And what would I tell him? That urine was constantly coming on its own or that I was urinating all the time? This message was not easy to communicate. But then, there was no way I was going to keep such a thing to myself. Keeping it to myself made me feel as if I were choking. I had to share it with someone.

When I finally gathered enough courage and told my husband, he was very understanding.

"What do we do?" he asked me.

It pleased me that he always said "we," even when it was my problem. It made the problem less heavy.

"I don't know," I told him.

Later, he took me to Kisiizi, a missionary hospital several miles away from our home. The doctors there were very concerned. They examined me thoroughly and discovered that during the prolonged labor and afterward when the doctors were trying to stop the severe bleeding, my uterus and bladder were badly injured. Let me tell you, I was hospitalized for seven months.

All the hospital staff came to know me and like me a lot. "She is a cheerful patient," they said, and I smiled more broadly. I almost told them that cheer had to be my major companion if I was to survive what I was going through. They made me a ward leader. In those seven months, I underwent three major operations.

I don't know what the doctors did during that time, but they were all long operations. And before I underwent the third operation, I developed another disease. Unbelievable, isn't it? I developed terrible pain in my lower back and limbs. The doctors tried but failed to diagnose it. Pain ate me up like a goat chewing its cud. I received treatment after treatment, but there was no change. Each doctor who came would look at the medicine prescribed by his colleagues and call them jokers. He would then prescribe his own, but they all came to the same end—more pain! The doctors agreed that I would not be able to pull through the third operation while still in that state.

So I lay in a pool of pain and waited.

I waited and waited, till one day someone told us that what I was suffering from was an African disease called *embasha*, a disease that attacks hip bones and the lower back. It could not be cured by the white man's medicine. Amid protests from the doctors, people started bringing me herbs and stealthily smearing the affected parts. The doctors, especially those who were not African, insisted that there was no African disease that could not be cured by hospital medicine. However, the more I used the traditional medicine, the more relief I felt. The pain eventually was reduced, and I went for the last operation. But I was never my old self again. The disease weakened me permanently. At only forty years of age, I cannot do some of the things I used to do, like going up the hill three or four times a day to carry sorghum during a harvest.

When it was time to leave the hospital, my bill was so high that I did not even try to think of where I would get the money. I did not even try to bargain, because when one bargains, one is asked to make an offer. So how could I bargain when I had nothing?

As if God had peeped into my pocket, the hospital management sympathized and waived almost everything. "This girl has gone through so much pain," they said. "Let the hospital assist her." I was grateful when I was asked to pay only eighteen hundred shillings.

I was discharged in June 1980. Women had planted and harvested while I was in the hospital.

My husband never deserted me. He slept on a mat spread on the hard, cold cement and forgot the comfort of his bed. By the time we left, he too looked thin and pale, as if he had been sick. At one point, one of my sisters came to the hospital to relieve him. She stayed for a few days; then her husband ordered her to return home.

"She is just using the hospital as an excuse to meet her lovers," he said. "If she still considers me her husband, she must return home immediately!"

My sister had no choice but to go back home. When she got there, her husband demanded to know the names of the men she had been sleeping with. She tried to explain and plead, but her pleas fell on a rock, and he showed her the door.

With a heavy heart, my sister went back to our parents' home. My mother and my brother were still alive then. They welcomed her and told her to keep calm if the man had decided that he no longer wanted her. She tried to settle down but could not, because her heart was where her children were. As if in response to her feelings, a few weeks later, the children pulled down the fence around their home and used it for firewood. They misplaced things in the house and burned food all the time or served it almost raw. They ran about the whole village and refused to bathe. It did not take long before her husband dragged himself to my father's compound.

"Please, come. Let's go," he said to her.

"Go where? You sent me away," she told him.

"To your home. It needs you."

"My home?"

"Yes. And your children need you. Who do you think is looking after them?"

"They have a father."

The argument went on and on for some hours, after which the setting sun shone on their heads as they walked to his home turned their home. All this happened while I was still in the hospital.

Before my husband and I left the hospital, we were given shattering news. Something had gone wrong with my system. It was irreparable. I could not believe it as I listened to the doctor blurt out the fateful words. What if I could never have children?

As if he could hear my thoughts, he replied, "You will never have a child. But thank God you are now healed and healthy."

For a moment, I wondered what sort of medicine they had studied if they could not save me from such a painful situation.

"We had to choose between letting you die and keeping you alive. But you are not alone. Many women go through the same thing."

I was not many women. I was Zayaga.

But, my mother's daughter, God has his ways of sorting out our situations. When we went back home, my husband gave me his shoulder to lean on. He never referred to me as childless or barren. We enjoyed each other's company a great deal.

In 1982, my husband surprised me when he suggested that we should formalize our marriage. There I was, childless, with no hope of ever getting pregnant again. There were many young and beautiful maidens in our locality. So how could he say this? Two thoughts occurred to me. Either he was mocking me, or he was just joking to make me happy. But I was already happy with him. He had already done everything possible to ensure I appreciated him. I did not take him seriously.

But he went ahead and informed my people that he had something to discuss with them. When they received the message, they quickly jumped to the conclusion that, because I could not have children, he wanted to demand back part of the bride-price he had paid.

My people were not ready for such rubbish, though. They prepared what they would tell him in order to send him sprinting out of their compound. However, they too were very surprised when he explained his intentions.

"I have come back to you for a favor," he told them. "I know I have not finished paying bride-price but—"

"So have you come to pay?" they asked him.

"No. I have come to request that you allow me to wed your daughter. I will not forget what I owe you."

"You have spoken well," they told him.

We married in the traditional way, where girls escort the bride at night under the cover of darkness to the groom's home. After a week or so, the groom and some elders go to the girl's home to report that they have their daughter. Then the father and other elders from the girl's side ask the groom for a cow, traditionally referred to as *obufumurarugo*. It implies that since the parents of the girl were not asked for their daughter's hand in marriage, the man must have broken into the home and stolen her. After that is settled, they ask for bride-price and arrange to go and see the home to which their daughter has gone. That was how we married. So my husband wanted to formalize the marriage.

They approved of our planned wedding and even helped us to prepare for it. It was a small but very beautiful wedding, and I was a stunning bride. It's a pity my father did not see me then. He died in 1977. It was very tragic, especially for my mother, who was left alone at home. All my other sisters got married before me. Our two stepmothers and their children had moved away, and the third one had already died.

My husband kept his word and completed paying the bride-price later. We were a happy couple. But of course I was not a child. I knew all that would soon end. The fact that we would never have a child together was not easy to deal with. Silent discomfort sat between us and hovered above us. I knew that our every effort at happiness was being mocked. I was not sure what my husband felt, but personally, I felt terrible about the fact that I was never going to give him a child. And I felt angry that society was never going to appreciate me as a complete woman and that his family would forever brand me a misfortune for not being able to make my husband's lineage continue.

While all these thoughts crowded my mind, my husband never stopped being good to me. For months, I thought of what I would do to help him. There were two things I could do. I could either leave him so that he could marry another woman, or I could urge him to get another woman to marry and stick around myself. I thought about the options and decided on the latter. The problem was how to tell him. It had to be done in a very subtle way.

One day while he was away in the fields, I prepared to break the news to him on his return. I practiced what I would say to him. As soon as he returned, I called to him.

"My dear husband, I think it would be a good thing for you to marry."

"Why? What do you mean? Aren't I married?" he asked me.

"You are, but many things have gone wrong," I told him.

"I have not complained. Has someone been poisoning your mind?"

"No. But we can't run away from the truth." I had not prepared myself for his numerous questions. All the words I had prepared to say escaped me, and a huge lump formed in my throat. My voice went hoarse. I tried to continue but failed.

After a while, I composed myself. We talked and laughed long into the quiet night. By morning, we had agreed that he should find another woman to marry. I allowed him to use the wealth we had accumulated together to pay bride-price. When he said that he needed to build first, I offered to give him my kitchen. He warmed to the idea, and not very long afterward, a bride walked into our home.

When she came, I treated her like the daughter I had failed to have. Although traditionally our mother-in-law should have taken care of her, I offered to look after her in order to create a close relationship from the beginning. Culturally, a bride is not supposed to be seen outside the house. So I fetched water for her, collected the firewood she used, and provided her with food to cook. I helped my husband in every way possible to make his bride happy. She was happy. My husband was happy. And I was happy that he was happy. He faithfully attended to the two of us as wives, visiting us alternately. Whenever it was her turn for our husband to visit, I would leave the kitchen very early. The next day, I would wake up early and go to the garden without going to the kitchen. This arrangement worked perfectly well until that woman showed her true colors.

My marriage, which had been the envy of many, crumbled between my fingers. However much I tried, I could not scoop it back. All the troubles in my marriage sprouted from her. Of course, in a marriage, there cannot fail to be a few problems here and there. But the disagreements my husband and I had were too trivial to make me leave. He was a very good man, and I tell you, my mother's daughter, we cared for each other. But it did not take her long to separate us. But even when I left him, a year did not elapse before he started looking for me and giving me some assistance here and there. He even apologized. He asked me to come back, but I did not want to place myself between them again.

The day I left his home, nothing too serious had taken place. It started like a joke, but soon they saw my back. After my co-wife had two children, both boys, she started looking down on me. She constantly reminded them that I was not their mother and they should not have anything to do with me. She told me that whether I worked hard or not, everything belonged to her sons. Yet I had wanted us to be one family, for the sake of peace and togetherness. She planted prejudice in their hearts at a very early age. I took everything in stride, as a strong woman should, but she did not leave me alone.

She finally succeeded in turning my husband against me. You know children are like a nerve. She used them to turn him against me. At first, she claimed that I had a lot of food and should therefore feed her children. Giving them food was OK by me, but being forced to give it to them was not. My co-wife and I were not on sharing terms. She had made it clear she did not want anything to do with a childless woman. Why, then, did she want something to do with the food that was the product of my arms?

My husband started calling me an evil woman who wanted his children to starve to death. He did not stop to wonder why his favorite wife was not working hard enough to feed her own children! I was not going to slave away for one who hated me. Whenever I asked the children to do something for me, she would stop them from doing it because, she said, I was a bad woman who could harm them. Then, later, she would shamelessly tell them to come to my house for food.

Our estrangement intensified. My husband found fault with the house or me every time he visited. I soon realized that these were excuses she was using to stop him from visiting me. One morning, he woke up and started quarrelling with me for no reason at all. I would have ignored him, as usual, but this time he locked my house and told me that he no longer wanted me as his wife. He said some abusive words to me and told me to leave his home and go to where I belonged.

Several thoughts went through my mind. Finally, I decided I did not want to end my marriage. So I went to the Local Council officials for help. I did not tell them everything, because I am not a fool who spreads my underwear next to a footpath. Even you, my mother's daughter, I have not told you all. I have left a few things in my stomach.

The LC officials called my husband and handled the case. I won, and they told him to open the house for me. We went home with some LC men. When we arrived in front of my house, my co-wife jumped out of her hut and stood in front of us. The sight of her made my heart somersault. My husband stood a few feet away from the group and looked at the hills.

The chairman called out to him, "Sebo Davida, we have arrived."

"So what if you have?" my husband answered rudely.

"Open for your wife."

"Never!"

"Aren't you lucky she wants to keep her marriage? She wants you!"

"Never!"

"Open your wife's house and let her enter."

"Never!"

"If you don't want to visit her, it's OK, but let the woman enter her house."

"This is my home."

They all shook their heads in disbelief.

"Our power stops here. We are leaving," the defense secretary told me.

I wondered whether the man swearing was the man I knew. I felt deeply hurt when my husband refused to open my house. I had a lot of food in the house because it was the harvest season. In a very huge way, my lazy co-wife defeated me, because she enjoyed everything I left behind. Anger scratched at my insides as I turned away from the house I had lived in for fourteen years. I could not beg him again. My mother's daughter, I am no daughter of the wind. I decided to go back to my people and leave him with his. Without a word, I turned, and my legs gained strength I did not know they possessed.

Suddenly I felt a strong happiness envelop me. A strong hand was urging me to freedom, and I obeyed it. After a short while, I was seated with my mother.

"This is a surprise visit! Are you well?" she asked me.

"I am well and not well," I told her. Then I explained what had happened.

"We know what has been going on in your marriage. You have made a good decision to come home," she said.

Our two lonely souls embraced and consoled each other. Finally, I was where I belonged, or so I thought. That was way back in 1991.

I went back for my clothes months later. His wife was there when I went. She popped out of her hut, the way she had done the day I left, and planted her body in the middle of the compound. When she smiled at me, I also parted my lips and showed my teeth. I greeted her, then entered my house to get what had brought me there. I knew she was feeling bigger than the world, so I let her continue deluding herself.

The years I had spent in my marriage were dead years. I had nothing to show for them except a few clothes, a wrinkled face, and, of course, a childless tummy. I did not get any of the things we had acquired together—I received no land, bedding, hoes, utensils, mats, chairs, or anything else. I emerged out of the house with only a small bundle of my few clothes. As I trotted home, I opened my imaginary life book and erased the marriage chapter.

My husband—I still call him my husband—and his wife now live far away from our village. They migrated to another part of the country. But whenever he comes back to see his people, he checks on me. When it is a long time between visits, he writes. He askes me to write and tell him how I am. I don't hate him. And I don't at all care about what my co-wife feels, because she was the source of all my problems. And she should remember that, by law, I am still his legal wife.

I am no longer with him, but he never gave me an official document to end our marriage. I am his legal wife officially, married to him in the Catholic Church. So we still have rights and privileges as husband and wife. You see, I learned a few things from women's groups and from attending public talks organized by parish and subcounty chiefs. But, well, she should feel secure! It is eleven years since I left him. I don't think I'll go back to him, or to them, to be more specific.

Before they migrated, they sold off everything that belonged to him. He even sold a lot of what belonged to me. But since we never officially divorced, I would not let him sell our matrimonial home. I know the law recognizes that separation and divorce are different. If a man has not divorced you officially, he is not supposed to leave you homeless. Couples always separate and come back together. I don't intend to go back to him, but neither do I intend to give him a divorce. That was not part of our arrangement the day I encouraged him to get another woman.

We hear that currently the law does not favor the woman in divorce. And by the way, when I married my husband, the land where his home was located was small. With my contribution, we bought the neighboring plot and added it to ours. So when I heard that he wanted to sell it, I swore to myself that he would not rob me blind! Someone must help!

Someone must support me! Someone must stop him! Indeed, when I went to government officials and explained, they helped me and stopped him from selling it.

Ironically, when I wanted to sell my own land, which my mother had given me, he said I could not sell it without his approval and that he was not going to give it away. My mother had given it to me to look after her in her old age. When she was giving it to me, I stupidly let him sign on the agreement.

But his signature was to show that he agreed to my looking after Mother. When things changed for the worse, he also changed its meaning and said that the land had been given to the two of us, and that was why he too had signed!

I wanted to sell the land so I could build a small house with iron sheets. My mother's hut leaks. Let me tell you, when it rains at night, in the morning I don't need to take a bath. When it rains during the day, I run to the neighbor's house, although I know I am not very welcome.

Now my husband says it is OK to live like that! Every time it rains, I carry muddy feet to someone else's home. They soon get tired of you! My mother's daughter, I was not like this! I used to be a person! Meaty and nice looking. These veins, protruding at the slightest opportunity, all have tales to tell!

When I left my husband, who had ganged up with his wife and children against me, I was glad to go back to my people. As a girl, I had been the darling of the village. Ha! I was a girl of the people. Although I never went to school, I was very intelligent. I taught myself to read and write, and I intimidated my age-mates. Later, I was asked to be the leader of a community club that taught girls and some boys to read and write. There was no village activity that took place without me as one of the main actors. In the club, we learned things to do with personal hygiene, farming, arts and crafts, and public speaking through storytelling. We organized exchange programs and visited other clubs. It was a very enriching experience, which girls of today miss because community clubs no longer exist. My team almost always performed best in the parish and other competitions.

In my village, I was the first girl to master the art of crocheting. Boys and girls from all the nearby schools came to me for school bags. I made quite a bit of money out of it. I made small ones for old people to carry their Bibles in when they went to church. I made hats with beautiful designs for men and elderly women. I also made rattles for school and church choirs nearby. My name became a household name. Why then wouldn't I be glad to return to my people after a failed marriage? But, my mother's daughter, when I got there, it was a different story. I wondered whether that was the old village I had left behind.

It's unbelievable, but when I went back to my home, the whole village turned against me. They looked at me suspiciously and never let me mix with them as freely as I had done as a girl. And they have a name for women like me—*ekishubaaka*, "the thing that has returned home." To make matters worse, in 1993, my half brothers and half sisters connived to sell some of our father's land, even the part of the compound where my mother was still living. She was old and ailing, and my half brothers said that she would soon die and I would take over what belonged to them. My father had distributed his property equally among his wives, but traditionally it is sons who inherit. Since my own brother had died, they thought they were entitled to what belonged to my mother as well. My mother was still alive, but she was too weak to follow up on the case. It was during that case that I came to know about the legal aid that KABNETO offers. When you are carrying a heavy burden, you talk about it to people who have not even asked. I was wondering about what to do, so I went to a friend and told her about my problems. She took me to her friend, and the friend took me to someone else who had at one time worked with the Legal Aid office. Together, they directed me to the KABNETO office. That was way back in 1993.

At the office, I met a woman who was introduced to me as the legal officer. I narrated my story, which she listened to attentively. It felt so good to have someone listen to me with interest. After listening, she gave me advice on how to proceed with the case, and she did not charge me any money. She told me that my half brothers and their friends—the LCs—should not be allowed to threaten me. She said that whatever happened, I should remain consistent and strong. She sent letters to the LCs and to the men who were buying the land and told them that if they did not give fair judgment, the case would be forwarded to the High Court and she would stand in for me.

"From your story, it is clear that your mother's things belong to you, and your sisters and you have a right to use them in the way you want. Together, you might later agree to sell them and share the money, or you can share them amongst yourselves. We do not have powers to enforce the law, but we have the power to influence it," she told me as she gave me the letters.

Her support and that information contributed so much to my winning the case in the LC 3 court. In 1996—sadly, a few weeks after we buried my mother—I got documents of the judgment, which confirmed that the land belonged to her and her children.

You know, when a girl gets married, and her marriage goes bad, people laugh at her as if she has no home to return to. When she goes back to her father's home, she is asked why she has left her home! Where do you and I really belong?

Frieda's World

WALTRAUD NDAGIJIMANA

Frieda is a young Mufumbira woman with a long history of physical and mental abuse. She "married" her husband when she was young and inexperienced. Her parents were not paid the customary bride-price and showed indifference to her suffering. They only tolerated her when she sought refuge in their home, but they did not actively participate in solving her marital problems.

Due to financial pressure, Frieda was always forced to return to her husband and endure his physical and mental abuse. But she finally left him, taking her children, when he went after all of them with a panga. *Frieda's father gave them one room in a small hut, where she still lives today. Her husband has started selling their joint property.*

She does not look any different from thousands of other Bafumbira peasant women. Frieda is only thirty-four years old and is small and strong. She has known years of hard labor in the stony fields of this part of the country. The land demands so much of the women and gives back barely enough for them to keep alive. Her rough hands grip mine firmly. The soil of the field she has been working on still clings to her skin, up to her elbows, like a thick coating. Her arms are thin like sticks and jut out from under her torn dress.

She looks at me uncertainly. I want to know what made her leave the man she lived with for fourteen years—the man she had six children with—and go back to her parents' home. But she is reluctant to talk. She lifts her hand and straightens her colorful head cloth. Her short hair is full of red dust. She has never been to a salon; her hair knows only the rough blue soap, expensive in the village but given free at the petrol stations in the city to those with cars.

"Now, what do you want to hear from me?"

She has become a bit more confident, pulling and brushing at her dress with her hands. In fact, she wears two dresses. The one on top is held together by an old string. It is supposed to protect the other, better dress from the dust of the field. She has put down her hoe carefully in a corner of my garden. We sit on an old mat. Cautiously, she pulls on the straw of her Mirinda. She has chosen a soft drink over a beer, urwagwa, *or* amamera.

No, no alcohol, not for many years. She has seen what it does to a man; it breaks him and turns him into an animal, she says. She will never touch it again in her life.

She does not raise her voice when she speaks. She comes from a little village at the foot of one of the volcanic hills. Her father's house was not any different from the other village homes, but it had never known extreme poverty, beatings, or abuse. Normally, she and her siblings lived alone with their mother. Twice a year, her father would come home from Buganda, where he grew tobacco.

She did not like school. She attended for a short time, but she did not have the head for it. Numbers confused her. When she was around twelve years old and about to be baptized, the local priest called all the catechumens for half a year to the parish. There they stayed in a big dormitory. In the mornings, they had classes and talked about Jesus and Maria and why they were going to be baptized.

"When I was there, I thought if I was a good girl and obeyed my parents and the rules of the church, and later became a good wife, nothing bad would ever happen to me," she says.

An old nun with a lot of experience and little patience taught her how to read and write. And what she learned there was enough. She can write her name, count her money, and calculate how much profit she can make from the tomatoes she grows.

After the time in the parish, she helped her mother in the fields. Early in the morning, they would go to the fields with their lunch packed in a small pot, then set about hoeing the land. *They planted their feet firmly on the stony ground and lifted their hoes to strike the hard soil.*

Oh no, the work was not easy. But they would go on laughing and talking, catching their breath from time to time while leaning on their hoes. Sometimes, when Frieda was boisterous and full of strength, she would lift the hoe high over her head in the Kiga fashion and strike a blow that sent lumps of earth and stones flying high in the sky. Yes, she had always liked field work; it was hard, but she never grew tired or got bored with it. As the young bean plants broke through the soil, her heart would swell with happiness and pride.

"When I was about sixteen, my aunt, who lives in the next compound, thought it was time for me to find a husband." She shrugs her shoulders. "I did not mind much. Some of my friends were already married, and two of them already carried children on their backs. I was not in a hurry, but it did not matter. I still liked my home, but if I found a man, I would go with him."

The man her aunt had her eye on was from a polygamous family. His mother was the third wife of some rather rich man who did not care much about his wives or children. Her father-in-law had what Frieda calls "a complicated character." Soon after their wedding, the mother-in-law went back to her home village, where she lived in a small house.

From time to time, the man she called her husband would come and spend a night with her, only to leave her alone again the following morning. After a few months her belly would swell, and, in due course, she would produce another mouth to feed. When she had four children, she told the man never to get near her again. She never wanted to see him again. He left her after giving her a thorough beating, a swollen eye, and a missing front tooth. This only reinforced her decision never to set eyes upon him again.

The next time she saw him, he was in his coffin, with a number of other wives sitting around it.

*F*rieda's husband grew up with a mother who did not have the energy to tame his moods and tempers and a father he hardly knew, because the father did not care about him and died early.

"My aunt did not know much about him," Frieda says. "But she thought he was as good as any. Anyway, what can you know about a man in a short time?"

Frieda was shown her future husband by her aunt on a Sunday afternoon, when they had gone for a walk along the main village road. Young men and girls were strolling along, and when they passed by him, her aunt gently nudged her in her side.

"He did not look bad and was laughing with one of his friends as we passed him. Actually, he was rather good-looking."

They never talked that day, but Frieda had felt the man's gaze on her for quite a while and giggled nervously.

The following Sunday, they followed the same route, this time with the sure purpose of seeing him again. And it did not take them long to meet him. This time, he looked directly at her, and she did not cast her eyes down as she had been told. She had wanted to get a really good look at him. He smiled at her, and that seemed to clinch the agreement.

She never talked to her mother about him—one did not talk to mothers and fathers about these matters, her aunt had warned her—but she found it quite difficult not to share her feelings with her mother, to whom she had been close all her life.

One Saturday night, not long after their second meeting, her aunt called her to her compound. They sat casually on a mat, and her aunt whispered that Sunday was the day for her to join her man. She was shocked and worried, but her aunt looked very confident.

She instructed Frieda to pack a few of her clothes and wait until it was dark, when one of her friends would knock on the window shutters of her room. Frieda looked doubtful—would she have the courage to leave her home just like that?

Of course her mother had to be asleep in her room, and so would her brothers need to be asleep in theirs. They would not let her go to some man and a new home where her labor would be exploited without brideprice being paid.

Frieda had often heard about this practice of girls joining their future husbands at night. In August, when the sorghum was harvested and the time for brewing beer had come, the drums that accompanied the young girls on their way to their future husbands would be heard nearly every night.

That night, she had gone home rather scared. Was she really going to get married the next day? She tossed in her bed from side to side, waking up the next morning to her last day as a girl in the security of her father's house. The whole day she stayed at home, not even going out for Sunday prayers. Secretly she packed her best dresses and tied them in one of her new head cloths. There was not that much to take.

When night fell, she locked herself in her room. She secured the door tightly with a bolt and sat on her bed, dressed and waiting for the promised knock. Her heart beat so loudly that she thought everybody in the house could hear it. She heard her mother go to her room and get in bed, the mattress creaking under her weight. Then the paraffin lamp was soon put out. Her brothers were still talking, but they too soon fell asleep, and all was quiet in the house.

She listened to the night wind outside and the rustling of the trees. Then, suddenly, she heard the faint knock. She looked around her room for the last time, picked up her bundle, carefully opened the window, and climbed out into the cold and unfamiliar darkness. Two girls were standing outside waiting for her. They took her bundle and put their fingers to their lips to indicate silence. Quietly, they disappeared into the darkness. Frieda followed.

They moved along the narrow path without a word, groping for the shrubs and bushes that might help them find their way. After what seemed like an endless journey, they reached the junction to the main road to Kisoro town. Here, they found more girls waiting for them. Some of the girls had drums, and when they recognized her, they started drumming joyfully and singing fast, laughing and cracking jokes as they made their way to Frieda's future home.

Frieda's husband was waiting for her somewhere near the gate; he was surrounded by friends. Pots of beer had been brought to the compound, but Frieda did not look at them. The man who had chosen her and with whom she was to share the rest of her life led her into a small house, opened a door, and entered the room with her. The girls stayed outside with the boys around the pots of beer.

Her husband approached her. Frieda was so scared about what was going to happen next, but she knew he would not be able to face his friends outside again if he did not have sex with her. She tried to concentrate on something else, such as wondering whether at home they had already discovered her disappearance.

The man drew closer. There was a faint smell of alcohol about him, and he was sweating. He looked at her, then slowly removed his clothes. Frieda sat down on the bed, watching him doubtfully. But he took her gently; while it hurt a lot, it was soon over. Frieda wondered whether that was all, but she soon fell asleep. She knew she had come to a good man who would look after her well.

Outside there was a lot of shouting and ululating. Friends and relatives welcomed her husband back from the bedroom, where for the first time, as they all knew, he had performed one of his duties to his wife. When he came to her again, long after midnight, Frieda was hurting all over. But she did not say anything. Perhaps that is what it means being married, she thought.

In the morning, she kept to her room. His sisters had brought her water to have a bath. She sat on her bed, not knowing what to do. Her husband had gone out earlier to talk to his mother, who had stayed away the previous night.

When she came to look at Frieda, she was kind but firm. Since her husband was dead, she had taken on the role of gathering information about her son's prospective wife to ensure that she was the right girl for him.

Physical beauty was not all that important, but a girl had to be healthy because a lot of hard work was expected of her. Modesty was another quality in a good wife and Frieda had it, in addition to being healthy and strong and having a well-developed bust, which was a sign of fertility. Also, she was not cross-eyed, nor did she stammer when she talked.

Was she very tall? No! Being tall would prevent her from working hard and carrying heavy loads.

So far so good. She is not a bad choice, Frieda's mother-in-law seemed to be thinking. She called one of her daughters to bring fresh food for Frieda, who sat shyly in what was to be her sitting room. A simple wooden bench and a low table were all the furniture that adorned it.

"It did not take me long to get used to the place," Frieda continues. "My mother-in-law is not a bad woman. Later in the week, my husband showed me the gardens that belonged to him; they were not many, but they looked fertile."

Two days after her disappearance from home, her husband sent over a pot of beer and an emissary to tell her people that she was not lost but in safe hands. Some weeks later, she went to see her family at home. They greeted her but did not show much concern. She told her mother that she was already pregnant, a fact that was neither welcomed nor abhorred.

Maybe they would have been friendlier if her husband had brought them some money as part of the bride-price, which he did in the same year. It was not much, but it made Frieda feel more appreciated in her husband's home, where she was now doing most of the field work and all the household chores.

Yes, Frieda was able to cultivate a piece of land successfully; she was not idle nor a gossip, who would talk away a full day's work at a neighbor's house. She started growing tomatoes on a small patch in her fields. She loved seeing the fruits ripen on the strong stems. She looked after her plants carefully, because she had good plans for them.

Her husband's house was located strategically close to a crossroads. Here she planned to put up a small table by the roadside and sell her produce. This would give her a bit of income to buy clothes for herself and the coming baby. She did not get any money from her man, though he was working as a porter at one of the big building sites. One day he would be a mason, he boasted, and make a lot of money.

Sometimes she wondered where he put his wages, but she never dared to ask him. He was the kind of man one would not ask too many questions, especially when he had had a drink or two.

Her womb was growing daily, and it made her uncomfortable sometimes, but she was determined that the child should not disturb her work in the fields and, through that, her financial plans.

The day she put her small bamboo table by the roadside and sold a full basket of tomatoes within a short time, she felt very pleased with herself. She felt she had achieved something great and wondered why her husband had instead looked at her with a dark eye and clenched jaw, which normally meant trouble.

This was the day she had felt would be the beginning of a new life for her, with a little bit of money to bring her some comfort. And indeed, it was the beginning of a new life, but it was quite different from the one she had envisaged. That evening, everything changed for her.

She had tied the little earnings she made from the tomatoes in her handkerchief and pushed it under her bra to keep it safe. There she would not lose it. While she was in her kitchen cooking the evening meal, she suddenly felt somebody behind her. She turned. In the doorway stood her husband, swaying from side to side. A repelling smell of stale, strong liquor came from every pore of his body.

"I will teach you tonight, not tomorrow—no, no, tonight it must be—to sell the fruits of my land, have you heard? Fruits of my land without telling me. Who do you think you are in this home that you can simply sell and buy what you want? Where is the money, bitch?"

Frieda sat in complete silence, too stunned and scared to look at the man darkening the kitchen entrance with his towering height. As the drunken voice came closer, Frieda moved from the small, blackened stool toward the corner of the dark kitchen. She stood very still as her husband approached her. His face was contorted with fury. She gazed at him fearfully, her eyes darting here and there. But there was no way she could escape.

The first blow fell on her right cheek. She cried out in pain, holding her face with both hands. But he pulled them away and hit her hard again and again. Frieda cried out repeatedly, but with a vicious blow he pushed her to the ground. She fell heavily. He was upon her in no time. He ripped open her dress and pulled it down. He fumbled in her bra and pulled out the handkerchief with the money in it. He held it triumphantly, then looked at her in disgust and gave her a final kick on her legs that made her wince. And this is how he left her.

She scrambled to her feet, hugging her belly that seemed miraculously not to have been harmed. But her face had already started swelling, and a little blood dropped from her mouth. She pushed her tongue along her gums and thought that one of her teeth was loose. She felt absolute terror. Could she go outside, or would he be waiting for her there? Her body shook violently. She peeked out. Everything was dark and quiet. It seemed nobody else had heard anything.

She sobbed hard and swallowed a mouthful of blood and spittle as she tiptoed toward the house. She half expected to find him inside the house, but he wasn't. She stood there, her hand on her throat, wondering what to do next. He had all her money now, enough to keep him in cheap booze for a whole week. And then what would be her fate? Could she expect this every evening, as long as he was in need of money and as long as she had a little of her own?

She sat down on her bed. No, she would not stay in this house, but it was too late to go to her parents' home. Tomorrow she would go there. Surely they could not turn their daughter away after all this. She touched her swollen cheek and eyes. What would they say about this?

She did not want to go to her mother-in-law. Mothers-in-law always stick by their sons and blame their daughters-in-law for whatever goes wrong. But this house was not safe. There was nowhere to hide. He knew all the corners. She got up slowly and took her blanket, packed some of her most treasured clothes in a black plastic bag, and wondered where she could go in order to be safe. She considered staying in the kitchen but discarded the idea.

She went outside and gazed around the compound. The granary was the only safe place where he would never imagine her hiding. Slowly and painfully, she went toward it. Every step caused her a lot of pain, especially where he had kicked her on the shin with his heavy boots.

It was not easy to climb into the granary; her belly got in the way, and her body ached all over. But finally she managed to get in, and she sank to her knees among the heads of sorghum. A sigh of relief escaped from her. She lay down carefully and spread the blanket over herself. This was not the most comfortable of beds, but it was safe and not too cold. She turned slowly and painfully onto her side, and after a while, she fell asleep.

Not long after that, she heard her husband coming from afar, shouting obscenities, his curses abnormally loud in the now total blackness of the night. He must have lost his way and was groping around in the darkness, stumbling over the sharp volcanic stones.

Her bed in the granary gave Frieda a feeling of security. Surely he would not find her there, but as the voice came nearer, she hardly breathed. He pushed open the door of the house and stumbled inside, still shouting. Had he realized that she was not there?

The door to his mother's house opened just enough for Frieda to see her standing there, listening. But nothing happened. The shouting in the house stopped, the door closed, and Frieda fell into a fitful sleep.

As the sun rose in the east, she woke up, shivering with the early morning cold, and painfully climbed from the granary. She brushed the dry sorghum stalks from her dress and pulled others out of her hair, trying to look a bit decent so as not to arouse everybody's suspicion on the way home. But God, the pain she felt, and the shame! How terribly humiliating to go home to her parents in such a state when she thought she had left her father's house for a better one!

Since it was still early, she met hardly anybody on her way, except for a few early risers coming from the nearby spring to fetch water. She ducked behind the bushes whenever she saw someone approaching, or she bent her head low, pulling her head cloth over her bruised face.

When she reached home, her mother was already up and about. She let out a shriek of pain and fear when she saw her daughter. She pulled the cloth from her face and touched the bruises. Frieda, for the first time, broke into painful sobs. She cried and cried until she had no more tears left.

Her mother led her to the sitting room. Her father came and looked at her but said nothing. Her brothers regarded her with disgust. They were men; she could not expect much compassion from them.

Her mother gave her some warm porridge to drink and water to wash with. A little later, Frieda fell asleep in her old room, which she now had to share with one of her sisters.

When she woke up in the afternoon, she heard a familiar voice in the sitting room, which, however, did not belong to her parents' home. She strained her ears for a moment and immediately realized that it was her mother-in-law talking. Then her mother told her rather roughly that a visitor had come to see her.

Reluctantly, Frieda got up and went to the sitting room, trying very hard not to look at the woman who had come to plead for her son. But when her mother-in-law saw her poor face, she gave a gasp of horror. Frieda's mother looked at her daughter with contempt and said, "It is the home you chose for yourself. You did not ask me or your father or brothers. It was what you chose for yourself. You must go back there." How she must hate me deep in her heart, Frieda thought.

At that moment, it seemed to Frieda that her mother-in-law regarded her more kindly than her own mother did. Her mother-in-law told her mother in a gentle voice, "Leave her here for a few more days. I will be sending her some food. By God, she has cultivated enough of it. I want to talk to my son first." A little later, she left without saying another word.

◎◎

It took Frieda a few days to recover from this first incident. Most of the time, she hid in the house, too ashamed to speak to her neighbors and relatives. What a mess things were now! But eventually she had to face some of them. While a few felt genuinely sorry for her, others grinned, thinking, Serves her right. A woman who has not been paid bride-price for is worth nothing and is not appreciated in a home. She is like a sack of flesh that can be sent back any time.

Frieda knew she was not really a welcome visitor in her parents' home now. So, on a Saturday afternoon, she made her way back to what she considered her own home. Her husband was nowhere to be seen. She got the key to her house from her mother-in-law's hut and sat down on the wooden bench in her sitting room. The house smelled unclean, the bed was unmade, and a heap of dirty laundry lay on the floor by the bedside. She blinked away her tears. What misery she had come back to!

When her man came home at night, there was only a faint odor of alcohol about him. He said nothing to her, and they ate their food in silence. That night, he made love to her like a savage, but she was scared and kept quiet, fearing that he would turn against her and their unborn child.

Two days later, she gave birth to their firstborn, a beautiful little girl. Frieda did not have any clothes for her, but the nurse at the local maternity center had a small heap of baby clothes for emergencies. She gave her a tiny little dress and a baby cap before Frieda carried her firstborn back to an unsafe home and an unsafe future. But all seemed to go well, at least for the time being.

In the months that followed, whenever her man came home drunk, he would push her a little, or slap her, but who did not know that a man who loved his wife had to beat her every now and then? And so Frieda kept quiet and thought she was maintaining peace in the home. But deep inside her heart, fear was always present.

After a month or two of relative calm, she started growing her tomatoes again, tending them and waiting for the time she could sell them.

But apprehension never quite left her, and when it grew dark and her man was not yet home, she sometimes felt cold desperation clutch at her heart.

As she cultivated his gardens again, she would always make sure to ask him what he wanted her to grow there. Sometimes he would growl an answer; at other times he would tell her to grow whatever she wanted.

Roughly half a year later, a big building project was started in the neighborhood. This time her husband was employed as a mason. Frieda was happy for him. It would mean he could earn two to three thousand shillings a day. If only he could use it well, they could improve so much on their home.

The first payday came, at long last. Frieda thought of cooking meat and some bananas, not the beans they ate every day. That evening, she waited eagerly for him. When it grew dark, she walked slowly from the kitchen to the house. She put her child to sleep. The evening chill spread throughout her body. She shivered. They had very nearly quarreled the previous evening when she had talked about his money. But she feared that any moment he might pounce on her again.

Now she was carried away by thoughts of what the night could possibly bring. She ate her food listlessly and waited. Nothing. No sound came from outside except the rustling of leaves on the eucalyptus trees. The silence now troubled her. She no longer felt safe in the house, but she had to stay on. There had been days when she felt like leaving, when she was full of fear after he had yet again raised his hand against her, but wondering where she could possibly go made her stay on.

She could not tell anybody about her thoughts or fears regarding her husband's terrifying temper and violence. And yet she had nowhere to go and no one to turn to.

That night, nothing happened, because he never came home at all. He was away for the next three days. He stayed away until he had spent all his wages with another woman in town who, it seemed, had thrown him out when he tried to hit her after his money was gone.

When he arrived home, he had a nasty smile on his face, probably expecting Frieda to do what other women do in those circumstances, which would be to call him all kinds of dirty names or try to burn his clothes. But Frieda kept quiet and went to get his supper.

He waited a little while for his food to come; then he ate ravenously. But suddenly, without any warning, he pounced on her like a wild beast. Only a foolish woman would try to struggle with a man in such a mood. So Frieda quietly stood there, trying to hold back her tears and the fear that gripped her.

He ripped her dress and pulled the money from her bra. He gripped her arm, and she turned to face him.

"This is not your money," she said, turning away.

His chest heaving in anger, he shouted at her, "Nothing here is yours, do you hear? Nothing, absolutely nothing at all. You came with nothing, and you will go with nothing from here."

With a calmness that surprised her, Frieda walked away to her gardens and sat down. She must start living differently, she thought; she must look after herself and her child and the baby that had recently started growing in her womb. Next time she would keep her money in a safe place, maybe a tin that she would bury in the garden. She would dig a deep hole under one of the trees or look for a hole in a big trunk. If she were lucky, nobody would ever see her get money from there.

"And that was what I did," Frieda says. "Next I hired a piece of land from someone else and grew onions this time. Someone sold them for me for a little commission, and I hid my money in an old tin. He never came to know about it."

For a time, life continued. Her man had his own money, but she never saw a coin of it. She had a little of her own that she never talked about.

When it was payday, her man would come home drunk, sometimes giving her a few slaps when she asked for some money to buy soap or salt. But he never gave her even a hundred shillings. One evening, he beat her when there was too little salt in the food; another time, when his clothes were not washed, he tried to beat her again, but she managed to escape in time. She kept quiet. When her bruises did not show on her face, she was happy. She could always cover the dark spots on her throat with a sweater around her neck. But as her second pregnancy became more visible, she started fearing for her unborn child.

One evening, when she heard him staggering on his way back home again, she felt she could not stand it anymore. She said a prayer as she opened the door for him. He tried to rush past her but fell flat on his face, right next to her feet. His nose was already bloody, his upper lip crusted with blood, his hair coated with soil, and his clothes wet and spattered with mud.

A wave of fear went through Frieda. As he slowly lifted his head, his face was a picture of fury and pure, undisguised hatred. He scrambled to his feet, supporting himself precariously on the hard bench, and finally gained his balance by tightly gripping the table. Anticipating what was coming to her, Frieda moved backward. His blow landed on the mud wall and sent a framed photograph crashing to the ground. The glass broke into a thousand small pieces. He looked at his fist in surprise, and fresh outrage surged through him.

Frieda took more steps backward. She had her little daughter tied onto her back and needed to protect her. But her husband had not quite finished with her. With agility she had not thought him capable of, he suddenly jumped forward with a thick stick in his hand. He hit her hard on the back twice. Then he hit her again. The third blow landed on her daughter, who let out a painful scream. Unconcerned, he tried to hit her again. Frieda cried out in agony and rushed from the house.

This time, she ran to her neighbor's house, and with all her strength, she banged on the door. She shouted and screamed, and the child, full of pain, cried with her. They let her in for the night, but the next day she went home again.

From then on, Frieda says, for the next fourteen years, the whole cycle kept repeating itself. The violence that started early in her marriage never stopped. She was beaten again and again, sometimes nearly to death.

"Now," she says, "I have to look after my five daughters and his son from another woman who came and lived with him when I had gone home for quite a long time. My husband brought this woman to his house soon after I had gone to my father's home again. But she could not stay with my husband. No woman can stay with this man. She left after a few months and later gave birth to a baby boy. When he was old enough, she just brought him to me to look after. Children belong to the man, you know. The boy is big now, nearly six years old.

"My last born is now two years old. I have made my bed in all the homes of the neighborhood; so many nights I would run with my children to seek refuge from this raving man, who would beat us with any

instrument that came his way. He never beat me alone. He went after
the children, too, who were really terrified of him. Every few months I
would spend some weeks at my father's home with all the children. Once
I stayed for nearly a year away from this batterer because he beat me so
much that I had to get treatment in the hospital. My father took pity on
me and took me in, together with my children, as I could not leave them
behind to suffer."

I ask what finally made her leave her husband for good. She tells me
that, about two years ago, she had enough money in her small tin in the
garden to buy a goat. How proud she felt when she bought it. She loved
looking at it, and her children would happily take it out to graze. It was a
beautiful animal, strong and healthy, and she was told that it always gave
birth to twin kids.

Her husband never commented on the animal, but he looked at it
reflectively. It was a period of relative quiet and rest. He did not earn a
lot of money, so he could not get soaked in booze in the evenings. To his
credit, he had started building a house before Christmas, but the work
had not gone further than window level by August.

Oh, how much Frieda wanted that house! Her five children could
have two rooms instead of being cramped in a single room. But when
progress on the building stalled for more than eight months, she became
disappointed but dared not ask him why he had stopped building. She
knew a question at the wrong time could be dangerous for her.

One Sunday morning, he suddenly told her that if she had some
money, she could continue building the house. Not trusting his proposal,
she kept quiet and waited a few more days to see what he would do.
When no tempests followed, she believed he sincerely wanted her to finish the job. So she started collecting the volcanic stones from her fields
that are commonly used for building. Her children helped her enthusiastically, even though this was not a child's job. They heaped big and
small stones near the building site. Although the work was hard, they all
enjoyed it because they knew it meant a better future for them.

Her man did not say anything, and they went on with the work. After
a few weeks, when the heap of stones had grown and their enthusiasm had
weakened, Frieda asked some people to help with the building. Finally,
after a month and a lot of secret trips to her garden tin, Frieda knew the

house was ready for roofing. She had already put in windows and shutters and often worried about thieves stealing them.

By some coincidence, it was her turn to get the money from the savings group she had formed with eleven other women. Every month, each woman would contribute ten thousand shillings and give the entire sum to one member of the group, who would use it to do something for her family, such as buy mattresses, a bicycle, or even land.

That month, it was her turn to receive the pooled money, which she planned to use to buy iron sheets for their house. Oh, how impatient she was! She waited for her husband to be in a good mood. Normally, he treated her kindly when he knew some money was coming her way.

When she told him, a light came into his eyes, and the following Monday they went together to the Indian shop in town and spent all her savings on the iron sheets.

They felled some trees in the garden, and the carpenters came and put up the roof. She did not have money to pay them, but there was an old kitchen to be demolished in their compound, and with the money the timber from the kitchen would bring, she could buy a door and pay the carpenters. Pulling down the kitchen was hard work for a woman, but she did not mind very much. Even if her man did not help her, she knew she could accomplish the task. She sold all the timber as firewood, paid the carpenters, and fixed the new doors. It was soon time for them to move into the new house. Maybe life would be better.

When the sun shone brightly on the iron sheets, her heart pumped with joy and anticipation. She waited for her man that evening when the house was complete, eager and excited, the key for the padlock of the new house hanging like a mayor's golden chain around her neck.

But when he came back home, he was so drunk, so utterly soaked in cheap liquor, that all her joy immediately vanished. She looked at him with unbelieving eyes. Her children had already stolen out of the house and waited behind the tree in the compound. They did not speak but just stood there, watching and fearing what was going to happen.

"Give me the money," he said.

"But I have no more money," she told him. "You know it all went into the new house. Even the door has been fixed."

"I want what is mine," he roared.

"But it is all ours, yours and mine," she replied.

"You seem not to understand that, in this compound, nothing has ever been yours or will ever be yours," he said in a deadly calm voice.

He had barely finished the sentence when he went to the bedroom, returning with a bright new *panga*. Frieda screamed in terror.

"I have no money, please, I have no money. You know I can't have any." She ran around the table as he held the *panga* high over his head, ready to strike her. Outside, her children shouted in panic while she screamed to them to run away and save themselves. They sprinted off.

Frieda was still trying to talk some sense into him while desperately looking for a way out of the room. Finally, she managed to escape through the kitchen door. She ran toward the tree where her beautiful black goat was still tied. But her husband came after her and hit her beautiful black goat with one vicious blow, splitting its head open and leaving it lifeless on the ground.

Frieda stopped dead in the compound. She knew this blow had been meant for her. She had escaped death by a hair's breadth. She looked at the man and her goat, turned around, and left the compound.

After that incident, she never went back. Next time he would surely kill her or one of her children. She returned to her parents' home. After hearing her story, they gave her a room for herself and her five children.

That night, her husband burned all her clothes and even those of their children; then he threw the dead goat on top of the fire. Nobody from the neighborhood dared to approach him in his madness. They all knew better than to put their lives at risk.

Not long after this, Frieda sent the children to visit their father on a Sunday morning, when he could not possibly be drunk. But he chased them away. They swore never to go back to see him or go anywhere near the house ever again.

Last year, she went to the local village chief to ask him to settle their case, but it was of no use. Her husband had bribed all the members of the council with beer. She was painted as a quarrelsome, money-minded woman who wanted to possess all her husband's property. She was not even given a chance to defend herself. Another accusation leveled at her was that she did not want to have her husband in her bed. To this she replied that he did not have to rape her so as to have sex.

This made some of the men laugh, which encouraged her to ask them where they thought she had picked the five children from if they were not his as well as why he had given them names and was registered as their father on their baptism cards.

A few days later, when she met the chief on the road, he took her aside and told her in confidence not to go back to her matrimonial home because her husband was a very dangerous man who might kill her next time. He was not telling her anything new. She turned and walked away without a word.

She could have gone to the police and reported that her man had tried to murder her, but would it have been any help? She had been embarrassed and humiliated often enough. Her throat still showed black marks that will never leave her, a reminder of the night he had tried to throttle her.

How can she divorce him when she was never properly married? She just left him like you leave an old dress that no longer fits you, that no longer means anything to you. She took nothing from the house. She left everything of hers there, and now it was up in smoke. She never spent a single night in the house she herself had built. Neither did her children. She knew she would never go back.

◎◎

Frieda receives no help from the man whom she once called her husband. There is often no soap in the home, no oil, no salt, no food. The children are nearly going naked.

She went to the probation officer, but her husband was faster. Money can make a government officer deaf when a woman talks. The probation officer had listened inattentively for a few minutes, then fobbed her off with some officious speech. She left his office in disgust.

She hears from neighbors that sometimes her husband brings women there—they spend a few weeks with him but eventually leave. Sometimes, when he has money, he spends a week in town and comes back home broke.

When he started selling his gardens, which he called his most treasured possessions, Frieda got scared that her husband's son would have nowhere to build a house in the future. So she tried to fight again for her own and her children's rights. She went back to the Local Council, who referred the case to the Magistrate's Court, but to no avail. Sore and dejected, she left the court. As she walked away, one of the court clerks winked at her and indicated that she should wait for him.

She waited patiently near a hedge that separates the court from the rest of the town till the clerk came. He took her a little farther away and whispered that there was now a Legal Aid clinic in Kisoro, which gave help to people in her kind of situation. He added that women frequented it with complaints about land and property conflicts, domestic violence, rape, and other social abuse and injustices.

"I had nothing to lose by going there," Frieda says. "There was no harm in going to Kisoro and trying to find out whether that office could help me."

So one rainy day, when she could not work in her fields anyway, she walked to town and quickly found the place.

"The man in the office was not difficult to talk to," she says. In fact, he seemed to be the first man she had ever met who could understand her problems. She told him everything, showed him all her papers. He, in turn, brought out a piece of paper and wrote, for a long time, everything Frieda said.

"Finally, it was nearly afternoon, and I was getting hungry. He gave me a letter, one copy for my husband and another for the Local Council 1 chairman. He wrote to them that, in all matters concerning the house and the land, particularly in case my husband wanted to sell anything, the Legal Aid office in Kisoro had to be asked for advice. On top of that, each party—that is, me and my husband—had to come with a witness to the office to discuss our case."

"Whom did you go with?" I ask.

"I went with the woman who used to give me and my children refuge at night when my man chased us from home."

"And your husband, whom did he go with?"

"His brother."

"What happened?"

"You see, my witness said that my man is a brute when he is drunk and that he tried to kill me. She said that I slept so many nights in her home that she had even lost count of the number of times."

"And your husband's brother, what did he say?" I ask.

Frieda laughs. "He said exactly the same thing—that my husband is terrible when he is drunk, that he harassed me and the children, and that I had suffered a lot at his hands. I don't think that the two brothers were on friendly terms after this for a long time. But I was happy—I was so happy because the man in the office gave my husband a letter, and another one to the chairman of the Local Council, forbidding him to sell anything, any land or the house, without my consent. That office is really good—at least for the women. That man in that office was the first one to help me. He told me if my husband sold anything again, I should not be afraid to report him. Then he would go to prison."

We sit quietly for a moment. Some of Frieda's problems have been solved, but not all of them. She cannot stay with her whole family in her father's house forever. Children belong to the man's home, and one day, when her son is old enough and can defend himself, he will have to claim his property—if there is any left by then.

Luckily, so far she has not seen any of his father's violent streak in him. "He is still a good boy," she says. She takes care of him although he is not hers and her own five daughters are enough of a problem.

Frieda is still breast-feeding her youngest child. Her husband does not give her anything for the care of the children. You cannot enforce a maintenance order when the man declares himself sick and unable to work and has no income. The officer at the Legal Aid clinic told Frieda that there was nothing they could do for her since her husband had no regular income, but they promised to coordinate with the local chiefs on the ground to ensure that he did not sell any land or the house.

Frieda does not have to apply for custody of her children, because nobody else wants them. She shoulders the responsibility alone but worries that the time will come when she may not be able to manage. She also worries about her health. Could her husband have infected her with some disease that he picked up from some of the cheap women in town or those he brought home during her absence? She knows about AIDS, but she will not take the test because the results would mean nothing to her. As long as she is still healthy, she will work.

How is she earning her living? Oh, she cultivates gardens for other families, and they give her money for a day's work, or they let her cultivate a piece of land if she digs one of equal size for them. She has put her husband's son in school. It was a struggle to get him the school uniform, but at least he is now learning something. She doubts whether he will ever go to a secondary school, because she will not have the money for that. She only hopes she will have the energy to make him abstain from alcohol.

"It is hard these days to bring up children alone. I wish I had someone to help me," she says.

I ask whether she has another man. She smiles. "Who would take a woman as poor as me with six big children? And I think I have had enough of men. You see, I am only thirty-four now, but I have seen enough trouble to last me a lifetime. No, I do not want another man. I want peace and quiet, some food for my children and me, and a bit of meat at Christmas and Easter. I do not really need more than that. If I can buy myself a dress once a year and some clothes for my children, it will do. Real problems will come when one of them gets seriously ill," she mutters, "because then I shall not know where to go for money."

She has not forgotten about all the pain and torture. Sometimes she wakes up at night sweating, waiting for the footsteps outside and holding her throat in apprehension until she realizes that she is safe. She wonders whether that fear will ever leave her completely.

Her eldest daughter is now fifteen years old and not at school. Sometimes she helps Frieda cultivate the land.

Isn't she worried that her daughter might make the same mistake as her mother did, marry early and become unhappy?

"Is there anything that has ever prevented a girl from getting married when she has got the idea in her head?" Frieda asks.

She rises to go: a small bent woman, going to a home, after a hard day's work in the fields, where she is tolerated but not loved.

Maria Demands Her Share

WINNIE MUNYARUGERERO

The story of thirty-six-year-old Maria Goretti is about her struggle to get a share of her dead parents' property for herself, her three sons, and her daughter. Maria returned to her birthplace in Bufumbira, Kisoro district, in 1994, after the geno-cide in her adopted country, Rwanda, occurred. With her Rwandan husband killed and his relatives either dead or scattered in exile, Maria and her chil-dren felt that they had no place in that country. But her brother, the male heir, insisted that Maria's sons could not inherit any of the family property because they do not belong to the clan.

We sit outside in the garden. It is quiet, except for the occasional two or three barefoot women who shuffle past, talking loudly. The footpath that runs along the garden is not a thoroughfare. It is narrow and only leads to some few homesteads a little farther up the hill. Only muffled sounds of the few vehicles in the town can be heard from that distance.

Maria coughs a dry, sharp cough. She has AIDS, known in African countries as slim. She digs for a handkerchief from the right pocket of her dress. She puts the handkerchief to her mouth as she coughs. Her hands look soft and beautiful. The tapering fingers end in nails kept short and clean. She notices me looking at her hands. She looks down at them also and smiles. Her teeth are white and even. She passes her hand over her hair, which is thin and wavy, probably due to her sickness. Her sharp, seemingly youthful eyes do not seem to belong with her prematurely aging face.

Maria asks a question: What is a woman in her position supposed to do with her sons? Throw them away?

*Y*ou want to hear my story? It is long. I hope you have the time to hear it all. Some of it takes place in Rwanda. That is the happy part. I wish I could forget the part that happens in Congo. It is the worst. From Congo, I came back to Bufumbira. I have faced only quarrels and conflicts ever since.

My childhood was very ordinary, except that I grew up partly in Bufumbira and partly in Rwanda. Maama was a Congolese, but before she met my father, she was married in Rwanda, where she produced two children with her Rwandan husband, a girl followed by a boy. She told me her first husband was not a bad man, but later misunderstandings developed in their marriage. If you are a married woman, madam, then you know that problems come to every marriage, even to the best.

Maama decided to leave her husband and follow her brother, who was at the time working at Mutolere Parish here in Kisoro as a teacher. She arrived here with her son, still very young, strapped to her back. She found her brother living at the mission. It was here that my father met her. After producing only two children, my mother was still young and beautiful. My father fell in love with her. The priests wedded them soon after. My parents had three children—another girl, a boy, and myself. The boy is the oldest. I am the youngest of Maama's children with my father.

The happiness in Maama and Daata's marriage did not last long. You see, my father was a womanizer. He loved many women. He brought some of them home and kept others in rented rooms. After only a short while, he would chase away one and bring another. Other times, the women themselves would leave when they realized that the man was not serious. Fortunately for Maama, all the women left before they bore any children. At least Maama was saved the burden of raising other women's children. Whenever she complained about his behavior, my father would beat her. He was not only a womanizer—he was a wife beater as well. Maama was not happy.

I do not work in the gardens anymore because of my sickness. Even as a young girl, I did not do much field work. When others went to work in the gardens, I did light work at home, like cooking and cleaning. I don't know what would have happened had I married a peasant. Hard work like digging makes my head ache. I was very lucky to marry an educated man who did not require me to work in the gardens. My husband was employed, and we had money to buy food and hire laborers.

When I returned to Bufumbira, the hard situation forced me to work in the gardens whenever my health permitted. I was very sickly all throughout my childhood with headaches, and later I suffered from stomach ulcers.

But I was telling you about my father. He did not pay fees for me to go to school. He was too busy chasing after women to have any time for anyone or anything else. He may have paid fees for my brother for a short time, I am not sure, but as for me, I never went to school at all. You know our people think that educating a girl is a waste of money. I can only write my name. I do not write very well, but at least I am able to sign agreements. I got tired of dipping my thumb in ink like an old woman. I learned to write my name as an adult in a women's group. Perhaps if I had gone to school, I would not be suffering the way I am now.

Maama's son, my half brother, was called Ntoni. We all grew up together here at my father's home. Later, when he was big, my mother encouraged him to go back to his father in Rwanda. There was property for him with his father. Ntoni went back and found that his father had since remarried. He lived with his father for some years. As time went by, quarrels arose between him and his stepmother.

He returned to Bufumbira and persuaded Maama to return to Rwanda. Because Maama was already very unhappy with Daata, she was only too willing to leave. She took us with her. Her Rwandan husband welcomed her back with open arms. I think he still loved her. He built her a house.

Problems soon developed between my mother and her co-wife over their husband's attention. The younger wife accused the husband of spending more time with a woman who had deserted him, only to return with a bunch of children from another man for him to look after.

Her greatest fear, though, was that these children would share her husband's property.

Quarrels between Maama and her co-wife became frequent. Soon my stepfather became overwhelmed by these fights and called in the authorities to intervene. The property was divided equally between Maama and her co-wife. Maama lived on her piece of land with all her children: Ntoni and us from our Bufumbira father. My half sister, Ntoni's sister, was already married and had children.

After some time, Ntoni started behaving strangely toward Maama and the rest of us. It appeared that he had all along used my mother to get his hands on the property. Now that his father's property was divided between his two wives, he wanted Maama and all of us out of the way. He started to nag Maama constantly to take us back to our father where, he said, we belonged. He was particularly harsh toward my brother, who was later forced to return to Bufumbira. But after he left, Maama worried about him. Who would cook for him? Who would take care of him? She, therefore, convinced me to follow him.

My brother and I lived for some time with our father, but he was not very good to us. I decided to return to my mother. My brother remained behind. I was about twenty at the time, but I was not very strong.

◎◎

I am feeling a bit dizzy. I slept very badly last night, and in the morning I cleaned out my stomach with vomiting. I put nothing near my mouth before I left home. Not even water. The troubles my children and I have gone through have united us. I am not just their mother. They are my advisers, companions, and friends. My third son in particular cares for me. When they don't find me at home, he is the one who dashes to the neighbors to inquire whether I have been taken to the hospital. Even today, he will be waiting by the roadside until he sees me. But I told them I would be here today, so they will not worry much. Yesterday I came here after they left for school. They were very worried when they did not find me at home. They were told that a car had picked me up. You see, my sickness hits like lightning. I may be well in the morning, but by midday, I am in Mutolere Hospital on a drip. My good health is like a mist. It is there one moment and gone the next.

But let me not talk about the children now. They come later in the story. I haven't even talked about my marriage. As I told you, I had returned to Rwanda when I was about twenty. I was old enough for marriage, and I soon met my husband. I remember that day well. It was a Sunday, and we met at church. My half sister's husband introduced us. They were friends. I was told his name was Jean Baptiste. He was handsome, with a very charming smile and very white teeth, like somebody who was fed on milk. I wanted him to smile all the time.

Later that day, we all ate lunch together at my sister's place. He sat next to me. I felt a wonderful, warm feeling talking to him. He touched my hand several times as he passed food to me. His were not the rough hands of a laborer but the hands of someone who works in an office. He appeared sophisticated and knowledgeable. I felt proud to be noticed by such a man.

Maama had some education in Congo, her country. She was a very neat woman. She brought us up well. We were always the cleanest and most well-behaved children in the neighborhood. I did not look like the typical Mufumbira peasant girl.

Jean Baptiste and I became friends from that Sunday. He became a frequent visitor to our home. Maama liked him very much. She felt proud that her daughter had caught the eye of a man who worked with pen and paper, not a hoe. He worked as a clerk in an office.

Soon he was talking about marriage. But he was not sure whom to pay the bride-price to. You can understand his confusion; my Rwandan father was not really my father. The journey to Kisoro, to my real father, was long. He therefore persuaded me to just move in with him.

Of course, he could not pay bride-price to my mother. My God, have you ever heard of such a thing? How could a woman accept bride-price for a fellow woman? It is never done. A child belongs to the father, not the mother. A mother gets her share, a special mother's gift. The bride-price goes to the father or the nearest male relative if the father is dead. Surely you must know that!

Jean Baptiste gave me sixty thousand Rwandan francs as a gift and later gave Maama two hundred twenty thousand, the mandatory gift to the bride's mother. In Rwanda, before a man pays the full bride-price, the children do not belong to him. They belong to the mother. Our children, therefore, were registered on my identity card. You know that in Rwanda, everyone has an *indanga muntu*. It is not like here, where only men have graduated tax tickets.

I lived with my husband, and we produced three boys. Sometime in early 1994, we started hearing rumors of war. Soon we saw people escaping from Ruhengeri, Kigali, and everywhere around us. One day, my husband rushed home unexpectedly, at about three in the afternoon, from the tea plantation where he worked as a clerk. He was very worried. He said we had to leave immediately because the situation was getting extremely bad. I quickly gathered the children and packed whatever belongings I considered valuable, and we joined others, thousands of people from other towns and from the villages nearby, all walking and carrying their things. We headed for Goma via Gisenyi.

In this moving sea of people, family members were unable to stick together. We assumed we would easily locate one another later. What was important was that we were all headed for the same destination. My husband and the two older children walked on ahead. You see, I was in early pregnancy and sickly. I could not keep pace with younger and stronger people. I walked slowly at the rear with my youngest son and my mother-in-law. I did not see my husband again after that.

My husband died a most painful and lonely death. He was a good man. You know, many of our men beat their wives. He was not like that. For all the years we lived together, I never suffered a slap from him. He was of course a man and demanded respect in his home, but he was not harsh. He was not the type who drinks and neglects his family. He was educated. That made a difference.

My husband died at the hands of Ntoni, my own brother. Ntoni was at first in the army but later, together with some others, was sent home. But when the 1994 war started, the discharged soldiers were recalled. Ntoni must have been happy to handle a gun again. He was a greedy man. I suppose it was the army that made him like that.

He had never forgiven my husband. As I told you earlier, my husband did not pay bride-price for me. Ntoni held a grudge against him for that. He had hoped the bride-price would go to him as the brother of the bride. He saw, in the prevailing confusion of our flight, his chance to carry out his revenge. He was stationed in the area we passed through as we fled.

He found my husband and the children and duped them into believing he was going to help them. My poor husband did not know how wicked the man was. At night, my brother tied him up and hit him repeatedly on the chest with the butt of a gun. He must have burst his lungs or heart. The boys watched helplessly. Later, their so-called uncle left my husband for dead. The frightened children sat next to their father as blood oozed from his mouth and nose throughout the night. As soon as the light of dawn showed them the path, they ran to the roadside to seek help. Passersby did what they could to help, but the damage was so bad that he died that same day. All this time, I was happily following behind, unaware of what had happened. I did not find out until much later, when I ran into the children in Goma town.

I had never been to Goma town before. Many of us fleeing had never left our villages before. It was just by sheer luck that I noticed my children sitting alone like orphans on the veranda of some building. I expected their father to be somewhere nearby. Then the children tearfully told me how their father was killed. I was horrified but not surprised. I had known the depth of Ntoni's wickedness for a long time.

In Goma-Gisenyi, we were heaped into camps. We would stay a few days—sometimes one night—in one camp; then we would move on. We stayed at Mugunga camp and at another one near Goma airport. My mother-in-law died in this camp. The next day, we just abandoned the body and continued. That was common. A person would die and would be left unburied as people continued fleeing. There was no time and nobody prepared to bury the dead. Everyone was trying to get as far away from the Rwandan border as possible.

We were later moved to a camp at Gatare near Sabginyo Mountain. We lived in this camp for over six months. It was a bad time for me. I was sickly even before I became pregnant. With the pregnancy and the bad conditions, I got worse. I was very weak, and yet, to survive, one needed to be strong. You should have seen the pushing and fighting of the crowds when rations were being distributed. It was not for those without strength. The children were still small. They could not fight in that crowd. It was very hard. Only Bikira Maria kept us from dying.

I would wait until the fighting was over and everybody had got their rations and left the compound before crawling to pick up the fallen grain from the dust, mud, or even human excreta. Surprisingly, the children did not fall sick. We could have died of hunger, dysentery, or any other disease. Do you see this rosary? It never leaves my neck. It kept us, my children and me, alive in that camp. All this time, I kept close to the relatives of my husband. I feared that if I died and the children were not near their relatives, they would be all alone. But you know what happens when things get really hard. People become bad. That is what happened in this case. It was clear that the children and I were a burden to them. They had to share with us the little food they got. I saw the bad feelings in their eyes. It was so unreasonable. They could very well see I was ill. I hated having to depend on other people. I always want to do things for myself. The situation was bad.

In the distance from the camp, I could see Mount Muhabura tantalizingly close. I knew that just behind it lay my home. Many an evening I would just sit and look at it and pray. It was hard to imagine that I would ever see it from the other side.

One day, when I had a bit of strength, I tied my husband's clothes together to make a small bundle, which I passed over my head so that it dangled down my chest. I got a stick for support and slowly, resting several times on the way, tottered to the village to try and sell the clothes. They were part of the few valuables I had packed as we fled. I had carefully kept his best shirts, ties, and suit all this time. But let me tell you, it was not easy keeping anything in the camps. Thefts were rampant. If you took your eyes off your belongings for just a second, something disappeared. One of my sons always stood guard whenever I left.

Anyway, I went to town. But when I returned, I found the children alone, crying. Their relatives had vanished. The children had looked and called for them everywhere in the camp until people told them not to bother because the relatives had moved on, to escape responsibility, I guess. That sort of thing happened fairly often. Sometimes husbands abandoned wives and children. Fortunately, I had managed to sell the clothes. That money helped to keep us alive. You see, after that trip to town, perhaps because of the exertion of walking some distance, I became very ill. The children and some good people in the camp did their best to nurse me. The children became mature overnight. They are wonderful!

Joseph, the oldest, is sixteen. He is in class six. He is the spitting image of his father. The one who came after him is fourteen and is in class five. Their youngest brother is twelve and in class four. The war in Rwanda interfered with their schooling. When we arrived here, it took time before they resumed school. They lost about three years altogether. As soon as I got some strength and knew my way around, I got them back into school. They had problems adjusting to a different school system, a different language, and new people. The girl, who is only seven, is in class two. I gave birth to her the night I arrived in Kisoro.

The situation was really bad in the camp. But God had not totally abandoned us. A distant relative of my mother heard about my state. His home was not very far away. He took us there, and we rested for some days. He and his wife were very good to us and later told me how to get to Kisoro from Ruchuro. The money from the sale of the clothes came in very handy for the journey.

You know, God is great. If we had remained in Gatare camp for just one more week, I would have delivered there, and I certainly would have died. My delivery in Mutolere Hospital was not easy. I was in labor for over six hours. I was weak, and the baby was big. The doctors had just decided to operate when, by some miracle, I delivered. I bled a lot after the delivery and received several bottles of blood.

You see, the taxi that brought us to Kisoro was the same one that took me to the hospital. I was so sick that the taxi driver did not have the heart to throw me out at the taxi park along with my little boys. All through the journey from Ruchuro, they huddled close to me, afraid that I might die. I prayed fervently all throughout the journey that if I were to die, I should die after reaching Kisoro. I dreaded dying on the way and my children being abandoned in a totally foreign country. At least in Kisoro they would eventually be traced to my people. I had provided my oldest son with some facts: he knew my brother's name, the name of the village of my birth, and the name of my late father.

I delivered that same night. I remember the date well. It was September 16, 1994. Later, some of the other patients recognized me, and a message was sent to my brother. He was very happy to see me alive. He had feared I might have been killed in the war in Rwanda. He took the boys with him. Afterward he regularly checked on me and generally took care of me. I was so sick; I remained in the hospital for over a month. But I am very grateful to God for one thing: my daughter was born strong and healthy. She is still a very healthy and happy girl in spite of the fact that she did not breast-feed. She was not born with slim. She has been tested a number of times, and each time she has been found negative.

As for me, I was informed soon after delivery that I had slim. I first became suspicious when I was told my daughter could not breast-feed. They said she was too weak. They would let me hold her only for a short time before they took her back. A nurse would stand by to make sure I did not feed my baby. I could see the baby was normal. I constantly begged to be allowed to feed her.

One morning, one of the nurses sat with me, and we talked generally about many things. She was very friendly and asked me many questions. Then she explained why the doctors discouraged breast milk for my baby. I was sick; I had slim, she told me. My milk could expose the baby to the disease. I was ready to do anything to save my daughter's life. The nurse told me many things about the disease and what to do to keep strong. She was very kind and gentle. She did not seem to blame me or think I was dirty.

At first I was shocked. My late husband was not a man who chased after women. As for me, I had not known any other man sexually. I was angry and felt betrayed, but later, as the same nurse talked to me some more, I learned to accept my condition and not to look for anyone to blame. My baby was taken care of by the staff of TASO. I was too sick to do much. TASO paid all my bills during the time I was hospitalized. I am so grateful for them.

When I left the hospital, I was still weak. My brother came to take me home. I noticed from the beginning that his wife was not happy to see me. She had not even once visited me all the time I was in the hospital. I could also see that my children were not happy. It was obvious that the woman treated them badly. But I was still very weak. I could do nothing.

My parents' house was old. It had recently collapsed. By the time I returned, therefore, I had no house to return to. The children and I had to squeeze into my brother's house with his wife and their three children. It was difficult. My sister-in-law harassed us constantly. She blamed my children for everything that went wrong in the home. It was so bad that my eldest son threatened to run away at one time. She took advantage of my being weak to beat me up sometimes. One time, she found me sleeping at night and pushed me off the bed to the floor. It is a wonder I broke no bones. Other times, whenever my brother was not at home, she would throw me out of the house with the little infant. I would spend the night out in the open.

A time came when I could not take any more of her cruelty. There she was, sauntering like a queen to where I lay. She stood above me and looked down at me as if I were nothing. I looked up at her and kept quiet. She started, as usual, to pour abuse on me. I was still weak at the time, but her taunts got to me. A wave of anger lifted me from the bed, and I stood facing her, ready to fight. Then I noticed a pestle lying nearby, where my son had placed it after pounding sorghum. I snatched it up and, with the kind of strength I did not know I possessed, brought it down. I missed her head by a split second. The bitch was young and strong and as agile as a cat. Instead I got her elbow as she scampered out. For a good three weeks, her hand was swollen and lame. It straightened out after treatment. But she has been scared of me since that day. She only abuses me from a distance.

My brother did not intervene. He did not wish to offend his wife. He was blind to everything. But the neighbors were not blind. They got concerned. What shocked them most was when they learned that I was sometimes forced to sleep out in the cold with a very young baby. The Local Council leaders of the village intervened. They believed that my sister-in-law tortured me because she wanted the children and me out of her house. They therefore ordered my brother to repair Maama's house for me to move into. He repaired the house out of fear of the authorities. We moved in, but the repair work was so shoddy that the house collapsed again in no time at all.

Meanwhile, the abuse by my sister-in-law continued. Moving out of her house did not seem to make much difference. She said I had no business being there. She wanted me to go back to Rwanda, where my home and property were. It did not matter to her that my husband was dead and his people were either dead or in exile.

One day, during one of the sessions at TASO, I shared my problems with the group members. One woman told me about the office in Kisoro town that helps women with legal problems. She told me how she had got help when the relatives of her dead husband wanted to grab her land from her. She directed me to the office. I did not know Kisoro town well. It had grown very large during the years I lived away in Rwanda. I asked around and eventually found the office.

At the office, a young woman welcomed me. She told me she was a lawyer. I narrated my problems to her, and she listened attentively. She wrote down everything I told her. She asked me many questions. I answered them truthfully. I explained that my brother and his wife did not want me to have a share of my father's property. She assured me that I was as much my parents' child as my brother and was therefore entitled to a share of their property. She then wrote a letter and gave it to me to take to the LC chairman of my village. She wrote letters to other important people. She promised that my problem would be handled soon.

Indeed, not long after my visit to the office, the LC 2 chairman, the probation officer, and the LC 1 executive committee held a meeting at our home with my brother and me. They ordered that our parents' property be divided equally between my brother and me. Any property bought by my brother was his, and I could not claim any of it. Only what had belonged to our dead parents was to be divided.

I was not the only one facing such problems of inheritance. Many women had returned from Rwanda with no hope of ever going back, because their husbands were either dead or missing. The authorities, I learned, had handled several similar cases before mine.

I think I need to lie down for a short while. I feel sleepy. I told you I did not sleep very well last night. Slim is such a bad disease. It does not allow me to do much work these days. I get tired easily. I depend more on the children to do most of the work. I used to have months of respite, sometimes as much as six months, but not anymore. I suppose the disease is growing. Without TASO, life would be very difficult.

TASO helps people suffering from slim. It employs good people who teach us how to look after ourselves, what to eat, and how not to infect other people. I told you I did not breast-feed my daughter. TASO people provided the milk I gave her for a long time. They taught me how to mix it and how to feed her. Even after I left the hospital, they continued to bring the milk and check on me at home. They got to understand my home situation and the problems I was facing. Besides giving me foodstuffs like sugar, beans, cooking oil, and maize flour, TASO staff regularly bring me soap and a little bit of money to buy paraffin and food. I sell the oil, some of the soap, and some of the sugar. My children like *bushera*. It is sweet and does not need sugar. We do not need all the soap. It is the same for the cooking oil; we do not use much of it. TASO also pays my medical bills. It teaches us how to prepare our children to manage on their own when we die. Even before this free education was introduced, my children did not pay school fees. So you see why I am very grateful to God for TASO.

You know, with this disease, I get hungry a lot. I need to eat often, but only a little each time. You are spoiling me, putting this flask of tea beside me like I am the wife of a chief.

I was talking about my brother and the property. The land was divided. I got a piece of it and part of the banana plantation. I also got Maama's house, but, as I told you, my brother had repaired it very poorly and refused to repair it again after it collapsed. He was bitter that I had got some of the property. His wife's attitude became even more hostile. But I ignored them as much as possible. Fortunately, at the time I was not very weak. I had enjoyed about two months of strength. I had even managed to work in people's gardens to earn some money. With this money I bought timber and paid men to repair the house. I made sure it was well done, not like the way my brother had done it. I wanted to show him and his cruel wife that I was not living at their mercy.

The house stands strong even now. It has become another cause of dispute between my brother's family and me.

The piece of land and plantation I got as my share continued to eat away at the heart of my brother and his wife. They continued to be nasty to me, and this disturbed me a great deal. I knew that with my sickness, I could die anytime. I did not want to leave the children with hateful relatives. I wanted so much to be friends with my brother's family.

One day, I called him. We sat alone and talked. He is not really bad. He is only weak and allows himself to be controlled by his wife. She poisons his mind against me. I said to him, "Child of my mother, you see I am sick. My sickness is not the kind that gets cured. I am in and out of the hospital all the time. One time, it will be my body that will be brought home. Tell me, my only brother, when I die, will you take care of my orphans?"

He did not hesitate but answered straightaway. These were his very words: "I will never mix my children with children of foreign blood. I will not have Banyarwanda on my father's land."

"What will you do? Send them out into the cold?" I asked him.

"They will go back to their country. To their relatives."

"But you know what happened in that country. They would not know where to go. They would not find any of their people. They are either dead or scattered as refugees in other countries."

"That is not my problem. I don't want your sons on my children's property," he concluded with finality.

Then I asked him whether, supposing my children lived on another property and not this one, he would care for them once I was gone.

"I am not asking you to feed or dress them," I added. "Suffering has made them mature beyond their years. They are able to fend for themselves. But without me, they would need an adult to guide them. Would you be an uncle to them? Someone they could turn to for help and advice? Would you receive them as children?"

"No," he answered. "With property of their own, your children would no longer be children. They would be men. They would be bigheaded and would not listen to my advice. If your children do not respect me now while you are still alive, would they respect me when you are dead? Would they respect me when they are property owners?" he asked.

That's when I realized that I had to do something to get my children away from my brother's compound. As I told you before, God is powerful. At Mutolere Hospital, there was a *muzungu* working with TASO. Remi was this white woman's name. She knew me as a member of TASO and knew my situation very well. She visited my home several times and became my friend. I told her how my brother had become more hostile after I got some of the property. I told her my children would not be safe if I died and left them with my brother. They needed to live away from that family. She explained that TASO did not have a lot of money. She advised me to pray. Later she returned to her country.

Remi was very good to my sons. When she returned to her country, I thought that was the end of our friendship. But she did not forget my sad situation.

One day, I got a message calling me to the TASO office at Mutolere Hospital. I was told that Remi had sent me a present. You see, when Remi returned to her country, she collected money from her friends. This was the present she had sent. The money totaled three hundred fifty thousand shillings. Remi sent it to me to buy a piece of land for my children. Madam, you cannot imagine my happiness. There are good people in this world, and Remi is one of them. May God bless her and give her a husband!

With the money, I bought a piece of land. I have a copy of the agreement. A relative of mine, a doctor, keeps the original at the hospital. I trust him. My enemies might take the agreement when I am very sick or unconscious and destroy it. Then, after I am dead, they could turn against my children and chase them off their land. I keep all original documents in a safe place at the hospital.

Now I had land, but no house. We could not live on empty land, could we? But where was I to get the money to build a house?

By God's kindness, the house got built. This is how it happened. Dr. Albert, also working with TASO, took pity on me. He also knew my story of harassment by my brother's family. He approached the principal of Nyakabanda Technical School. He explained my situation and asked if the students, during their practical lessons, could build the house for me. The principal agreed. They built a big three-bedroom house with a store in one of the main rooms. It has an iron roof. My greatest wish is to add a fourth bedroom. Then each of my four children would have a room to himself. This would prevent quarrels later, when they are living without me.

I have a home for the children now, but that does not mean my problems are over. My brother and his wife still regard the piece of the family land that was given to me as theirs. They still don't agree that a daughter has a right to inherit. They insist my share of the property is in the home where I married. My brother's wife still harvests bananas from my part of the plantation. When I send the children to harvest from my gardens, they are attacked, and the crops are taken away from them.

I went to the Legal Aid clinic again for help. This time I wanted my sister-in-law arrested for assaulting my children when they were harvesting from their own garden. I was very sad when I was told that the woman officer who had helped me before had left. The person I found there said she was only keeping the office. She did not know anything about legal matters. I went there several times after that but found it either closed or occupied by the same woman.

There is another problem. I told you how my brother refused to repair Maama's house for me again and I had to do it myself? When I moved to my new home, my brother wanted to simply take it over. But I would have none of it. Not after the way they had treated me, my brother and his wife. These are the same people who made me sleep out in the open with a one-month-old baby. They wanted to rent it out, to operate it as a shop. Why should those greedy dogs earn money from my mother's house when they had refused to repair it after it collapsed? And they are the very same people who do not even want to look at my sons!

Where do they expect me to put my sons? Throw them in Chuho River? They would not make any fuss if the children were daughters. They would instead be examining the buds on their chests, longing to see them open before they could rush to get bride-price. Would they hesitate to demand bride-price for the "foreigners," as they refer to my children?

Let us continue with the story. I was telling you about the house. I locked it up when I left, and it will remain locked until they give me the money I spent on its repair. That is all I am asking for.

After failing with the women's office, I reported to the LC 1 chairman of the village. He has not done much to help. He said that if my sons are attacked again when they go to harvest, they should raise an alarm. They have done that a number of times, but nobody has answered their calls for help. The neighbors say they do not wish to get involved in family matters. What I fear most now is that the children might fight back one day. They are growing. They are becoming men. What if one day they are goaded into hitting that woman? She could even be killed! Can you imagine that? This could easily happen when I am not alive to keep them under control. Now, I warn them to hold their anger. But who will restrain them when I am gone? The problems with my brother's family are not yet over. And the constant quarrels and lack of peace are not good for my poor health. I should try to end the conflicts, and with God's help, I will.

Quest for Freedom

PHILOMENA RWABUKUKU

The minibus rolled down the hill, sliding, skidding, and squeaking until it slithered into a ditch. It stopped halfway across the road, the tires on the near side dangerously off the ground and the body precariously leaning against the steep incline. Overhead, a huge chunk of earth, loosened by the heavy rain that still intermittently fell, threatened to collapse. Every passenger's face was grim, eyes filled with foreboding. Lips were pressed together as if each person was afraid of uttering the word that might send the chunk of earth crashing down.

"Get out! All of you get out and push!" the conductor yelled unnecessarily. Everybody got out of the taxi slowly, carefully, afraid that the slightest movement could send it rolling.

"All right! Puuush!" the man shouted. The taxi zigzagged across the road, and everybody screamed and scampered as it suddenly turned and faced the direction we had come from. The male passengers pushed, tugged, and cursed until the old taxi was cajoled into facing the right direction.

By silent, mutual agreement, all the passengers walked behind the taxi without anyone suggesting that we board. It groaned up the hill slowly, moving like some drunkard, staggering and veering until it stopped about half a kilometer away from where it had veered off the road.

From that point on, we moved with less difficulty as the slopes became gentler. Every now and then, the vehicle would have to stop to allow the herds of cattle that crisscrossed the road and dotted the landscape to pass. Sometimes there would be a man with a stick on his shoulders guiding the cattle. Other times it was a little boy, or the cattle grazed by themselves. At one herd, the driver hooted and raved, threatening to run over a calf that adamantly stood in the middle of the road. Startled, the calf leaped and fell, its eyes glazed.

"Oh! How heartless!" the old man screamed at the driver.

"Maybe he's a Mwiru. Have you ever seen such cruelty to a calf?" The other passengers joined in ridiculing the driver. "Get up, brother, and may you live long!" they said, addressing the calf as they would a beloved person.

Slightly after seven, I was in Buhembe village, Kazo county, seated next to Nankunda in her father's compound. She is the firstborn of six children, some of whom are still at school. She was educated up to primary seven before she dropped out, owing to lack of school fees. Her family boasts of a strict Christian background, which groomed Nankunda into a well-disciplined girl.

Nankunda Mbarara of Kazo is twenty-six years old. At eighteen she married Kanyesigye, a possessive and cruel man who battered her constantly. She left him after two years and now lives with her parents. She wants a divorce from him, citing cruelty and adultery as her reasons. Her husband and his family are against it, although the church, the local officials, and FIDA have all recommended nullification of the marriage. But due to Ugandan law on divorce, which favors the male spouse, and the slow judicial system, the chances of Nankunda getting legal redress soon are hanging in the balance.

*N*ankunda began. "We saw each other. We fell in love. We wanted to wed. Hmm . . . I first saw him at Rwemikoma church during a Sunday service. That day, I felt, rather than saw, someone watching me. I could not turn to look because I was seated next to my mother. Surprisingly, she had already noticed how distracted I was and kept pointing out the verses the pastor was quoting. And then . . . then . . . the pastor told us to wish the nearest person peace with an embrace instead of the usual handshake. From my mother's embrace I turned to my left, and there he was, waiting for the godsend embrace. It was the warmth in his eyes that was my undoing! For looking into them felt as if I had suddenly walked from a chilly room into early morning sunshine!

"Strange emotions assailed me. I felt so confused. It was an experience I had never had in all my eighteen years. From that Sunday, Kanyesigye became a regular worshipper at our church. I began to desperately look forward to Sundays. Soon I realized that after every service, Kanyesigye would create an opportunity to meet and greet me. Then it occurred to me that he was attracted to me, too. The good girl who had been accustomed to hurrying home soon after church found herself looking for excuses to remain at church a little longer or walking slowly, hoping that Kanyesigye would come round for small talk. And he always did, accompanied by a friend of his from our village. My heart would burn with a fire hitherto unknown to me. At times I would feel guilty about my feelings, but soon I got accustomed to them.

"Then one Sunday, I did not see him. As we left the church compound and I desperately looked around, praying it was just a matter of time before he showed up, the friend tapped me on the shoulder and told me that he had a message for me. 'It's from Kanyesigye. He greets you. And he says that you should reply to this letter,' he said as he slipped the letter into my hand."

Nankunda hurried home and immediately went into the kraal, pretending to check on the calves. And there, behind the calves, she savored the words in the letter. For several minutes, she stood among the animals, rubbing her sweating hands together. Later that night, she wrote a short letter to Kanyesigye.

"I just told him that his letter was very good but that we needed some time to think about it."

Three months later, Kanyesigye sent a *kateerarume* to Nankunda's father to start marriage negotiations. Nathan was very pleased about his daughter's marriage prospects and sent the *kateerarume* to say that he was ready to receive his daughter's suitor.

In May 1994, an introduction ceremony was arranged. Kanyesigye, accompanied by his father and relatives, came to Nankunda's home to be officially introduced as a prospective son-in-law. Nankunda's family and other people of her clan gathered for the occasion.

"That day," she said, "is one I will always remember despite what has happened to me!

"My in-laws came carrying two pots of local brew, one of which was placed in the middle of a circle of low stools that had been arranged earlier. As if on cue, the elders, who had been hovering around, came and occupied all the twenty stools. Each elder carried a walking stick."

These elders had been invited by Nathan to help him discuss the *enjugano* with his in-laws. The drink was to help keep the elders' throats wet as they deliberated on such important matters. Though in Kazo-Nyabushozi bride-price involves paying about fifteen cows, Nankunda's parents settled for a token payment of only five cows, because Nathan said that he was not inclined to turn his daughter's marriage into a commercial transaction. The second pot of beer was placed before the elders as soon as the bride-price was settled. This is called *ensiima*—appreciation for the acceptance and sealing of the marriage agreement between the two families.

A few days after the introduction ceremony, Nankunda's father's brothers accompanied him to Kanyesigye's home. There, they were led to a kraal from which they selected five cows that they considered suitable for the bride-price. After this, they were entertained with a great feast before they left to take the five cows to Nathan's kraal. The week that followed saw Kanyesigye and his relatives returning to Nankunda's home to communicate the date of the wedding. It had been scheduled for August. Nathan reciprocated by treating his in-laws to a luncheon.

On August 27, 1994, the eve of her wedding day, Nankunda's parents held a give-away ceremony, locally known as *omuhingiro*.

"This was the day my family bid me farewell and presented *emihingiro* to my husband," Nankunda said. When I asked her what *emihingiro* is, she explained, "These are gifts every bride must receive from her parents at her wedding, or she will be ridiculed by her in-laws."

Nankunda paused as if she was reflecting on some profound issue. And then, with her eyes shining, she told me about her dowry. "My parents did me proud. They gave me a colorful send-off. My going-away gifts included a double bed with its mattress, bedsheets, a blanket, a bed cover, cups, plates, and other household items. It all cost 1.5 million shillings!"

With pride, Nankunda pointed to a raised platform, which was decorated with gray and black patterns made from ash and soot. On the platform were several black milk pots and gourds with beautifully woven lids, which were also done in different patterns and colors. After washing and polishing the milk pots and gourds, Nankunda covered them with a white netting, which had beads around the hem, making another attractive pattern around the platform.

"Do you see all that? Those are items a Muhima wife must have. They are essential for the preparation, preservation, and serving of milk and other cow products. Such items were among my *emihingiro*. Then there's that!" she said, suddenly bursting into hearty laughter and pointing. "*Engyemeko!* Ha, ha, ha!" Her mirth making me very curious, I encouraged her to tell me about the *engyemeko*.

"Oh, it was so funny!" she continued, laughing. "My aunt carried it in soon after the other gifts had been presented. Holding it aloft, provocatively swaying her hips, she shouted, '*Emihingiro, emihingiro!* The most important of all gifts is here! Ladies and gentlemen, I bring in the Marriage.' Aunt was carrying a special earthenware pot specifically made for married women. Traditionally, I am supposed to collect and boil herbs in that pot and use them to prepare myself for sex with my husband. Everyone present accorded its presentation a standing ovation."

Nankunda further explained that handing over the *engyemeko* to Kanyesigye was the symbolic declaration of his conjugal rights, which are considered the core of a marital relationship. Without *engyemeko*, the man and his people have a right to reject the *emihingiro* and say no to the marriage.

"Addressing my in-laws, my father said, 'Kanyesigye, my newly born son, and all of you, my dear in-laws, I have given you your wife, Nankunda. Keep her well. The *emihingiro* you see there are signs of our love for her and respect for you. From today onward, she belongs to your clan. When she comes here, she will be a visitor. May she live with you in peace.' There followed a lot of clapping and ululating, as the guests were now sure that I belonged to them. In order to further celebrate that day, a sumptuous banquet was set before the in-laws and the invited guests."

The following day, August 28, 1994, at St. Peter's Church in Rwemikoma, a pastor joined Nankunda and Kanyesigye in holy matrimony.

That was a historical event in Kazo, because Kanyesigye and his younger brother held a double wedding.

"I tell you, ours was the wedding everyone talked about for a long time. Imagine two brides coming into the same homestead. Big personalities attended; two bands played at our reception at Bugarihe! The cameras kept clicking and flashing until we were almost blinded! It was a wedding beyond my dreams."

Nankunda showed me two large albums of photographs taken at the church and at the wedding reception. She was a happy bride in white, with her groom smiling as he looked into her eyes. Their happy faces promised a bright future.

Soon Nankunda began to settle into the routine of married life. She so much wished to please her husband, to make him happy. But it did not take her long to realize what a difficult task it was going to be. She was supposed to do all the domestic chores as well as graze and water the cattle and milk the cows. She wondered why her husband was not helping. She was also expected to till the land and grow crops for their food.

Frowning, she recounted, "During the day, I would wander with the animals looking for pasture, after which I would take them to water. Milking would follow; then I would have to prepare meals. At night I would collapse into bed, exhausted. Still my husband expected me to satisfy him sexually. 'You turn this way!' he would demand. Though I obliged most of the time, I could not match his vigor. And the stench of his breath from the local brew always made me sick! We disagreed almost every night and barely had enough time to rest. The following morning I would be very angry with him, but he would behave as if nothing had happened. He would drink just as heavily and return home stinking. We would quarrel; then he would force me to have sex with him. 'Is there another husband in this home? Otherwise how do you explain not wanting me!' he would shout at me. Then one day he decreed, 'Never leave this home without my permission. If you ever dare to do so, count yourself dead.' From that day on, I could neither attend church services on Sundays nor go shopping. Even when I fell sick, the man would escort me to the health center to ensure that I interacted with no one.

"After he was away from home for long hours, he would start quarrelling from the time he got to the gate. 'Tell me whom you have been entertaining during my absence!' Kanyesigye would demand. To this, I would answer, 'Nobody, husband. You also know that I do not see anybody except you.'"

Her husband would insist that she account for the footprints or bicycle tire marks in their courtyard. "It did not matter to him that our house was so close to the road! Or that I had the heavy chores that left me with neither the time nor energy to entertain anyone!"

Nankunda's husband started beating her regularly in order to make her reveal the identities of the intruders. She wondered why her husband was so possessive and unnecessarily suspicious. Shaking her head, she said, "My husband had jealousy stored in a huge granary so that every time he returned home, he threw off the lid and unleashed it on me! He would beat me up, and most of the time no one would know about it because he would lock me up in the house and pay a health worker to treat the bruises, wounds, and swellings until I recovered. He would guard the house to ensure that no one saw me and that I saw no one except that damn health worker. Then I would go back to work like a donkey, as if nothing had happened."

By the end of their first year of marriage, the battering had become so severe and frequent that Nankunda could no longer keep quiet. She needed help, urgent help, or else one day people might find a dead body and fail to trace the killer. That was when she started reporting the cases to the Local Council chairmen.

"The first time I went to the LC chairmen, we were counseled and told to reconcile. Kanyesigye told everybody that he would not touch me again. We went back home together, and I was feeling reassured. However, before a week elapsed, he jumped for my throat again. I went back to the LCs. When they called him, he said that he had been tempted by the devil. This time he begged me for forgiveness, and the LCs told me that marriage was all about forgiveness. This soon became a routine. I started getting angry with the LCs for not taking any action against Kanyesigye. You see," she said, pointing to a pile of documents, "all these are letters to and from the LC officials about our cases. This one, dated August 27, 1995, says that I was beaten very severely. This other, of November 4, 1996, describes how I was battered. This one, of March 2, 1996, states that I was severely battered and in bad shape. And so on and so forth. You can see the heap, and they are all about the severity and frequency of the battering."

Nankunda said that other times she would run away to her parents, but it would not be easy. "Often my sisters-in-law or my husband's aunts or uncles would help me escape. They would hide me for a few days or accompany me at night."

In each case, Kanyesigye or his father would follow her to bring her back to her marital home. Some elders would sit and discuss the problem. Kanyesigye and his father would apologize to Nankunda and her people, after which they would leave with her or give her time to recover from the beating, then fetch her. During these meetings, Kanyesigye never once came up with a specific reason for his behavior, which forced Nankunda's mother to sternly demand, "Tell us what you want to kill her for. Is she dirty, sloppy, or disobedient? Does she not fulfill her wifely duties? Hmm? Does she deny you your rights or what? Eeh? Why do you treat her so?"

Kanyesigye did not make any accusations before his in-laws. Nankunda mimicked how he used to answer these questions: "I do not want to say anything about it. I just want my wife back." The people who heard him were convinced that Kanyesigye loved his wife and that the conflicts would lessen as the couple grew closer in marriage.

But that was not to be. As soon as they got back to their home, he would batter her heavily, as if to compensate for the many days he had spent without beating her. By the end of 1996, Nankunda felt she could not endure it any longer. She went away to her parents and stayed for a year, testing the possibility of a separation. It was when she was still there that she had her firstborn, a girl. Though her parents loved and sympathized with her, she found staying with them rather uncomfortable.

"I had lived in my own home for two years. It was not easy to fit into my parents' home again. Our relatives who came home made it more difficult for me. They ridiculed me, saying that I had failed to sustain my marriage." She wondered what was to become of her. What a burden she had become to her parents! They had been so good to her all her life, and now she felt she was becoming a big problem to them.

Thus, when her husband came for her toward the end of 1997 and begged for her forgiveness, she readily agreed to return to him. He claimed to be a changed man since he had become a born-again Christian. He told her how he had stopped drinking, which had been the main cause of his violence. Seeing Kanyesigye so humbled, begging and crying, had convinced her that God had heard her prayers to provide a home for her child.

However, Nankunda's faith and hopes were short-lived. Soon after her return, her husband reverted to his old self. He again started selling their cattle and spending the money on alcohol and women. Whenever he sold an animal, he would drink copiously until the last coin was gone. He was not bothered by financial obligations to his wife or daughter. One time, he returned home after three days and commanded her to name her lovers. He said to her, "Today you will tell me the men who were here while I was away. You will tell me what they were doing here!"

Enraged by his unfair accusation and broken promise, she shouted back at him, "What kind of husband are you that you should stay away for three days and come back to make such demands? Look at you, drunk again! Is this what you were talking about when you begged me to return to you? Eeh? Our last cow—see what you have done! Is that the piece of land we agreed to buy? Drinking has become your wife! Tuh! Let me spit you out lest you make my mouth stale!"

"You woman, if you don't shut up, I'll show you real manhood today," he said as he approached her threateningly.

"And what do you call real manhood? This drunkenness, hopelessness—this stench! Tuh! Let me spit again before I puke," she shot back, blinded by rage.

"Wife! That's what you are. A woman! How dare you insult me! Do it again and you will see the man in me!"

All caution gone, she spat into his face and jeered at him, upon which he grabbed her and pulled her toward the bedroom.

"Tonight you'll tell me about whoever has given you this confidence!" he shouted as he tossed her against the opposite wall and bolted the door.

As she recalled this incident, Nankunda trembled, and her eyes brimmed with tears. "The man killed me that day. He descended on me like a heavy hailstorm. He punched and pounded and hammered until my body was a bleeding mass." She showed me the scars left on her body by the injuries he inflicted on her.

"See here? My ankles are now permanently swollen because of the stick he lashed at me with, like a warder's baton! Hmm. See my head? This scar and this one and this. They are so deep! No hair will ever grow there! See my arms? Were I to undress, you would be shocked. My whole body is like some cruel traditional healer subjected it to excessive incisions. And here! That's where my fingernails used to be. He pulled them out. And look! Do you see any toenails? He got a pestle, grabbed my right foot, and pounded it until all the nails were loosened from the toes. I screamed and begged for mercy, but he wouldn't listen. He grabbed my right foot, and I thought my heart was going to fall out. I yelled and shrieked. By the time he was through, my body was dead to pain. And he talks of love! I swear in God's name I will never set foot in Kanyesigye's house again. Never!"

More than four years after that battering, Nankunda's left knee remained swollen as if it had an abscess. Both her ankles were abnormally plump. There were two ugly black scars on her left breast, looking as if they had been freshly opened. She kept fragments of the *enkoni*, which she extracted from her body after her husband beat her with it. After that terrible battering, Nankunda reported the case to the Local Council chairman, but he referred her case to the police. The police in turn sent her to a doctor to get a medical report. The severity of the injuries prompted the police constable in charge of Rwemikoma's police post to order the arrest and prosecution of Kanyesigye. Unfortunately, a relative tipped Kanyesigye off, and he escaped to Mbarara.

To Nankunda's chagrin, the medical examination also revealed that she was two months pregnant, at which she shed tears. "During the four months I spent recovering I hoped and prayed that I would miscarry. But I did not. I carried the pregnancy to full term, though every day my prayer had been centered around one thing: a miscarriage. I am now glad I did not miscarry, because my baby girl became such a consolation during those very difficult times."

After she recovered, she vowed to seek a divorce from Kanyesigye no matter what. She no longer cared about the stigma and labels that people attach to women whose marriages fail. She now knew that Kanyesigye could easily kill her. She had to find a way to annul that marriage so that she would be free of him forever.

Nankunda's parents helped her follow up the case with the Local Council court at Buhembe, which later forwarded it to the two courts at Burunga. All three Local Council courts concurred and recommended that Kanyesigye and Nankunda dissolve their marriage. They endorsed a letter, which in part read, "This woman E. Nankunda has been beaten and battered so many times that we have lost count. It is the concern of all people here to see that she gets redress. . . . We recommend that this marriage be annulled."

Nankunda did not stop at that. She also went to the church where she had been wedded and presented her case. The pastor and the church council were acquainted with the Kanyesigye affair and had earlier been involved in counseling and reconciling the couple. Now they too realized that Nankunda could easily be killed. After a lengthy meeting, the council authorized the pastor to write a letter recommending that Nankunda be assisted to file for divorce. Part of this letter read, "They started their quarrels and fighting as soon as they started their marriage. E. Nankunda was always cruelly beaten by Kanyesigye, the husband, and everybody here knows that. . . . Moreover, Kanyesigye has been engaged with another wife with whom they have one child. . . . I advise this couple to be parted if there is any legal means that can be undertaken to secure life and freedom."

This letter was also countersigned by the church leaders at Kazo archdeaconry, who further recommended that Nankunda should see the Diocesan bishop Kyamugambi in Mbarara for further assistance. Nankunda sadly recalled, "I even traveled to Mbarara to see the bishop. The bishop sent me to a lawyer who handles church cases. Do you know what that man told me? To pay half a million shillings! A friend had sponsored my trip to Mbarara. Could I even tell him that I had only ten thousand shillings? With my burden weighing heavily on my back, I went back to my parents frustrated and discouraged."

Meanwhile, Nankunda's father-in-law came to her home regularly seeking to settle matters between her and his son. According to him, Nankunda was "their" wife whether her husband wanted her or not. They, as a family and as a clan, had married her, and he wanted her back. He insisted he would not settle for anything less. Tradition and custom demanded that Nankunda return to her marital home. She felt helplessly trapped in a marriage turned foul. Although her parents supported her all the way, she was worried that she might be forced to return to Kanyesigye.

In 2000, the International Federation of Women Lawyers went to Kazo. These FIDA legal officers went to Rwemikoma subcounty to educate the local community about their existence and functions. They held meetings with both local and church leaders. This is where Jovia, Nankunda's mother, learned that FIDA offered legal advice and assisted people, especially women who had legal problems. Moreover, there were practically no legal fees involved.

Of course, many people in Kazo had heard about FIDA, but they had shunned it because it was associated with women activists and the campaign for the emancipation of women. Most people in the area perceived it as a negative force that sought to dismantle the established order of things. Many women had been warned never to heed the nonsense preached by FIDA. Wives had also seen FIDA as a threat to the stability they enjoyed in their homes and relationships.

After interacting with the visiting officers, people's attitudes toward FIDA changed, and their hopes were raised. They heard that, besides counseling and reconciling people, FIDA also helped disadvantaged women to understand and use the law for settling conflicts.

Talking about what she felt like then, Nankunda said, "As I listened to those people, I saw a new dawn come for us women of Kazo. My hope of divorcing Kanyesigye was revitalized."

When Nankunda approached the group leader, she was advised to go to the FIDA offices in Mbarara, because the officers had already been away for three days and had to return that day.

The following week saw Nankunda in Mbarara seeking whatever help FIDA could offer. When she presented her case, FIDA officials thought they should call her husband and talk to him before proceeding.

"This seemed like delaying issues to me," complained Nankunda. "But then I said to myself that if this was going to speed up the process, I had better comply."

She found Kanyesigye in a suburb of Mbarara town and delivered to him a letter that FIDA had written to summon him to their office. Instead of reporting to FIDA, he followed her to Rwemikoma to threaten her.

She remembered that day, saying, "When the taxi got to Rwemikoma, there was Kanyesigye, ordering me to alight."

He said to her, "You woman, get off that vehicle and explain what this letter is all about!"

Looking at him with contempt, she screamed at him, "Can't you read for yourself? Did you have to come all the way from Mbarara to ask me, or are you looking for an excuse to batter me again?"

Her voice rising a bit and her nostrils dilating, she continued, "I refused to get out of the taxi. How could I be sure he hadn't come to finish me off? Let me tell you, I *fear* that man. Up to now, he has never gone to FIDA. Several other letters were sent to him, but he ignored them all."

Instead, his father is the one who showed up to confront Nankunda. These two could not reach an agreement because she wanted her freedom, and he insisted that he wanted her back in her marital home. She recalls with resentment how her father-in-law angrily shouted at her, "If you think I will allow a divorce, then you have a long time to wait. And don't you imagine I am interested in the *enjugano*, either. It's you, our wife, I want back."

She pleaded, "Sir, all I need is to be released. To be free to continue my life. Surely you know how much I have suffered at your son's hands."

"Woman," he replied, "we married you, and you will remain our wife as long as we still want you."

She wondered what he meant by "we still want you." Though she could see that he was getting more adamant, she sought to make him see reason. "Sir, do you want me dead? I wish to see my children grow. I want to be able to look after them. Your release will enable me to work. Maybe I will run a shop. Perhaps I could do—"

He rudely interrupted with such force that she thought he was going to hit her. "Woman, I have already said no! And let me warn you, if you stock that shop you talk about, it will mean your death. You will die in that shop, I assure you."

Seething with rage, frustration, and despair, she shouted back, "You do not understand at all, old man. Don't you realize that your son does not want me anymore? Are you going to marry me?"

It took the intervention of two FIDA officials to calm the two down and prevent an exchange of blows.

They discussed the possibility of Nankunda getting a divorce and tried to make her father-in-law understand that if she wanted to leave the marriage, she could. She had a right to freedom. The law was on her side. The husband had been treating her so cruelly, so crudely, that even the church had recommended a nullification of the marriage. The church seldom talks of divorce and rarely allows couples to separate, its focus being on counseling and reconciliation in order to keep the spouses together for life.

But Nankunda's case was unique, and it was treated as such. The old man was asked if he was aware of all the accusations against Kanyesigye. For instance, hadn't there been occasions when Nankunda had run to him for redress after a battering? What about Kanyesigye's infidelity and promiscuity?

At the mention of promiscuity, Nankunda asked her father-in-law, "Aren't you aware that your son has started sleeping with Luusi, a widow whose husband died of AIDS? Do you know that Luusi has been down several times and clearly shows signs of HIV/AIDS? Have you so soon forgotten how your dear son pounded my toenails and fingernails? Do you want me back so that he can chop off my toes and fingers and then my limbs? And why should you be the one to come for me? Don't you know your son deserted me? I have been living at my parents' home for almost five years now, and your son has never stepped in my father's home!"

The FIDA officers agreed with her, saying she had the right to leave her husband and to have custody of her children if she proved to the court she was capable of looking after them. They explained that Kanyesigye could be ordered to provide for her and the children even after their divorce.

Nankunda was thrilled to learn that all these conditions weighed heavily in her favor. She said to her father-in-law, "Sir, I intend to file for divorce now that I understand what the law says. I shall be free yet."

"Go ahead and file for divorce," he threatened. "I shall be ready for you. I will make sure you don't win the case." She feared he might use his wealth to influence the court, knowing that she was penniless.

She now said, "I felt intimidated, but I did not give up. When I went back, I asked the lawyer to help me get out of the miserable marriage.

Kanyesigye, in addition to beating me, had had numerous affairs. He even had a child with another woman! I provided the lawyer with all that as evidence against him to support my quest for a divorce."

But the lawyer's response infuriated her rather than calmed her. The lawyer said, "In Ugandan law, when a man proves his wife's sexual involvement with another man, she can be charged with adultery, and the man is therefore entitled to file for divorce. On the other hand, a man can only be charged with adultery if he is proved to have had sex with a married woman. And even then, if a man were proved adulterous, a wife would not sue him for divorce. The law does not recognize a man's adultery as grounds for his wife to divorce him."

After many discussions with the lawyer, Nankunda planned a new strategy. She remembered what the lawyer had told her: that a man could sue for divorce if he could prove the wife's adultery. She said, "That's when I decided to have a relationship. It would be adultery, and surely he too would be disgusted and perhaps grant me a divorce. And I am also human. I have feelings, too. I had been at my father's home for almost five years. And as luck would have it, I conceived! I was so happy. Now there was all the reason for him to get rid of me. But he has not shown any signs of wanting to give me a divorce."

◎◎

After narrating all this, Nankunda, her eyes full of hope, said, "But you have given me hope. I will go back to the FIDA offices and resume my quest for freedom. Don't you think I stand a chance?"

I told her that she did have a chance. I also told her that FIDA works in collaboration with the Legal Aid Project, another organization that handles court cases for disadvantaged people, especially women like her. Her interaction with me finally brought her to Kampala to see lawyers at the Legal Aid Project headquarters, where a file has been opened for her. Her hopes were revived when she learned that the Legal Aid Project was ready to pay her legal fees. She was told to find a lawyer who was willing to take on her case.

"I hope this will be soon," she said, knowing that in the slow Ugandan judicial system, cases can drag on and on for years. "Kanyesigye is still legally my husband and can walk in any time and make demands on me as his wife. That's partly why I have resorted to living with my parents until I am more certain of my circumstances."

Meanwhile, the law on divorce remains vague and slow, with many limitations that leave a woman with no clear escape from an unwanted relationship. Nankunda's hopes are hinged on the promises of the Legal Aid Project clinic. In the meantime, all she can do is wait—wait for that moment when she will win back her freedom.

Taste of Betrayal

Margaret Ntakalimaze

Bibiana Kanyamihigo offers me a wooden stool to sit on, taking one opposite me under the mango tree in front of her house. The house looks spacious from outside, with the usual durable corrugated iron sheets for a roof and walls made from volcanic stones of different shapes and shades, which form a beautiful pattern.

Dressed in a yellow skirt and a white blouse with an oversize blue pullover on top, she tugs at the neck of her pullover and squints at the sun overhead. It is an exceptionally warm afternoon for Kisoro. I smile at her, and she smiles back tentatively.

A tall middle-aged woman with an oval face and neatly braided black hair, Bibiana has soft skin, like that of a younger woman. When she was young, she put all her energies and resources into ensuring a better future for her family. But after the death of her teacher-husband of twenty-seven years, she discovered that he had had another family tucked away, to which he had given part of their land and other properties earned through her diligence and sweat. Now Bibiana finds herself struggling to regain what legally and morally belongs to her.

She turns her small dark eyes on me. They are sharp and compelling, and she has a way of staring without blinking, which I find quite unnerving at first.

"I hear you have suffered a lot," I say gently after she greets me. "Tell me about it."

She stiffens and is silent for some time. The light in her eyes dims, and her face creases with lines of pain.

"Where do I start?" she says eventually, not asking a question but thinking aloud. Then she falls silent again. There is a faraway look in her eyes.

My husband was Kanyamihigo, Aloysious Kanyamihigo. So I am Bibiana Kanyamihigo, and before my marriage, I was Bibiana Nyirankariza. Now I prefer to be called just Bibiana.

I got married when I was a young woman of twenty. Many young men wanted to marry me, but Aloysious was my favorite. He was very handsome, and every girl in our village wished he could marry her. But of course he could not marry them all; he chose me. I remember the envy the other girls felt when he asked me to marry him.

My parents did not know about him yet, I mean, not as my suitor, you know. His parents were our neighbors, so naturally our families interacted a lot. But Aloysious and I kept our friendship secret. But then he kept urging me to tell my parents so that he could come for an introduction. I felt a bit shy about telling my parents, because traditionally this is not the way it is done. But one evening, when no else one but my mother and I were at home, I gathered the courage to talk to her about him.

"Should I get married to him?" I asked her.

My mother looked at me for a moment and then replied, "Yes, my daughter, you couldn't have chosen better. He is a nice young man, he is educated, and he will treat you well. But don't you want to complete your studies first before you get married?" she asked rather sternly.

I had only one year to complete primary school. My parents wanted me to go to a teacher training college and become a teacher. I did not know how to tell her that I did not want to go on with schooling or that I did not want to become a teacher. At the moment, all I wanted was to become Aloysious's wife.

"Does it matter?" I asked my mother.

She looked at me as if I were out of my mind, and I hurried to explain that I was not really interested in further studies. "See, I can make children's and women's clothes," I assured her. I had always liked working with my hands and had won many prizes for my handiwork at school. And anyhow, how could I continue studying at the school where Aloysious was teaching?

My mother agreed that it could cause talk if people came to know that he was interested in marrying me. She also thought that it was high time I got married, anyway. So she promised to talk to my father about it.

I waited patiently. Eventually my parents agreed and made preparations for the wedding. On December 27, 1967, I got married to Aloysious Kanyamihigo. It was a memorable occasion—the wedding of the year, they called it. I received many presents from my parents, relatives, and friends. I lived with him happily, with our twelve children—five girls and seven boys—for twenty-six years. God has also blessed me with wonderful grandchildren from both my sons and my daughters. They usually come and stay with me, especially during Christmas.

At the time of our marriage, Aloysious Kanyamihigo, who was a grade two teacher, was the headmaster of Mutolere Primary School. A few years later, he left for upgrading at Ggaba Teacher Training College, leaving me behind to care for the family. We were staying on the school premises at the time, and my only activity, apart from taking care of my children and generally looking after the home, was sewing dresses for children by hand. When my husband eventually realized my great interest in tailoring, he arranged for me to take a course. His school was the ideal place to get customers, and many parents wanted me to make dresses for their children. Christmastime was the busiest, with every mother wanting new dresses or shirts and shorts for her children. Everybody in those days used to buy a new dress for Christmas, you know. Now Christmas means nothing to children or adults.

So for three months I learned how to use a sewing machine and cut dresses using paper patterns—things like that. When I finished the course, I was an expert dressmaker. The number of customers increased, and so did my speed and output. I was now confident enough to make ladies' dresses as well. Eventually I became exclusively a ladies' dressmaker and became well-known throughout Gasiza.

My mother had been a bit doubtful as to whether I could really make money from sewing. She was so happy now that she brought a piece of cloth for me to make her a dress. Since it was the first time for her to put on a dress made by her daughter, she decided to wear it at Christmas and tell everybody she met at church that her dress had been made by me, her daughter. After that, women flocked to my house to have dresses made just like my mother's. She made my tailoring business boom even more, I can tell you.

My business continued doing well, and I was able to rent a house at Gasiza trading center. I worked hard and sent money to my husband in Kampala to purchase cloth of different prints for me. I sold these to my customers, who then asked me to tailor them into dresses for them. Those were busy but happy times for me. With the profits I made from my tailoring business, I later bought a very big piece of land in Gasiza and a plot in Gasiza trading center.

When we were planning to start building a family house, my husband had to leave me alone once again, this time to go to Makerere University for further studies. However, this did not stop me from carrying on with our plans, despite the saying in Rufumbira, *Umugore tiyubaka inzu cyangwa akaba nitaka*, meaning that a woman does not build a house or own land. I went ahead and built the house you see now. I love this house, this place. I never get tired of watching this beautiful view. When we first moved into our new house here, the first thing I would do every morning was to open the bedroom window and gaze across and drink in that breathtaking beauty. My husband used to tease me, saying that I was like a *muzungu*, a European or white person. "You act as if you've never seen a mountain or a hillock before," he would say impatiently.

Even now, when I am besieged with all sorts of problems, gazing at that wonderful scenery somehow soothes me. And these people think they can banish me from all this to some hole in Mutolere-Gasiza!

But I am giving you the tail of the story—where was I? Yes, I was telling you how I came to build this house. Most of it was built while he was away pursuing further studies. Of course he came home for holidays and inspected the progress on the house and gave advice. You know how men tend to look down on women. Whenever the workers became big-headed and refused to follow my instructions, I would call him to come and sort out things or simply threaten them with his coming.

In 1985, he was promoted to the post of principal of Kisoro Teacher Training College, a position he held till his death in 1993. Later on, we bought more pieces of land in Gasiza and Muganza, my husband's birthplace. That is where most of our land is now. After the family expanded, we started developing the land and growing cash crops like Irish potatoes, peas, sorghum, and many others.

I plowed all the fields using the money I made from my tailoring business; it paid for hired labor. I bought the seeds and did the planting. Whenever I could, I would work with the porters planting and harvesting. I encouraged my children too to take an interest in the land, and they liked participating in harvesting the crops, which usually coincided with their school holidays.

My husband's job as a schoolteacher and, later, as a principal of a college, took up most of his time. But he contributed a lot in other ways to the development and welfare of the family, although teachers in those days, even head teachers, did not really earn a lot. It is the same thing today; two of my children are teachers and are always grumbling about the low pay.

Anyway, the harvested crops were stored in the house we built on our land in Muganza, but because the house was vacant, we decided to take in a tenant as a security measure against thieves. At first we rented the two rooms out to a certain driver. But later the Parent-Teacher Association of Muganza Primary School expressed their wish to rent a room for one of their teachers because they had no staff houses. My husband and I agreed and signed a tenancy agreement with a female teacher called Molly Rukundo.

Five months after Molly moved into the house, she gave birth. We did not know she was pregnant when we allowed her to rent our house. This kind of thing was frowned upon in those days—I mean, an unmarried woman, especially a schoolteacher, giving birth before marrying. Anticipating that she would be sacked from her job, my husband asked her to vacate the house.

But she apologized to the PTA and was allowed to continue teaching. So she stayed in the house as well. She later produced two more children, but no further action was taken against her.

Meanwhile, my sister-in-law, who was married to a man in Masaka, lost her husband. She sold her land and all her property there and came back to live in Kisoro. She bought a small piece of land near ours. When my husband and I realized how small her piece of land was, we decided to give her part of our land free of charge, for good.

It was the land I bought, but I did not think of it that way at the time. It was our land, my husband's and mine. Everything we had then belonged to us jointly. You know, you always become wiser after something like this happens. If I had known what a snake that sister-in-law of mine was, she would not have seen even an inch of that land, I assure you!

When I think of how I toiled to buy that land! How I denied myself so many things, how I would sometimes work the whole day without lunch in order to make enough money to buy more land so that our future and our children's future could be secure! You, Mutwarekazi, said you come from hereabouts, so you must know how scarce and precious land in Kisoro is.

My sister-in-law got greedy and wanted a bigger share of what she called her brother's land. When he refused to give her more, she took her complaint to the local authorities, claiming she was entitled to the family land. Family? What family? This was not clan land left behind by her father when he died. This land was bought by my husband and me through our sweat. She lost the case and was warned against raising it again.

I wouldn't say my husband was very close to her, but she was his sister—his only sister, actually—and you know about all this clan own-ership of land in Kisoro. People can't distinguish between ancestral and acquired land. As soon as you buy land, people think they are entitled to it just because they are family. But I wouldn't have minded if she had asked nicely and not demanded. She is not a good woman really; she never liked me from the beginning.

Then tragedy struck. My husband fell sick with a disease known in Bufumbira as *uruho*. It is a terrifying disease that makes the stomach swell so much that it looks like a drum. We took him to Mutolere Hospi-tal. He was there for a very long time, weak and in so much pain. I could not bear to look at him. But he tried to be cheerful for my sake and kept saying that he would get better soon.

After he had been in the hospital for about a year without getting better, he said he wanted to come back home. I talked to the nurse who was attending to him, but she told me that my husband was too weak to travel and would never get home alive. "Your husband is dying," she said brutally.

I could not believe or accept it. I prayed to God every night to make him better—oh, how I prayed, Mutwarekazi! But on September 14, 1993, my dear husband passed away.

The next day, his friends and relatives came to the hospital to take his body home. The arrangements for his funeral started, and it was agreed that the body should be taken to the ancestral burial grounds in Gasiza-Nyakabande. So we buried him there.

But even before his body was cold in the ground, my sister-in-law unfurled her claws. She ganged up with Molly, who was still renting our house in Muganza, to steal my property and land. I know it was my sister-in-law who incited Molly to claim that she was my co-wife and therefore entitled to retain the house she was staying in and the land on which it was built. I had bought that land with my own money, my savings made with sweat from my own body.

They did not stop there. They wanted to confine me to Mutolere-Gasiza, where I had only a plot—one I could not even use to grow enough food to feed my family! And who were they to tell me where to live and where not to live?

I did not have a will from him. I knew that when he died, all his property, including the many pieces of land we had bought together and all the other property, would be mine. He never said anything about anybody else being entitled to it, did he? My husband and I had built our home together, and we had never said, "This is mine, this is yours." Moreover, he was an educated man and never behaved like those who despise women and think that they cannot own land or property. But as soon as he died, all these troubles set in as if to mock me for believing I had a secure future.

When these people realized that I was determined to fight to the end for my rights, Molly, the so-called co-wife, sued me in the magistrate's court of Chahi in Kisoro. I was outraged by the audacity of the woman! Who was she to sue me? What contribution had she made toward acquiring the land she was so bent on snatching from me? That woman had impudence!

I do not accept that Molly's children are my husband's, as she was claiming; he never told me about them. Anyway, that was not the point. The point was that Molly was occupying my land and house illegally, because I was the rightful administrator of my husband's estate. Surely even these people at the Legal Aid clinic could see that.

Of course I was worried by the summons; in fact, I was deeply disturbed by the letter they sent me. I had thought that the letters from the administrator general giving me authority over the estate would end the matter, but apparently these people were determined to keep on disturbing me. I did not know what these officials at the Legal Aid clinic would do, and that worried me. Supposing they decided to take my land and other property away from me and give them to Molly, what would happen to my children and me then? Why were they on Molly's side when the facts spoke for themselves? Had she bribed them? I could not put it past her, especially with my sister-in-law's connivance. But even then, I vowed that I would not give up without fighting for what was legally and morally mine. I would go to the Legal Aid clinic and explain my side of the story.

Before I went, I made inquiries about this Legal Aid clinic, and I was told that it had just opened to provide legal advice and counseling to women with problems like mine. Few women knew about it, and so many did not make use of it. I can't imagine how Molly and her fellow conspirator came to hear about it, but then they were determined to move even mountains to take away everything I possessed.

While talking to people about the summons I had just received and seeking their advice on how to deal with that particular problem, I learned that the clinic had the reputation in Kisoro of being fair when helping people to resolve their conflicts. It was even responsible for saving some marriages by knocking some sense of responsibility into some men's heads, I was told. But that had never been a problem in my marriage. While my husband was still alive, we never had any quarrels about money and things like that. He paid school fees for the kids and gave me money for food. All my problems stemmed from those two women's greed after his death.

The next day after receiving the summons, I went to the Legal Aid clinic. I woke up very early in the morning in order to walk the three-kilometer distance while it was still cool. I had thought over the matter deeply as I lay in bed the previous night, and I knew that despite whatever lies Molly had told them, when they heard the truth, they would change their minds about threatening me with legal action.

I was fortunate enough to find the legal officer on duty already in the office. It was just before ten in the morning. After greeting me, the officer asked me what my problem was, and I showed him their summons.

"What do you say to the charges, then?" he asked.

I emotionally related my story and the machinations of my so-called co-wife and my sister-in-law to deprive me of my land and my husband's property. The officer listened attentively to my story. When I had finished, he said, "This is a court case. As the lawful wife of the late Kanyamihigo, you are entitled to inherit and administer his estates. But first, some investigations must be carried out by the Criminal Investigation Department of Kisoro to establish the facts. I will send them a letter to this effect."

He seemed to know what he was talking about, which was reassuring. I felt my spirits soar with hope once more. As I listened that morning, all I could think about was that I had been right to come, because it looked like this would help me to finally solve the problem. The official of the Legal Aid clinic appeared to agree with me that, as the lawful wife, I was entitled to administer my late husband's property. The law was on my side.

Little did I know how much suffering still awaited me.

I walked out of the place thoughtfully. My watch told me it was one o'clock, the time my younger children would be home from school for their midday lunch break. I quickened my step, but at the back of my mind the question of what had prompted my so-called co-wife to turn to the Legal Aid clinic kept nagging me. It must be the influence of my sister-in-law, I thought, and I vowed to defeat the two of them in court.

As I prepared supper for my family that evening, I pondered my problem further, and I knew that I was not alone in that kind of situation. If your husband is from Kisoro, Mutwarekazi, you will know the kind of situation I was pondering.

Actually, many women thought I was better off than they, and so did I at one time. But now? Life is so unfair, isn't it? How can women who toil so hard to develop the land be denied the right to own it? Men have absolute control of it, including its use. And then, after the poor woman has toiled and sweat, the man just waltzes over and takes all the proceeds from it, leaving the poor woman empty-handed. It is high time these laws were changed. Let women be allowed to own the land they till. If the man wants money to drink or buy prostitutes or to leave to his concubines after his death, let him work for it or find it elsewhere. Many conflicts in homes are not only about the battering of women; they are about disputes over ownership of land and its use between married couples, family members, and neighbors.

As I pondered my problems and those of other women in general, the food burned. My daughter noticed my pensive mood and asked me what was the matter. I did not want to worry her unnecessarily. The older children, already young men and women, some of them with families of their own, knew what was going on and were very supportive. But they were not living in Kisoro, and I did not want to disrupt their lives by dragging them into these wrangles. This was my problem, and I intended to deal with it myself.

One evening, when I was working in the fields, my youngest son came running and told me that there was a man at home who wanted to see me urgently. I went home, and the man—whom I recognized immediately as the information secretary of our area—gave me a letter summoning me to a meeting of elders the following day.

"What is the meeting about?" I asked suspiciously before reading the letter.

"I am just a messenger," he said rudely. Then he left.

I opened the letter and read it. It stated that the meeting was being called to discuss the dispute between Mrs. Bibiana Kanyamihigo and her co-wife, Molly Rukundo, regarding the late Aloysious Kanyamihigo's estate. It was copied to all the members who constituted the council of elders. I did not need to search far to know who was behind this meeting, but the matter had already been settled in court! I wondered what they wanted with me and could not help cursing the day that my late husband and I first set eyes on that evil woman Rukundo.

Before I went to bed that evening, I visited my mother and briefed her on the latest development in the saga. She urged me to be firm and to trust in God. My mother is a zealous Catholic. I have never known her to miss Sunday mass in her life.

The elders' meeting was scheduled for three o'clock that Saturday, October 26, 1994, at the council hall, which served as a meeting place during the day and a dance hall at night. I was there on time, but somebody else was there before me—my so-called co-wife, Molly Rukundo. We eyed each other like cocks about to jump at each other's necks. I took the seat farthest from hers and tried very hard to ignore her presence until the meeting opened.

The meeting was chaired by the district executive secretary and was attended by fourteen members. The chairman read the letter from the administrator general's office authorizing me to administer my late husband's estate to members of the council. Other letters—such as the one from the district executive secretary to the magistrate, one with the magistrate's response, and one from my lawyers indicating that matters had been settled in court and judgment passed in my favor—were all brought to the attention of the members.

Molly was asked to explain why she had gone to the court before going through other channels. Her response was that by the time Kanyamihigo died, she had had three children with him, her own home, enough land, one cow, houses for rent, and banana plantations, whose proceeds helped her to provide for her family. She disclosed that after the court's ruling, all this property and land were grabbed by her co-wife—Mrs. Bibiana Kanyamihigo—who also tried to evict her from the house and leave her and her children helpless. That was why she had gone to seek assistance from the magistrate's court.

I denied any knowledge of Molly as the mother of my late husband's children. My late husband had one home and several other houses that he was renting out, and, as far as I know, that woman calling herself my co-wife was just a tenant in one of our houses. My husband never told me about her or her alleged three children.

"That was why I evicted her from my land. I based my action on the court's ruling," I told them.

I said that as far as I was concerned, she was a mere tenant, and I had a right to evict her. I showed them a copy of the tenancy agreement my husband and I had signed with her.

I can't say that anything I said made any impression on the elders, although they did not seem to agree on whether the deceased had had two wives and two homes. Some claimed to have known about Molly as the late Kanyamihigo's wife and Muganza as his second home, while others professed ignorance. But since the majority supported the first view that Molly's claim was legitimate, it was decided that I was the wrongdoer. They further observed that it was customary in Bufumbira for a man to have more than one wife, and in the case of Molly, her status had been legitimized by the payment of bride-price to her parents. They, therefore, concluded that since Kanyamihigo had died without making a will, Molly had every right to hang on to the land and property that the deceased had put at her disposal in order to enable her to look after her children. That was the custom of Bufumbira, they claimed. I wondered why culture and customs are always invoked and become sacred and unchangeable only when women try to fight for their rights.

The resolution of the council of elders did not surprise me in the least, since Molly seemed to have every man in her pocket. But if they thought that I was going to follow their unfair judgment meekly, then they did not know the type of woman I was. To make matters worse, when I was sent a copy of the proceedings, the facts had been so distorted that I was compelled to write to the district executive secretary who had chaired the meeting and dispute the content. You see, a copy of the minutes had been sent to the administrator general in Kampala. I feared this could bias him and make him reverse his earlier decision that I be the sole administrator of my late husband's estate. Because, according to the version of the copy of the minutes I got, I had agreed to share everything with Molly and her children, which was not true.

I suppose you think I am a hard person? Well, I knew I was doing what I believed was right. That gave me the courage to go on fighting. But I became prone to bouts of depression, and although they say that we should never think ill of the dead, I even started to blame my late husband for burdening me with the consequences of his adultery. If I had known he was living a double life, I'd not have trusted him so much.

You know what they say about troubles coming in bundles? I had not recovered from the distorted report of the meeting, which Molly had received with jubilation—she was now going around telling everybody

that she had defeated me—when my sister-in-law dragged me back to
court again. She claimed that I had refused to give her part of her father's
land. She lost the case. Then she resorted to cutting down the banana
trees on my plantation and was arrested for trespassing and willful damage of property. She was remanded in prison for a year and a half. While
in prison, she got a lawyer who managed to have her case referred to the
High Court, and she was released on bail.

When I went to court to check on the case, I was told to wait for the
High Court summons. The High Court was in Kabale at that time. But
in the meantime, my sister-in-law and Molly were forbidden to trespass
on my land.

I waited to be summoned by the High Court for a long time. After
a year of waiting, I received the summons and consulted a lawyer. The
lawyer demanded a high payment to take up the case. I could not raise
the money. So I went to court with no legal assistance. The case dragged
on and on and was later adjourned till further notice. After another year
of waiting, I went back to the High Court in Kabale to check on the case.
To my surprise, there was a notice on the board informing all concerned
that my land case had been dismissed. I could not believe this. Nobody
had called me to hear the judgment.

Apparently it was news to Molly and my sister-in-law too, because
they went around telling people that they had defeated me once again,
burying me for good. I felt extremely bitter that after toiling over the
years to ensure my future, I should end up fighting for what is legally
and morally mine. I have suffered, Mutwarekazi; I have been tortured.

For a long time I tried to direct my anger against Molly and blame her
for everything I have endured since my husband died, but his infidelity
is the cause of most of this. I wonder why men who commit adultery are
not treated by society in the same way as adulterous women! Are they
condemned? No. They always veil their misdeeds in ancient customs and
traditions! But my husband is dead, and Molly is not. She is, therefore,
the enemy I must fight. I don't intend to give up for as long as I live.

I am tired of courts. There is no justice there. I know that now. But
I will make Molly pay one way or another. That land she is occupying
illegally, that house she calls her own, will never be hers. Never!

Not Until I Find My Daughter

∞

BANANUKA JOCELYN EKOCHU

Winnie Kirabo stands in the middle of her shop in disbelief. Someone removed some louvers from the window, entered the shop, and stole her most expensive fabrics. She is devastated. She has just returned from Kampala, where she had gone to follow up on the case that has turned her life into a nightmare.

A thirty-two-year-old mother of three, Winnie is tall and has dark skin and even teeth, whose whiteness is enhanced by her dark gums. Her beauty is even more pronounced when she smiles, something that, unfortunately, is becoming a rare occasion. She wears her hair short, a style that is favored by women from her part of the country.

She comes from Kenshunga in Rushere subcounty, Nyabushozi county, Mbarara district. Kenshunga is well-known for its abundant milk and vast grazing fields. The green pastures cover the hills, and the cattle, which graze at will, are the only interruption to the lush scenery.

Winnie never had the privilege of going to school. At a very young age, which she does not remember, she found herself in a very bad polygamous marriage. When her husband became violent, she left him, took her children with her, and started a new life. Winnie managed to build a comfortable existence for *her children and herself through enterprise and hard work. She was determined to ensure a future for them by giving them an education. However, through her eldest daughter, fourteen-year-old Anita, fate dealt Winnie a blow, turning her fortunes completely around.*

This is a heartbreaking tale of a mother determined to get justice—including appealing to the highest office in the country—against her daughter's defilers and kidnappers who use their might to deflect the course of law.

"I could not go on any longer. The man was a womanizer. On top of having many wives, he had other women outside. There was no happiness at all in the marriage, so I left," she says, her face showing the satisfaction of an achiever. She had a hard time coping alone, with three young children to feed and no source of income. However, Winnie was not going to allow hardship to dampen her spirits.

"People did not understand why I left my husband. They all said that there is no easy marriage and I should stay and make it work. Nobody wanted to help me. I was on my own, but I was determined to survive. My children needed food, shelter, and school fees. The realization that I was the only one who would provide them with these things gave me the strength to work hard," she says, recalling the hard times she went through to reach where she is now.

Not only was she determined to feed her children, but she was also going to give them what she herself had missed—an education. She was convinced that only those who were educated could get well-paying jobs, and she did not want her children to miss out.

"I am a living example. If I had had an education, I would not have had to struggle the way I did. I would have got a job like other educated women. I never went to school because my parents did not value education. I would not make the same mistake regarding my children."

She started by selling small items, like ghee, which is abundant in Nyabushozi since the people there keep cattle. She would take the ghee to Mbarara, Lyantonde, and Kampala, where it was in high demand and could therefore fetch a good price.

"I did not know any other way of earning money. Making ghee was something that I knew very well. I grew up seeing my mother make it. By the time I was twelve years old, I could make it perfectly well. So I decided to start with it. With time, I knew I would learn more about business, and then I would see how to expand it."

This way, she fed her children and paid their school fees. However, she wanted more than that. She was not going to be satisfied with living hand to mouth. She wanted her children to have the best. They needed to have the good things in life, which, to rural people, may be luxuries but are actually basic necessities, such as shoes.

"I did not want people to think that, as a woman, I could not buy good things for my children. I also did not want my children to covet what others had. I therefore worked very hard and expanded the business to include other items like plastics and cosmetics. As my business grew, I started saving some money. When I had saved enough, I built myself a shop, and within a year, my daughter, Anita, joined senior one at Kaaro Secondary School in Rushere."

It was from this shop that someone had taken advantage of Winnie's absence by removing the louvers and stealing her fabrics. She explains why she used louvers instead of the usual windowpanes, which are not easy to open from outside unless they are broken: "I did not want to have what everybody else had. I wanted something different so as to show those people who thought I would not make it that being a woman doesn't mean being a failure."

Winnie's shop is in the Rushere trading center, near her birthplace. It is a nice permanent building, which she divided into two parts. She works in one and rents out the other. The building is decorated with tiles, and from a distance it looks like a drinking joint because of its two front arches, which give it a posh look. She has stocked it with women's clothes, plastic chairs, plastic plates and mugs, handbags, shoes, and many other items.

Apart from the shelves, the shop is furnished with two locally made stools, one for herself and the other for the occasional visitor. As Winnie sits on her stool and narrates her story, she keeps her legs together, a style of sitting that, in this part of the country, is a sign of decency in a woman. A woman who sits with her legs apart or with one leg on top of the other is looked upon as loose and immoral.

One day in February 2001, the headmaster of Kaaro Secondary School came to her shop looking for her daughter Anita. She was missing from school, and he wanted to know if she was safe. But Anita was not at home either. Both Winnie and the headmaster got worried, because some soldiers had been sighted at the school the previous day and the headmaster thought the girl could have gone with them. It was well-known in the area that soldiers were luring schoolgirls into sex.

"At first I didn't think much of it. I thought she was at school and that the headmaster wasn't well informed. But he assured me that she was not there. That's when I started to worry," Winnie says.

At that time, Anita was only fourteen years old. The headmaster went and reported her missing at Rushere's police post. The officer in charge came to the shop to try and find out if Winnie had any idea where her daughter could be.

"Could she have gone to visit some friends or relatives?" the officer asked. "Are you sure she hasn't been here?"

"No. I don't think so," Winnie replied.

"Maybe you sent her somewhere and you have forgotten," he probed.

"I wouldn't forget something like that. In any case, I would have gone to the school to ask the headmaster for permission to send her," Winnie said, irritated.

"Where would you expect her to be, under normal circumstances?" the officer prodded on.

Winnie, however, did not have any inkling of where her daughter could be.

As they were still worried about Anita's disappearance, an employee from Step-In Lodge in the trading center came and informed Winnie that her daughter had booked into the lodge with a soldier. More specifically, they were in room 7.

Winnie did not want to believe that she had heard right. "I could not believe it. My daughter was too young to be involved in sex. She must have been somewhere else, not in the lodge with a man. She could not do it." Winnie was in denial.

"It was your young girl, Anita. She booked into the lodge with a soldier, and I saw them with my own eyes," the employee insisted.

Winnie had no choice but to believe that it was true, since the lodge employee knew Anita very well. As the truth began to sink in, Winnie's legs, which could no longer carry her weight, started trembling; her heart was beating so fast that she thought she was having a heart attack. She collapsed to the ground as she tried to grab for a stool to sit on.

"The officer in charge went back to the police post and returned with two policemen and one policewoman. I wanted to go with them to the lodge, to see for myself if it was really true, but they did not allow this for fear that I would start a fight," she recalls, staring into space.

After moments of restlessness, she could not stand it any longer, and she followed them. Still the police would not allow her to enter. She went back to her shop, agitated and angry. In a flash, Winnie had changed from a cool, self-controlled woman into a frantic person.

At the lodge, the police officers knocked on the door, but the man refused to open. They threatened to break down the door, but it was not until they cocked their guns that he complied.

"Here is thirty thousand shillings; you can have it, but please, let's drop the case," he pleaded with the officers, realizing that he was in trouble. They refused the bribe and arrested him, handcuffed him and the girl, and took them to the police post. One of the policemen informed Winnie that the man had been identified as a soldier whose home was only two kilometers away from the trading center. Winnie rushed to the post to see the man who had ruined her daughter's life. When she saw the man, she lost her calm and started wailing uncontrollably. The man had all the symptoms of full-blown AIDS. His eyes were large and white, and he looked emaciated. His lips were blood red, and he had sores all over his body.

"Go back to the lodge and find out if he used a condom," the officer in charge said to his officers when he saw the physical appearance of the man.

This time, nothing and nobody could stop Winnie from going to the lodge. She had to find out if the man had at least attempted to protect her daughter. But there was no sign of a condom in the room, used or new. Instead, there was a towel and bedsheets that were spotted with blood. The officers took the exhibits to the police post as evidence.

When the officer in charge saw them, he could not hold back his tears. It was a saddening sight. Here was a fourteen-year-old girl, who, judging by the stained linen, must have been a virgin, and all evidence pointed to the possibility that she could have been infected with HIV.

"The police should allow us to handle him," one onlooker suggested, hinting at a public desire for mob justice.

"They can't. They will take him to prison in the morning and release him in the evening," fumed another. "Then he will come back and infect more innocent children."

Winnie, however, did not believe that a criminal with such incriminating evidence and witnesses against him could be allowed to walk free.

"I thought that it was only in cases where there was no clear evidence that a crime has been committed that such people were let free. But this man had defiled my daughter and been caught red-handed. I did not think there was any way he could escape justice. There was physical evidence and eyewitnesses, including the police officers he had tried to bribe. What else did a judge need in order to send him to jail?" Winnie says.

Anita gave a statement, revealing that the soldier had defiled her. The following morning, the brother of the accused, who is a major in the army, tried to persuade Winnie to settle the matter out of court. His concern was that his brother was ill and could die in prison. Winnie would not hear of it. Her argument was that her daughter's life had been jeopardized, and the culprit had to face the full force of the law.

"What about my daughter, who was exposed to HIV? Didn't her life mean anything at all? Much as the deed had already been done, there was no reason why that man should have been allowed to walk free. His being in jail would protect other young girls on whom he might have had designs."

Other people, though, advised her to accept the major's proposal: "You are a mere woman; you cannot stand up to a major." "If you had a husband, it would be a different matter. But you are alone—you can't manage." "Drop the case, Winnie—otherwise you are putting your life in danger." "Let the man marry the girl—she is already his wife, anyway." "Whatever you do, the girl is already infected. Why bother? Why create enmity?" "If the girl is old enough to sleep with a man, she is old enough to get married. Let him marry her." "Whether she goes back to school or not, the fact is she is already a woman. Why are you bothered? It will not change anything." "Ask for money and forget the case."

Winnie listened to all they had to say, but she stuck to her decision to pursue the case until she got justice. Only the officer in charge of the police post advised her against dropping the case. "Don't drop the case, Winnie. If such people are not punished for their crimes, they will never stop committing them," he said, adding that there was enough evidence to convict the soldier.

Both the accused and the victim were taken to Mbarara Central Police Station. Anita was taken to the hospital for a medical checkup, after which she gave a full statement to the police.

"She even fell sick, I believe, because of the sexual encounter. You see, she is very young. After I had nursed her back to health, I took her to Kakungulu Memorial School in Kampala. I could not take her back to her former school because everyone there knew about the affair," Winnie says, tears running down her cheeks.

The soldier was remanded, and this did not go down well with his brother, the major. He therefore devised other means of securing his brother's freedom.

"I don't know how, but he found out which school I had taken my daughter to. He lied to the school authorities, saying that he was Anita's uncle. He said that I was very sick and he wanted her to come and see me. They released my daughter to him, even though they did not know him," she moans.

The major rushed Anita to Mbarara Police Station, where she changed her statement, denying that she had had sex with the man. Winnie learned about it late at night, when the officer in charge of Rushere's police post at the time of the defilement rang her. (He had been abruptly transferred to Ntungamo.)

"He told me that the major had turned up with my daughter and that she had changed her statement. I did not sleep that night."

She did not know how to proceed with the case. She knew that she needed a lawyer, but she could not afford one. Her daughter, a minor, had been withdrawn from school, and she did not know where she was. What could she do? To whom could she turn? Then she remembered that, at FIDA's Mbarara branch, they provided free legal advice to people who could not afford to hire lawyers. She had learned this from a friend.

"I thought of what people had told me, that unless I dropped the case, my life would be in danger. But my daughter's life was already in danger if the major had already got her out of school. I could not abandon her.

Moreover, I did not know how he had managed to trace her. I was sure that at that time, she needed me, and I had to do something."

Early in the morning of the following day, she boarded the first bus to Mbarara and went to the FIDA office, where she made a statement. In her statement, she raised the concern that the major could be using her daughter sexually, since he was keeping her in an undisclosed place. The legal officer at FIDA responded by writing a letter to the state attorney of Mbarara municipality, asking him to investigate.

Winnie went to the police station to talk to the investigating officer, who was bound to know more about the alleged change of statement. As it turned out, however, the officer had not been consulted on anything concerning the case. Winnie was shocked when she told her that she saw the girl with the brother of the man who had defiled her. The officer further revealed that she thought that maybe Winnie had given in to pressure to settle the matter out of court. When the officer asked the girl if her mother knew that she was not at school, the man shouted at her, saying that they didn't want her mother to be involved in the case. Later, the investigating officer learned that she had been taken off the case. She was baffled at the way it had been handled.

Winnie went ballistic. She went back to the FIDA office and related the whole story to the legal officer. The legal officer listened attentively, after which she escorted Winnie to see one of the officers under the inspector general of police, who told them that the case would be investigated. The legal officer at FIDA, though, was not satisfied. She insisted that Winnie should go to Kampala and meet the inspector general of police in person. She believed that he was about the only person in the police force who could not take a bribe.

"I boarded a bus to Kampala, and my first stop was at my daughter's school. I was told then that she was not in the school. I was also told that soldiers were always hanging around, and it was suspected that Anita had gone with them. I was at least glad to learn that the gatekeeper was fired, as it was believed that he had helped her to escape," Winnie says.

From the school, Winnie proceeded to the office of the inspector general of police, where the receptionist told her that she could not see him. Winnie, however, was determined to see him. She wanted justice and no longer trusted the junior officers to help her get it. Fortunately, he walked in during this hot exchange and invited her to his office.

"After I narrated my ordeal, he assigned me to some police officers, and they took me to the school. By the time we arrived, my daughter had returned. We went through her suitcase and found four hundred thousand shillings and the major's telephone number. We took her to the inspector general of police and introduced her to him. She told him her side of the story, but she lied," Winnie says, looking shattered.

"The major is my uncle, and he has found me a place at Dynamic Secondary School," Anita shamelessly told the inspector general of police.

Winnie was riled by this response and denied that her daughter was related to the major. The inspector general called the headmaster of Kakungulu Memorial School and asked him to explain on what grounds he had released a student into the hands of someone who was not known to him.

"Ever since the girl reported to the school, she had been withdrawn and keeping to herself all the time. When the major turned up with another female relative and informed me that her mother was seriously ill, I thought that it must have been the cause of her unhappiness. I therefore had to let her go," the headmaster said.

The inspector general of police also called the major to get his side of the story. He used the number that was found in the girl's suitcase while Winnie looked on.

"I'm not related to the girl. I did what I did for my brother because blood is thicker than water. After all, the girl is known to be very loose. My brother was just unfortunate that he got caught with her," the major said.

The inspector general decided to counsel the girl and to enlighten her on the dangers of cohabiting with a man. When he was told that the girl had been taken to Dynamic Secondary School, he sent his officers to check it out.

"They reported back, saying that the school was substandard. It lacked facilities, and more important, the school was in the major's neighborhood. They also found that the girl was not staying in the boarding section of the school, as she had claimed."

Winnie reasoned that if she was not staying in the school, it was likely that she was staying at the major's residence, although she would not admit it. The inspector general of police tried to have her transferred from the school.

He invited Winnie, Anita, and some elders whom Winnie chose to his office, and he asked Anita if she was willing to go to another school. Anita said she would be, as long as she would not be made to go back to Kakungulu Memorial School. The inspector general decided to help find another school for Anita.

When I went to interview the inspector general of police about Anita's case, he confirmed Winnie's story and recalled, "I sent my officers to Mukono Town Academy, an upcoming private school affiliated with Brigham Young University in the United States. They secured a place for her, but after one week she left the school, claiming that it was in a village."

Meanwhile, the inspector general of police wrote a report and sent it to the director of public prosecutions. When Winnie went to the DPP's office to check on the progress of the case, the state attorney told her that the file on the abduction case had been sent back to Mbarara for further investigation. However, he asked her to drop the abduction case and proceed only with the defilement case.

"Since I did not know what it would mean to drop the abduction case, I went back to the inspector general of police for advice," Winnie says. "He was completely against it, saying that it would be wrong to withdraw the case. He added, 'The defilement case, for which the soldier was put in prison, is different from the abduction case. In any case, these are two charges against two different people. The abduction case is against the major, and it has nothing to do with the defilement case, which is against the major's brother. There is no sense, therefore, in leaving that case to try and pursue the first one.' He went on to say that he had done all he could and that the DPP had the authority to pursue the case from there, since the file had been forwarded to him."

Winnie went back home to Rushere and tried to recapture her life, which had been rudely disrupted by the circumstances surrounding the case. She was still getting advice from people who thought that unless she dropped the case, her life would be in danger. But she was adamant.

The case was later taken to court. The police officers from Rushere and the eyewitnesses, including the lodge employee, were summoned to appear at the trial. Arriving at the court, however, Winnie was told that no one other than the victim, Anita, would be allowed to testify.

"But the girl has disappeared; I don't know where she is. How then is she going to testify?" Winnie asked, not understanding what it all meant.

"You don't have to worry about it. The child will turn up," the state attorney said.

"These people will not allow her to come and testify against them. I'm quite sure they are the ones keeping her in hiding," she said.

"You cannot be sure that they are the ones hiding her. But rest assured that she will come to give her evidence in court. Believe me," the state attorney said.

"What about the witnesses?" Winnie asked.

"There are no witnesses," he said.

"There are several witnesses. There is the lodge employee who saw them entering the room and the police officers who arrested him on finding him in the lodge with the girl. He even tried to bribe them, which is more evidence that he is guilty," she said.

"What the witnesses saw or did not see does not count. Only the girl is in a position to tell the court what happened. After all, she is the victim, not the witnesses."

"But the witnesses saw what happened. Isn't the important thing what really happened? Whatever the girl says, as long as the crime was committed, isn't that what matters?" Winnie queried.

"Only the girl will be allowed to testify. If she was really defiled, as you claim, then she will say so in court," the state attorney insisted.

Winnie did not like this turn of events. She was already aware that her daughter had changed her original statement, saying that she had given it under duress. She therefore wanted to make sure that other witnesses would be allowed to speak and produce the exhibits.

"But what about the exhibits? The stained linen?" Winnie demanded.

"Those are not necessary," the state attorney said.

"And the doctor's report?"

"All those things are irrelevant. Only the girl will testify."

Winnie gave up the argument and decided to wait for the outcome of the trial.

Later in the day, Anita turned up in court with the major, his sister, and his brother. They sat on the bench opposite Winnie, who had come with the legal officer from FIDA for support. Anita would not even look at her mother, let alone talk to her. Winnie was saddened.

"My daughter was behaving as if I was the enemy. She refused to talk to me, but I'm sure she was acting on instructions. She was now allying with the people who had exposed her to the danger of HIV/AIDS," she laments.

She cannot hold her tears as she tells this part of the story. Her face contorts with bitterness and rage as she relives the scene.

"I felt ashamed and betrayed that my daughter had joined my enemies to fight me. These people had decided that I was the bad one because I had refused to settle out of court. The talk going around was that I wanted the soldier to die in prison, and therefore I was an evil woman. It hurt me that they considered my daughter's life worthless. What hurt me even more was the knowledge that they were using her to hurt me and laughing at her behind her back. But I believed in my heart that I would be able to reason with her. Moreover, I'm sure they will kick her out once the man dies, because then he will have escaped from the law and Anita will not be needed anymore."

Just as the state attorney had said, Anita was the only one who was called upon to give evidence at the trial. Nothing was said about the exhibits or the eyewitnesses who had come to help convict the soldier.

"Is it true that you were found in the lodge with the accused?"

"Yes."

"Did you have sex with him?"

"No."

"What about the bloody linen? Where did the blood come from?"

"I was having my period. That was my menstrual blood."

"What were you doing in the lodge with a man?"

"My mother had beaten me and chased me away from home. I had nowhere to go. This man just helped me and paid for the room in the lodge. But he never touched me."

Winnie was shocked and frustrated. She could not believe what she was hearing. After all the trouble she had gone through—now this! What frustrated her even more was that she was not given the chance to say anything, if only to point out a few truths about the whole saga. No one was given a chance except the girl, who, according to Winnie, had been coached on what to say.

"If they had allowed the rest of us to testify, I would have asked her about her original statement. There were witnesses who would have confirmed that she had given it freely, without being forced or threatened by anyone."

Winnie sat in the courtroom and watched her dream of getting justice drift away.

"It pained my heart as I listened to my daughter defending her defiler. Not only that, but she accused me of beating her and chasing her away from home. This was a lie. She was at school. That is where she came from to go to the lodge. I don't know how he did it, but the major had turned her against me completely."

The case was dismissed shortly afterward, and the soldier was released. As Anita headed for the major's car, the FIDA legal officer tried to talk to her. But Anita did not give her the chance. "Just leave me alone," she rudely retorted.

The major, his sister, and his two brothers drove off, taking Anita with them. Winnie was at a loss for what to do.

"I had hoped that I would talk to her after the court proceedings, try to make her understand the gravity of her situation, but I couldn't. This hope crumbled as she got into the car. I was left with the legal officer from FIDA. I just followed their car with my eyes."

When talking to me, the FIDA legal officer commented on Anita's rudeness to her mother, saying, "I couldn't believe the hatred that was evident in her eyes. I don't know exactly what happened, but whatever it was, it turned her completely against her mother."

Winnie returned to the DPP and asked him to enlighten her on the direction the case had taken. He told her that his office had nothing to do with police cases. He insisted that the victim's evidence was all that mattered; all the other witnesses and the exhibits were irrelevant.

"But I did not agree with him. People go to lodges because there is no other place to go. If there was no other intention other than to provide accommodation for my daughter, why didn't he take her to his home? His home is only two kilometers away from the trading center.

Isn't it clear that the only reason he took her to the lodge was to have sex with her?"

But the DPP insisted that the court could only listen to the victim and no one else.

An officer at FIDA's Kampala branch, however, was of the view that the state attorney could have put in more effort. "Once it is on record that a crime has been committed and there is overwhelming evidence to that effect, the state attorney can declare the witness hostile, then ask the court to disregard the witness's evidence and instead cross-examine her," she told me, commenting on Winnie's complaint that the case was mishandled. "In Anita's case, this wasn't done."

Winnie did not want to give up. She was determined to fight for justice. "What is going to be done to the major, who withdrew a child from school without her mother's knowledge and consent? Isn't that a crime?" Winnie asked the DPP.

"You should be angry with your daughter, not with the major. She went with him of her own accord. He did not force her."

"Whether he forced her or not, isn't it a fact that she is a minor and therefore cannot make her own decisions? In any case, in what capacity is the major keeping her? As his sister-in-law or something else?"

"If you fail to control your daughter, you shouldn't blame other people for her behavior," the DPP told an infuriated Winnie.

Winnie may not have gone to school, but she knew that an offense had been committed against her daughter, and she decided to fight on.

"I could not take it anymore, so I decided to get help from the highest authority. I was very lucky to get an audience with the president himself. This was in April 2002. He was very patient and listened as I poured out my heart. Then he advised me to go back to FIDA and request that they look into the case more closely and advise him accordingly." Since Winnie knew very little about the law, the president could not act based only on what she had told him. He needed to understand the legal aspects of the case.

Now, Winnie has almost lost faith in the law. She is baffled by it. As she narrates her story, she keeps on wondering what the law is for if it cannot protect underage children who are confused and defiled by adults.

"I'm not even sure that it is money that has turned her against me. They could be threatening her with death. What kind of law allows a man to withdraw a fourteen-year-old girl from school, in unclear circumstances, and keep her secluded from her mother?" she asks, unable to understand how the overwhelming evidence could be ignored, just because the girl changed her statement. "Suppose she decided to go and get married. Would the same law turn around and have the husband arrested? What if she was found cohabiting with a man but denied it—would the law let the man go free?"

Winnie wonders whether it is because she is not rich that the case has not been given the serious attention that it deserves. "Suppose Anita was the daughter of a rich person. Would they have handled the case the way they did? Would the major escape punishment for staying with a fourteen-year-old girl whom he has withdrawn from school? I don't think so. Which leads me to conclude that the law works only for the rich."

Winnie stares hopelessly into space. "People are advising me to drop the case. They say that Anita is an undisciplined child who should be let to suffer the consequences of her behavior. But what kind of a mother would I be if I gave up on a fourteen-year-old girl? I still believe that my daughter is too young to know what she is doing, and she needs guidance. She may have decided to support her defiler against me, but that proves that she doesn't know what is good for her. I will do whatever it takes to get justice and have my daughter back. I will not rest. Not until I find my daughter."

11

I Dare to Say

Facing HIV/AIDS with Courage

"Many of us celebrate our 'Africanism' and heritage by praising our sense of community, our extended family relationships, and our togetherness. We hail our openness and love of sharing stories, but how many of us can feel free and comfortable talking about HIV/AIDS, let alone give testimonies of our personal experiences? I call upon you to . . . learn and build a community of support where a culture of sharing and discussion remains one way of looking HIV/AIDS in the face and vowing to live and fight on. It would be a pity if we as women do not learn from others' experiences and realize how important it is to know our HIV status."
—Angelina Wapakhabulo, Positive Women Leaders of Uganda

HIV/AIDS is still a real and present threat in the world. This is particularly true in Africa, south of the Sahara, where the incidence of the disease is very high. The UNAIDS Report of 2004 states that three-quarters of HIV-positive Africans between the ages of fifteen and twenty-four are women. Until there is a cure or an effective vaccine, everybody is vulnerable, especially women and girls. It is therefore necessary to give HIV/AIDS a woman's face in order to create more awareness about the vulnerability of women and make them the centerpiece in the ongoing fight against the disease.

We hope these testimonies of women living with HIV/AIDS will help to increase awareness of the condition, leading to behavioral changes among both men and women. We hope these stories will help to fight the stigma of living with HIV/AIDS and encourage other infected women to come out in public so that they can gain access to medication, accept their status, and start living positively, thus improving their health and lifestyle.

This section presents the testimonies of four courageous women who at one time stood on the brink of death, hopeless and despairing, but had a complete turnaround when they came out in the open. Many women infected with HIV/AIDS don't have enough information about the disease and are afraid to reveal their HIV status because of the risk of being abandoned by their spouses and stigmatized and rejected by society. One woman whose story is presented here sends this message to her sisters living with HIV/AIDS: "AIDS is not the end of life. You are more important than the disease. Be open to members of your family, ask for advice, love yourself, and work hard to live. Hating yourself is the beginning of your grave, but accepting yourself starts you on a new life."

VIOLET BARUNGI

The Second Twin

GLAYDAH NAMUKASA

The bumpy road winds up into a mess of narrow and wide drains. Nakato is the first to jump off the boda boda, and I follow suit.

"Over there," she says, lifting her skirt to jump to the other side of the wide drain. This is the easiest route to her house. She jumps over the drain frequently. "My home is behind that wooden house where they show films." She raises her voice against the blare of music escaping from within its wooden walls. The song playing must be one of her favorites; she sings along, her lips moving in unison with the lyrics, "Ekitooke kifa nsalira . . ."

Two half-naked little girls are seated at the edge of the drain, casting stones into the foaming water. They are engrossed in their game, watching as the stones form ripples and bubbles in the dirty water.

"That one with plaited hair is my three-year-old daughter," Nakato says, smiling with parental pride. "Come and greet the visitor, Brenda."

I jump over to the other side to meet Brenda. She throws away the lot of stones she had in her palm and hurries over to me. I hold out my hand to her, and she extends her small dirty one in return. I take it. Her fingers are unnaturally rough for a three-year-old. She has large eyes that dance in their sockets, almost unceasingly.

As we head for the path bordered by narrow drains, a boy emerges from behind the wooden house, dancing to the rhythm of the music and singing along. He stops the moment he sees us. Brenda calls out to him, "Tongo, Aunt has come from the city."

"His name's Katongole, my firstborn. We call him Tongo," Nakato says, pausing in her steps. She doesn't mind the fact that we are standing beside stinking drains. This is the air she breathes every day, and this is her children's playground, but the stench is threatening to burst my nostrils. I turn my attention to Tongo, who is walking toward me. His stomach bulges through a ragged shirt that has no buttons. Unlike Brenda, he is a real picture of his mother, with the same red, tear-washed eyes.

After I shake Tongo's hand, which is sticky with jackfruit sap, we walk on. The path leads to a clutter of small mud-and-wattle houses partitioned by still waters and garbage heaps. We make our way around a heap of rubbish and the wooden house, where a group of teenagers are holding a conference. We go past two small houses, bent toward each other as if whispering into each other's ears.

Finally, we have reached Nakato's house. It is a large house with dilapidated walls and torn polyethylene acting as windowpanes. The wooden door shows evidence of many ant feasts, with paper wedged between the uneven edges.

Nakato points at a section of the house and says it is the room she is renting. It is only a humble extension of the big house and seems to have been a store, back when the house was still in good shape.

"We can't talk here, as you can see. For now I can't afford a bigger room, but I know one day we will be out of here," she says.

"We will go wherever you want us to," I say. I am amazed at her and her hope of one day shifting from this filthy place. As we walk away, I am left only to imagine what this pathetic tiny room consists of, but my imagination doesn't go beyond a small mattress for the three of them, a small heap of clothes, plates, and cups. I wonder if the size of the house would accommodate her height if she were any taller.

She leads the way back via the same route we came, away from the clutter of houses and onto a patchy football field. We sit down under the shade of a muvule tree standing adjacent to the field.

"Here it is better," she says. "At least I am sure no one will listen to what I have to tell you."

As Nakato begins her tale, we are both transported as if by magic back and forth in time. She has been between places for twenty-eight years: a miserable traveler on a quest for love, forever searching for a hand to wipe away the bitter rejection that has settled on her heart, like an inkblot on white linen.

*N*akato was born in 1976 in Kalonge, deep in Mityana district. Kalonge was known for a famous traditional birth attendant, Nambi, who, people claim, could communicate with the gods, mainly because her deliveries were always successful. No delivering mother had ever been reported to die in Nambi's hands, and none had ever failed to deliver normally. Nakato's was the first abnormal delivery to be recorded, and it almost tarnished Nambi's reputation.

Nakato was born a twin—a "stubborn" second twin—and almost killed her mother while still in the womb. Babirye, the first twin, came out of the womb headfirst, just like normal babies do. Nakato delayed, staying back for two hours after Babirye was born. The two hours were a time of absolute torture and pain for their mother, during which she bled profusely. She would have lost her life if it had not been for the extraordinary Nambi, who administered herbs that forced the stubborn baby out of the womb. Nakato came out feet first, a rare phenomenon; her head followed with difficulty.

"*Ono kasowole ajja kutambula nyo ensi eno*"—"she will walk the world because she has come to the world by her feet first"—Nambi had said.

Nakato's two-hour delay in her mother's womb seemed to decide her fate; at least that was Nakato's belief. It robbed her of love and attention and transferred them wholly to Babirye.

The delay also gathered the misfortunes of all unfulfilled future twin rituals, which became exclusively Nakato's. Among the Baganda people, on the birth of twins, the required rituals start as soon as the second twin is out of the womb. On hearing the news, Ssalongo, the twins' father, should climb onto the rooftop of his house and shout obscenities that reach the farthest corners of the village, tearing through all the coffee trees and the plantations and the mud-and-wattle houses. The second step involves the father's *ekigali*, into which money is dropped for the twins by everyone who comes to see them. This money is used solely to meet the twins' needs. No one else is supposed to use the money lest the twins "burn" that person in their anger.

A function to dedicate the twins to the gods is meant to follow as soon as possible. This ceremony revolves around the breaking of taboo, a sign that the mother and the father have become a little higher than other mortals.

In Nakato's case, these rituals were never fulfilled; at least that is what Nakato heard. As a result, Nakato suffered a great many misfortunes, such as recurrent, puzzling disease throughout her childhood, slow growth, and a rebellious character. All of this contributed to her rejection by her relatives, leaving her almost destitute.

Nakato tasted her first sting of rejection immediately after her birth, when she was not breast-fed. Nambi told Nakato's mother that stubborn babies had to be punished by being left hungry for some time. So while Nakato was left to starve for six hours, Babirye enjoyed the breast as soon as their mother was able to recover from the difficult delivery.

When the twins were one year old, Ssalongo and Nalongo separated. Nalongo went away and left Ssalongo with the twins, after which Ssalongo took the twins directly to Jaaja, their grandmother, who lived in the neighboring village.

At Jaaja's home, Babirye, the first twin, was the good granddaughter, quick to learn and obedient—a blossoming white rose in Jaaja's compound. Nakato, the second twin, was the opposite—impudent, slow to learn, sickly, and greedy. She had the stubbornness she had developed while still in her mother's womb, a stubbornness that grew as she got older. She was the bane of Jaaja's old age. To Jaaja, she was never Nakato by name; instead she was a demon, a snake, a goat, a fool—*musota, mbuzi, musiru.* Sometimes she was even a murderer—*omutemu*—because she almost killed Nalongo while still in the womb.

Nalongo never visited at all. Jaaja said she had found another husband and lived with him in Kiwawu, where she taught at a primary school. Ssalongo's visits were rare. On the few occasions that he came, he brought Babirye roasted maize; sometimes he even brought her a biscuit! Nakato, on the other hand, never received a single thing, because Jaaja always told their father what a bad child she was. Neither Jaaja nor Ssalongo ever loved her. They both even said they were tired of her unexplained illnesses. Her sickly nature alienated her further from her father and drew him even closer to Babirye, who rarely fell ill. But when she did, Jaaja would rush to inform Ssalongo, who would then rush to his sick daughter's bedside with sugar and bread. Nakato always looked on from a distance, envying Babirye as she was lovingly held in Ssalongo's arms. Ssalongo would then say to the child longingly looking on, "If you were a good girl, I would carry you, too."

She tried to be good, but her efforts went unnoticed. Most times, whenever she and Babirye went to the well, Nakato would hurry ahead in order to be the first at home. But then Jaaja would shout at her, "Why did you leave my grandchild alone?" When they went to collect firewood, Nakato would carry the heaviest bundle back home, but even that would fail to endear her to Jaaja, whose comment would be, "You deserve to do heavy work; after all, you eat a lot."

It was as if Nakato's struggle to get out of Nalongo's womb at birth had tied her brain in a knot so tight that it couldn't be undone, even at school. By the time Babirye was in primary seven, Nakato was only in primary four, and she had only been dragged through classes as if she was meant to have a taste of each class, regardless of her poor academic performance. In any class she joined, the pupils called her Granny. She was an object of derision both at school and at home.

While in primary four, Nakato made two decisions: one was to stop going to school, and the other was to disappear from home. She decided to stop her schooling because she felt that she was not making any progress at all. The teachers, who were no better than Ssalongo and Jaaja, always reminded her of how dense she was. She decided to disappear from home because she was tired of battling for affection.

Nakato was not sure of her age then, but her breasts were budding. She went to Kiwawu to look for her mother and found her with four children and her new husband. But even at her mother's home, Nakato was still considered the stubborn second twin. She was as welcome as the breath of death, because her presence only made her mother appear old to her new husband. So rather than being her mother's child, Nakato became the caretaker of her four children. Nalongo never forgot to remind her how she almost killed her at birth. Life with her was as worthless as a dried-up spring.

◎◎

Four years as the caretaker of her mother's children were all that Nakato could handle. Although her age was still a mystery and no one had ever told her the year she was born, she regarded herself as grown up because her breasts were fully developed. They were big enough even to breast-feed twins, as her mother once said during one of their daily arguments. Nakato knew she was too old to let her mother trample on her as if she were a fallen yellow leaf.

She disappeared from her mother's home to try out life again with her father. Because her illnesses had long since ceased, she thought that perhaps her father would love her. It was a gamble, but so was the life she was roaming through. Nakato was a polyethylene bag flying in midair, searching for its destination on the ground.

Ssalongo had a second wife and five children. They lived in the suburbs of Mityana town, in a congested neighborhood where houses were separated by barely an arm's length. To her father, Nakato was totally unwelcome.

"Just as you walked out of your mother's womb is how you are walking the earth, you stupid girl!" he told her when she reappeared. "You left your Jaaja without saying good-bye. I know you did the same to your mother, and I am sure you will do the same to me."

Her stepmother, unlike her father, welcomed her because she was Ssalongo's daughter, she said, but Nakato later learned that her stepmother wanted her around only to use her as a working machine in her booming shop and a caretaker of the five children.

Like Jaaja, her father never called her by name. He instead referred to her as "that fool," adding that she shouldn't call him Father because he didn't father fools. He said his eldest daughter was Babirye, who was now in senior three at one of the best boarding schools in Mityana.

Living her life as "nobody's child"—in which no one noticed she was a teenager who needed Vaseline to make her skin shine like that of the other girls in the neighborhood, a teenager who could no longer bear to go to the market barefoot—was depressing.

One lucky evening marked a turning point in Nakato's life. Her stepmother had, as always, sent her to the market to do the week's shopping.

The roadside was as busy as every other market day. It was lined with baskets of tomatoes, onions, and green peppers; sacks of yellow and green oranges and passion fruits; and mountains of avocados and paw-paw. The chorus of sound was heavier than usual as men, women, and children moved up and down. Nakato heard a honk tearing through the noise and saw a trailer parked behind a pile of sweet potatoes. What she saw was a miracle: staring through the windshield straight at her was love. She loved the squint of the narrow eyes that searched her face, per-haps seeing the good in her. No man had ever looked at her in that way. Among all the women and girls crowding to buy foodstuffs, this man had noticed her! She knew at once that the man seated at the steering wheel of the trailer was her stroke of good luck, life's gift to her.

He smiled and winked at her. She smiled back at him and immedi-ately responded to his beckoning. She made her way toward the trailer through throngs of people, trying her best to balance her footsteps, like good girls walk. Now that luck was knocking on her door, she had to open it wide.

"Beautiful young woman, where exactly do you live?" the man asked. His loving smile was directed at her eyes.

"I live just near the Gombolola quarters," Nakato said, lowering her eyes lest he scrutinize her and recognize her as the bad second twin. For the very first time in her life, someone had called her beautiful! At last, it was not only Babirye who was beautiful.

"Please get inside the truck so we can talk some more," he said.

While seated in the truck, Nakato learned that his name was Paddy and that he owned the truck and was in the transport business. She learned that he had seen her on many market days and admired her; above all, she learned that he loved her and that he wished to see her another time.

On every market day, she stared love in the face and touched love with her own hands. She heard words that had previously been audible only to Babirye's ears. He told her she was a good girl and that he wished to marry her. Paddy looked as old as her father, but the two men were completely different. Paddy loved her. Her father did not. Paddy always gave her money, which she used to buy herself Vaseline, a pair of shoes, and a new dress. He met every need that her father never bothered about.

On one of their secret meetings, Paddy said he wanted to take her away. She eloped with him, and they went to Nyendo, one of the semi-urban areas of Masaka town. It was hundreds of kilometers away from Mityana. They lived in a one-room apartment with two bamboo chairs and a table in the middle of the room. The bedroom, screened off by a heavy curtain, contained a small well-made bed and a wooden suitcase for her three dresses.

"Everything in the house is yours," Paddy told her, never forgetting to smile. "You are my bride, and I will formally marry you as soon as possible." He said he was constructing a house for her somewhere nearby and that as soon as it was completed and they had moved in, he would officially marry her.

And so Nakato's new life began. Every morning, she only had to wake up, cook, eat, drink, and wash dishes, after which she could just lie back on the bed or relax in her chair. Unlike all the other homes she had lived in, this one was surrounded by love, and everything that happened to her was a component of that love. Paddy never quarreled with her, never beat her, and never called her by any insulting names. Instead he reminded her every day that she was good and that he loved her very much. Her hopes of becoming a wedded wife blossomed each passing day, as Paddy always promised he would organize their wedding soon. Nakato, the bad second twin, had been plucked from the miserable life at her former homes and permanently placed in a home lit by rays of love. She felt certain that she was better off than Babirye.

Nakato's first pregnancy occurred within six months of moving in with Paddy. "My young bride is going to give me a child; finally I'll be a father!" Paddy rejoiced. But all she knew about the soon-to-be father of her unborn child was that he owned a truck, which he used to travel from one place to another, and that he was her husband. He never spoke of his relatives, and she never asked. She never argued with him or even opposed anything he said; she felt she had to be careful lest he get disenchanted with her.

But right then, life was sweet, although at times it could be hard, like when Paddy went away on what he called business trips. But even then, he always left her enough money to cater to her needs. It was a sweet-sour, sour-sweet life, but it was worth living.

After nine months, the terrible labor pains came. "It is important that we avoid the hospital because they may decide to operate on you, in which case all your deliveries will henceforth be by operation," Paddy said. It was believed that women who were operated upon were naturally weak and therefore not good wives. Nakato agreed, because she was determined to never make the mistake of being anything bad again.

She delivered at a traditional birth attendant's place that was deep in Matanga, twenty miles away from Nyendo. She had a baby girl who weighed 2.5 kilograms. Nakato's delivery was normal, except the baby's head tore her, leaving a big wound. The birth attendant said the wound would heal as long as it was taken good care of, especially if it was washed with *kamunye* herbs.

Paddy was always available to help. For a full month, he didn't take any business trips. He remained a loving man, and Nakato remained his submissive wife. She never objected to his desires, even when he decided to sleep with her before the wound was completely healed. "It helps to quicken the healing of the wound," he always told her. Somehow, she tolerated the terrible pain whenever he slept with her because, somewhere deep inside her heart, she believed physical pain mattered very little if it was the result of love. The wound, however, got worse each day. When it started discharging pus, Paddy stopped sleeping with her, but he remained the same attentive, loving husband as before.

The sour part of Nakato's present life was emphasized when the baby was one month old. Due to sores in her mouth, she couldn't breast-feed. She also had a fever, a cough, and diarrhea.

"The baby will be well," Paddy said, always comforting Nakato. "Some babies get sickly in the early stages, but later they get better."

Nakato totally agreed with Paddy. She believed that just as her own childhood had been tainted with illnesses, so would her baby's. The illnesses would go away, just as hers had.

Paddy said they shouldn't take the baby to the hospital. He brought tablets, which he crushed and gave to the baby. At times he brought herbs and said they would help, that the baby would get better.

The baby never got better. Two weeks later, she died. Nakato was unable to go to her daughter's burial; her wound was still in such a bad state that she couldn't walk to it. She would have tried to hobble there, but Paddy consoled her and said she should stay at home and that he would explain everything when he returned.

It was very difficult for Nakato to accept that her little girl would be wrapped in bark cloth and laid alone in an inaccessible dwelling. Her hope of becoming a loving mother drowned in the sea of tears she cried that day. When Paddy returned that evening, he told her that the baby had been buried in his family's graveyard. Then he reminded her that he loved her. He said everything would be all right and that, as soon as her wound healed, she would become pregnant again.

Her wound took two months to heal, leaving a big hole in what used to be her teenage womanhood. Paddy said it was all right and that her future deliveries would be easy because the birth passage had enlarged. She failed to conceive for the next two years, but everything was fine, just as Paddy had said it would be. Even with the threat of infertility, life was worth living because it was colored with love. Being a wife gave Nakato a sense of purpose in her life. Paddy painted her hope with fresh colors, and every time he did so, she saw that second twin—the one who was never loved, who came to earth tumbling on foot—ebb and fade out more and more, like a dying flame.

◎◎

In Nakato's third year of living with Paddy, life cracked. Sickness came and grabbed Paddy. Several ailments, such as fever, cough, and diarrhea, made their dwelling place in his body and clutched him in their jaws for a month or two before letting him go. The most stubborn was the cough. While the others would relent, it persisted. But Paddy was strong. He said the cough would one day realize he was unbeatable. He never went to the hospital. Just as he had done with the baby, he bought tablets for himself, sometimes herbs. He always said he would get well as long as she was there to nurse him. He said that one day he would be strong again, and then she would get pregnant and finally become a mother and a wedded wife!

Four months later, the crack in life enlarged when the cough planted itself firmly in Paddy's chest. It turned into explosive bouts that threatened to burst his lungs. The cough held on for a full month, weakening him more every day. Still he insisted that he would be well. He was completely bedridden. In one month, his body had started shrinking like a dried mushroom.

One rainy evening brought a stranger to their home. This was the first time in three and a half years that Nakato saw a visitor there.

"So you are the fool who's been keeping my brother away from his family," the visitor said.

She was a tall woman, far taller than Paddy, but with the same high forehead and narrow eyes. Paddy had never talked much about his family, but neither had Nakato. Their conversations had always been based on their future together, not their past.

Nakato watched as the visitor walked past her and parted the heavy curtains to the bedroom where Paddy lay, too weak to talk.

"Look what you've done to him," the visitor shouted. "Imagine what would have happened if I hadn't come. What you want, little woman, is to see him dead so that you can take everything that belongs to him."

Everything is already mine, Nakato wanted to say, but that was not the issue. The issue was that he would be well, and so she told the visitor.

"Why haven't you taken him to the hospital? My brother is going to die because of you!"

"I don't know where the hospital is. He won't die; he will be well."

"Idiot! Murderer! Now do exactly what I say."

The visitor advised Nakato to pack a few clothes in a bag, and they took Paddy to Viira Hospital. He was admitted for a week, after which he was referred to Entebbe Hospital because the doctor diagnosed tuberculosis. The visitor left them in Entebbe, returning to wherever she had come from. In Entebbe, they spent six months in the hospital. Each day Paddy received an injection and tablets. Despite the fact that his breathing was always labored, he tried his best to remind her that he would be well.

The visitor came on a few occasions to bring money. Each time she came, she had whispered conferences with Paddy that Nakato couldn't make out. During one visit, she came with luggage. Nakato learned that the luggage contained her clothes and transport money to take her back to wherever she had come from.

"You won't be needed anymore," the visitor told her. "You appeared from nowhere, and now you have killed my brother. What you should do is disappear just as you appeared."

"But he's my husband. I've not killed him. He will be well, and then we'll get married. He's building a house for me."

"He's never been your husband, foolish one. He's someone else's husband and a father to eight children and a grandfather to three children now. Leave today, because tomorrow his wife and children are coming for him."

◎◎

And so the unfortunate second twin was reborn. Hope and love were nothing more than components of the dust that blew past her as she stood trapped at the edge of life. She could not go back to her mother or her father. Neither could she go to Jaaja, not after having left their homes without saying good-bye. She couldn't face any one of them after her four years of mysterious absence.

The blowing wind sent her crawling to her paternal uncle's home in Masaka, seven miles away from Nyendo. Hope whispered to her when her uncle welcomed her with a smile. The smile wasn't as soft and wide as Paddy's, but it calmed her fluttering heart.

"We knew that someday the world would vomit you out. We knew you would come back looking for your relatives; that's why no one bothered to look for you," her uncle said. "The world is not as wide as you think. For four years you've lived just three villages away from me, but you never bothered to visit. A stupid girl you've always been, a stupid girl you'll always be."

Besides learning that she would always be stupid, Nakato learned that her uncle had discovered her whereabouts two years ago. He even knew the man she had been living with. She also learned, two weeks later, that Paddy had died of "the disease."

The little Nakato knew about AIDS was that "the disease" could be acquired by witchcraft, or one could get it if it found one's body to be a favorable dwelling place. If one's body wasn't a favorable dwelling place, then the disease would not stay. And people said that if one had the disease, one would be sick on and off, get skin rashes, and become skin and bones—slim. That was why the disease was referred to as slim. But, Nakato thought, of course Paddy had been sick on and off, but he never got any skin rash. As for becoming slim, it was the tuberculosis that made him so, not the disease. It was the tuberculosis that killed him.

Nakato spent three months alone in her uncle's home, in the confines of her shell. She was a "stupid girl" again, the one to blame for everything that went wrong. She was even blamed when her uncle's eldest son, who was twelve years old, was discovered sexually experimenting with his seven-year-old sister, a game they must have started playing long before she came to live with them.

Her uncle's wife referred to her as a widow. "Your husband died. Don't expect us to take care of you when the disease puts you down. I can assure you, I won't be the one to wash the sheets you shit on when you start having diarrhea and vomiting."

What would people say if they found out that they had a sick person in their home? After all, she wasn't even their daughter.

It did not take long for Nakato to find another man. This man told her both his names, Kyakubali God, and he told her he had a wife but wanted to take Nakato as a second wife. Nakato knew this man loved her. He didn't see her as a stupid widow but as a beautiful young woman. She believed that, unlike Paddy, God was honest because he told her things she never asked him. She definitely knew it was all right to be a second wife. After all, even Ssalongo had a second wife by the time she left his home, and he loved that second wife more than he loved her mother.

Nakato had learned to be a person of the present and the future. She taught herself to reveal nothing about her past life. The most she revealed was her name and place of origin, Kalonge village in Mityana district.

She ran away from her uncle's home one month after meeting God. God lived in a two-room house alone, with nothing more in the house than a bed, two small saucepans, and a few plates and cups.

He told her his real home was in Kampala and that he had come to work as a building contractor in Nyendo town. He was not as loving as Paddy, but he had saved her from the abuses in her uncle's home. During her seventh month of living with him, Nakato became pregnant.

"I don't need any more children," God told her when she broke the news of her two-month pregnancy to him. He said their relationship had to end, that he could never take her as a second wife because she had a fault on her body. She came to understand that the fault on her body was the hole in her womanhood that had been left after the birth of her first child.

God left her alone in the house without saying good-bye, and she never saw him again. She never argued with any of these men. She had learned to swallow her opinions from childhood, because no one ever listened to her anyway. Unlike Babirye, whom everyone listened to, her own speech was nonsense, what Jaaja referred to as *majaani*. Now, with God gone, she stayed alone in the house, staring at the walls, the walls staring back at her, thinking of where to go next, her thoughts closing in on her.

The next man she got was called Bernard, but he told her to call him Nad. Nad appeared soon after God disappeared. Men were always available for her, and she took every opportunity as it came, making herself as available to them as they were to her. She hadn't lost hope of one day finding a destination. Nad could have been watching her all along and admiring her, but he didn't say so. All he said was, "Call me Nad. That's what my loved one should call me."

Nad was also married and looked as old as Paddy had. He told Nakato that he already had two wives; they lived in that same neighborhood. She had never seen him during her seven months' stay with God, but what mattered was that he was ready to take her on as a third wife.

"In a few weeks I'll be leaving for Kampala. That's where I am going to start work in a garage. I am an engineer." He promised to take her with him to the city, but it would have to be their secret so as to avoid having his relatives find out.

Nakato told him neither that she was already pregnant nor that she had already had, and lost, a baby. She explained the fault on her body to him as an accident that had occurred two years earlier. Still, one of the mysteries in her life was her exact age, but she had learned to lie. To Paddy, she had been nineteen years old. To God, she had been twenty. And now, to Nad, she was twenty-five.

Nad took her to Katwe, in Kampala, where he had already rented a tiny room. Like God, he had only a bed. They bought two plates, two cups, and a saucepan the day they arrived.

"We will start a home," he promised.

Nad was as loving as Paddy. He got her a job in a nearby hair salon, where she learned how to plait hair. She decided that she would stay silent about her pregnancy until it started to show, because she was convinced Nad would believe he was responsible.

The truth, however, manifested itself six months later, when the labor pains began. Nad was away at work. By the time he returned, she had already delivered a baby boy in a nearby clinic. The look on Nad's face when he entered the clinic was enough to tell Nakato he wasn't happy. He looked down at the baby and without a word went to see the midwife.

When he returned, he said to Nakato, "The baby is not mine. We've only been together six months!"

"I was three months pregnant when I met you," she confessed.

"I was warned about you, but now I know I made a big mistake," he said, then marched out of the room. She never saw him again.

◎◎

Ssalongo was the first person Nakato decided to go to for help. She never did much thinking because she didn't trust her brains. Even when she thought about something before putting it into action, it always turned out to be irrational. Everything she said and did was wrong. If she did something right, it was always turned around and interpreted as wrong. She knew it was wrong to go back to her father, but she went anyway.

When she went back to the home of Ssalongo's second wife, back in Mityana, she found that he had long ago left her and was staying with a third wife five miles away. She followed him.

"It's because you are my blood that I will accept you here," her father told her. He made it clear he wanted her away from his new wife as soon as she was well enough to take care of herself and her baby.

She was lucky enough to spend a full year in Ssalongo's third home. After one year, he decided to take her baby away from her to the village to stay with Jaaja. He then told her to leave his home and go and find work. He suggested that she could go to Babirye's home to see if she needed help in the house. And he said that he never wanted to see her again.

Nakato's twin sister, Babirye, now a teacher, accepted Nakato into her home while she looked for a job. Babirye lived in Kassanda, one of the rural villages in Mityana.

Babirye never treated Nakato as her sister. None of her relatives ever regarded her as part of their blood. To Ssalongo, she was an enemy. To Nalongo, she was a foreigner. Even Babirye, with whom she had shared a womb for nine months, treated her as if she were an alien. They all regarded her as one who had chosen to cripple her life. During those three disastrous years with Babirye, Nakato learned one thing: her age. Babirye confirmed that she was twenty-five years old.

This was the longest time she had ever taken to find another man. When Christopher came along, she immediately opened her arms to welcome him, because all she wanted was to be saved from Babirye's coldness. She thought this time things would be different because he was a young man, twenty-three years old, as he told her, and he was looking for a woman to marry.

After one month of meeting secretly with Christopher, Nakato was convinced that he loved her because he had never complained about the fault on her body. She became pregnant during their second month of secret meetings. When she told him, unlike the men before him, Christopher was completely delighted and promised to take her to his parents as soon as possible.

"If this is the woman you have been seeing, my son," Christopher's mother said when he took Nakato to meet her, "and if she's pregnant, as you say, my son, then you have already killed me. She's the twin sister of Madam Babirye, and I know everything about her. She has seen half the world and reaped fruits of her own stupidity."

Nakato knew with certainty that it was Babirye who had already spoiled her name, both in the village and at her workplace. One of Christopher's sisters was Babirye's fellow teacher. Babirye had already published and sold Nakato's biography to the world. This was the day Nakato also realized that she had been on the front pages of the gossip charts in the village for a long time now, because she had the disease. Had she been someone who opened up to people and to whom people opened up in turn, she would have known earlier. But she had never had a knack for making friends. Everyone despised her.

In response to the news, Christopher disowned the pregnancy and threw Nakato out of his house, where she had been living for a month. And so yet another door of love had slammed in her face. She was back in her midair position, a useless polyethylene bag flying aimlessly, with no hope of finding a destination. Babirye had always said that Nakato had taken a slippery slope that had destroyed her life, but Nakato believed otherwise. Her parents' failure to fulfill the twin rituals was what had pushed her down that slope. Now people said she had the disease, but could she have it when she had never fallen sick, not even for one single day? How could she have it and still give birth to a healthy boy, who was now three years old? And who was it who could possibly have bewitched her with the disease? People said she was a killer, a "born murderer." The village was rife with stories of the men she had infected, of how she had fled village after village, leaving her victims dead!

After Christopher sent her away, Nakato, the killer of men, went back to Babirye.

"The regret of my life is ever sharing a womb with you, Nakato!" Babirye said. "You are a nasty, stubborn idiot! No wonder you almost killed my mother at birth."

Babirye remained as unloving and cold as ever, but she supported Nakato throughout the nine months of pregnancy, childbirth, and the first year of the baby girl's life.

In the same month that Nakato's baby girl turned one year old, Ssalongo fell ill. By this time, he had already taken a fourth wife, and he fell sick while staying with her. His fourth wife took him to Mityana Hospital, where he was admitted. When she learned that he was to stay in the hospital for months because he had severe stomach problems, she informed Babirye, then disappeared.

Babirye sent Nakato to Mityana to look after Ssalongo. "Be useful to us for once, Nakato," she coldly said to her twin before sending her off.

During his time in the hospital, Ssalongo had no choice but to love his daughter. But Nakato had already resolved to harden her heart against his love. Nonetheless, she cared for him and listened to him talk about how he had been bewitched, most likely by Nalongo.

She stayed with him in the hospital for four months, during which time she met another man. Of all the men she had been with, Denis gave her the most money and promised to start a business for her. She soon abandoned her father in the hospital and went to live with Denis.

◎◎

Life with Denis was unlike any she had ever led. He had a shop in the center of Mityana town, which he let her run. Nakato touched lots of money with her own two hands. But happiness with Denis was as short-lived as a flash across the sky. One month she was well; the next she was down with a cough. At first she thought it was just like other coughs, which come and go, but she later learned that it had come to stay. Its claws dug deeper and deeper into her chest, draining the energy and health out of her body.

She remembered Paddy and realized that, just like him, she was getting evening fevers, coughing uncontrollably, and losing a lot of weight. Yes, she thought, she had been bewitched because of the shop she owned! And it was very likely that it was Babirye trying to harm her out of jealousy, just like her mother was bewitching her father. Denis, too, was convinced that she had been bewitched.

They went to a shrine to see a witch doctor. After hearing her story, the witch doctor requested to see both Nakato's parents. He told Denis and Nakato that her problems were all the result of unfulfilled twin rituals—because Babirye and Nakato had not been dedicated to the gods at birth, the gods were now demanding the necessary rituals. Nakato's condition was deteriorating with each passing day, and the situation was desperate, but Denis was too afraid of facing her parents. He opted, instead, to take her to Mityana Hospital and abandon her there.

By this time, Ssalongo was out of the hospital. Nakato stayed alone in the hospital for a week, after which Ssalongo and Babirye came to see her. What Nakato expected was not what happened. She expected them to disown her immediately for having abandoned her father in the hospital three months earlier. Instead, Babirye was a loving sister and only asked about how long she had been sick.

Nakato was miserable, and her body was a harbor for all kinds of ailments. The doctors diagnosed tuberculosis and prescribed a course of expensive drugs. Ssalongo insisted that Nakato had been bewitched and that they should get her out of the hospital. He had no money to buy the expensive drugs.

It seemed as though getting ill was the best thing Nakato had ever done for her father and sister. They were loving and attentive to her—even happy, perhaps. This baffled Nakato so much that she drew deeper into the confines of her usual shell and let them do whatever they wished. She thought they wanted her dead!

Nalongo came four days later and took her away to Busunju, many miles away from Mityana. She told them she knew what was wrong with Nakato and that she had friends in Busunju who could help her. By this time, Nakato had declared her life a wasteland and surrendered to any hand that touched her.

Nalongo took her to a clinic in Busunju. A nurse there talked to Nakato and counseled her about testing her blood to rule out "the disease" with certainty. Nakato refused. Even though her life was a wasteland, she decided she would rather believe she had been bewitched than that she had "the disease." But the next few days proved otherwise. As her body continued shrinking, her brain began awakening. The counselor managed to untie the twenty-five-year-old knot in her brain.

Shortly after her decision to have the test done, Nakato was informed that she did, in fact, have "the disease." Some of the numerous questions that initially came to her mind were: Where did she get the disease from? Why was it that other people didn't have it? Why was it that the disease found her body a favorable dwelling? Why was she born a second twin?

According to the normal state of Nakato's mind, she would understand the disease to be the result of the unfulfilled twin rituals, therefore putting the blame on her parents. But now that her mind was clear, she thought otherwise. She managed to connect her sexual life to what the counselor had explained. And then she made the connection between her condition and Paddy's ailments. That was when she realized that not only had she been given the disease, but also that she had spread it to at least ten people.

It was a hard truth to live with. It shook her to the core and turned her life around.

◎◎

Nakato pauses and chews her upper lip, and I am suddenly thrust into the present. I rub my eyes and watch her reaching for the leaf that had fallen from the *muvule* into her lap. She says, "I may have been a 'born murderer' as people say, but I don't believe all that anymore. It's ignorance!"

She considers ignorance to be the grandfather of all HIV infections that have happened in the past twenty years or so. Ignorance: an inevitable rainstorm that first invaded Rakai district and washed away thousands of people. Then slowly and quietly, like a pool of blood leaking through a closed door, it spread to the whole nation, producing sons and grandsons.

"Maybe I got the disease from Paddy; maybe I didn't. Maybe I spread it to all of these men I've been with; maybe they, too, already had it. After all, the majority of them already had more than one wife. None of them used condoms. Well, they didn't know about condoms anyway." She still doesn't look at me. She keeps turning the leaf over and over in her hands.

Nakato believes hers is a story of a lifetime. She wonders how she could have been so desperate and so ignorant in those days. What bothers her is that ignorance still remains. Her father is one of the greatest victims of ignorance today. Chances are that he has the disease, but every time he gets ill, he still blames it on witchcraft.

Nakato finally lifts her gaze to look at me. She says, "Father's third wife died a year ago. By the time she died, he was already back with his second wife. Christopher, the second-to-last man I had, remarried. Their first baby died. If that woman had known, she would have had their blood tested first before getting married to him."

Testing blood before getting into a sexual relationship was unheard of at that time. But now, thanks to each and every voice that has spoken out to enlighten people about HIV, people are cautious. They respond to the voices of HCT, HIV Counseling and Testing, and go on to enroll in VCT, Voluntary Counseling and Testing, in order to know their status. As a result, whoever is found free of HIV in their blood strives to remain free forever, and whoever is infected is empowered to live a longer, positive, and constructive life.

Nakato believes the disease will soon disappear, just as it appeared. She is now a member of TASO, the AIDS Support Organisation, where she is surrounded by love, real love. Her fellow clients in TASO are her family, perhaps the destination she was looking for all along. They share experiences and encourage and edify one another. Above all, hope is the oxygen that keeps them breathing.

"Let me reveal something to you," she says, almost whispering in my ear. "I believe that these drugs we take can completely kill the virus!

Maybe the doctors haven't yet announced it officially, but I think they will at any time. Just look at me now."

I look at her as if I hadn't been seeing her all along. Her face is disfigured by swollen parotid glands. Her sparse hair is patched with what looks like a ringworm infection. She tilts her head upward to give me a clear view of her hollow neck. She sits completely still, only moving her arm to scratch the patches on her head.

Nakato's hope centers on ARVs—antiretroviral drugs—which came into circulation in the late 1990s. At first they were inaccessible except to the rich, but now Nakato extends her sincere gratitude to the Ugandan government for its great efforts to make ARV drugs available to even the common person who earns very little.

I ask Nakato whether she has plans to marry again.

"No," she answers, shaking her head. "I have no plans to marry again. It still hurts me to know that I spread the disease like that. As I said, the grandchildren of ignorance are growing up now. I can assure you, still, some of those men don't want to use condoms, and some people still don't test their blood. I am not ready to extend my list now that I know where and how I stand. And I don't wish to add on any virus from anyone else now that mine is beginning to die."

She tells me that her counselor said the virus of today is even more deadly than the virus of those days. Today's HIV has greater resistance to the ARV drugs than that of yesterday. Nakato's prayer is that whoever is free of HIV today remains free forever, since it is preventable.

Nakato loves her children very much, and she puts all the energy she has into looking after them. "The only problem is that my income is so low. I plait hair and get a few coins to buy food and pay the rent," she says. Her firstborn, Tongo, is now eight years old. She is saving to buy him a school uniform so that she can register him in a Universal Primary Education school.

"I haven't taken my children for a test yet. But I'll do it very soon. I now know that children have chances of escaping the disease at birth, even if their mothers have it."

She knows about the recent project that has been introduced, called the Prevention of Mother-to-Child Transmission of HIV, or PMTCT. According to the PMTCT program, an HIV-positive mother takes a tablet, Nevirapine, at the onset of labor. Nevirapine is an ARV drug that helps to stop the multiplication of the virus and makes it inactive. This reduces the chances of mother-to-child transmission. And after delivery, the baby is given a Nevirapine syrup within seventy-two hours; this helps to inactivate any virus that crosses to the baby. And when it comes to feeding, the recommended period of breast-feeding, without any other foods, is three months.

Nakato says she delivered both of her children in the hospital. The project had not been introduced yet, so she never had a chance to take the Nevirapine tablet. However, she believes that the midwives took good care to minimize the chance of infection. After all, they did not even have to cut her to enlarge the birth passage. That means there was less contact of her blood with her babies' blood. Of course, her babies never had the chance to have the syrup either, but as far as feeding is concerned, they breast-fed for less than two months.

Tongo and Brenda are healthy despite the conditions they live in. Nakato says, "But even that is not a guarantee that my children are safe. I will have their blood tested."

When I expect Nakato's face to crumple into tears, it softens into a smile instead. She says she will face whatever results come of her children's tests because she believes they will live as long as her TASO "home" exists.

"Let's say I got the disease from Paddy; well, it's been fourteen years now, and I am still living. I'll live to outdo this dying virus. We've joined hands in our 'home' to fight the disease. Our counselors tell us the fight is already on, right from the top to the roots."

Nakato is totally proud to be among the mighty women fighting the spread of HIV. Her only wish now is to continue fighting, to completely eradicate the disease before another generation is born in ignorance.

Key to a New Life

BETTY KITUYI

I have an appointment with Juliet at the Mildmay Centre, but I have no real mental picture of her. I imagine she must be thin and have rough skin spotted with rashes and scars, common characteristics of HIV/AIDS sufferers.

I approach the information desk and ask for Juliet. The receptionist points at a crafts shop at the end of the hall and says, "That is Juliet."

I turn and see a slender woman about my height, five feet tall, putting a dress on a hanger. I approach and introduce myself as the writer from FEMRITE. She smiles broadly and extends her hand for a greeting as she introduces herself as Noel Juliet. We suddenly move toward each other and embrace, happy to finally meet.

She leads me to a bench, and we sit down. I am surprised at her appearance. She is a beautiful woman. She looks smart in her bob-styled nana braids. Her dark skin is smooth and glossy. She looks healthy, apart from her red lips, the only visible sign of the virus running in her blood.

Before we have a chance to talk, another woman interrupts us. She gives Juliet what appears to be a medical report. I politely wait as she reads the report and discusses it with the woman. Juliet asks her what her CD4 count is. The *woman tells her, and Juliet reassures her that it is not as bad as she thinks. I look on in admiration as Juliet encourages the woman to continue taking her drugs and to keep her next doctor's appointment. Juliet explains to me that she acts as a role model at the center, encouraging patients to take their ARVs. She continues to explain that she receives these drugs free of charge from the center. I immediately appreciate her openness and forthright manner.*

Juliet proudly guides me through her crafts shop. I see many things I admire. I decide on an album made of recycled paper for my son's photos. Juliet tells me it is her design; designing is a natural talent for her, which gives her a lot of inspiration. She explains that the crafts are products of an AIDS support group at the Mildmay Centre. I am impressed by the creativity and positive energy these people exhibit.

We decide to talk on the lawn where we will have little interruption. Juliet seems happy. Her eyes are bright, her lips expressive. She cannot stop talking about Mildmay. I learn from her that the center, a branch of Mildmay International, based in the United Kingdom, was opened in 1998. It effectively combines clinical outpatient services with resources for the training and development of people involved with HIV/AIDS care and management. Since its opening, the center has treated more than ten thousand patients. Children receive free care.

Juliet begins her story in a slow but confident voice.

*M*y name is Noel Juliet. I am the fourth born of twelve children by my mother. I grew up in a large polygamous family in Ndese, Bugerere county, in Jinja district. My father had many children from many wives. I remember being told when I was a baby that there were three other half siblings of the same age in our homestead. My father managed to send all his children to boarding school, a rare privilege at the time. I studied catering at college. In my family, there are doctors, medical assistants, and engineers. I have lost many family members. My mother, two sisters, and my brother all died within a period of six years.

Ours was a closely knit, loving, and supportive family. I had a special relationship with each one of them. Mercy, my sister—there was nothing I couldn't tell her. I miss that openness and sharing. I value my Catholic faith, which I learned at home and in the Catholic schools I attended. I wear this rosary around my neck because it reminds me to talk to the

Blessed Virgin Mary. I am a fan of the popular Radio Maria. Although I had such a strict religious upbringing, I had my first child while I was in senior five, at the age of eighteen. The father of my daughter, Chris, was my first boyfriend, whom I met when I was in senior three. Chris was my best friend Catherine's brother. I met him when I went to visit Catherine at their home during one school holiday. We were shelling beans in the courtyard when he rode up on his bicycle. He was a slender boy then, with an athletic body, and he looked so attractive when he smiled to greet me. But he did not keep his eyes on my face for long. He looked down and turned away to enter the house.

Their house was the best of its kind in our village. Their father, a high-profile lawyer, had built a big bungalow that matched his status. Villagers regarded him with awe. I counted myself lucky to be associated with that family. I felt different every time I remembered Chris from that day. Ours was love at first sight.

◎◎

After we reported back to school the next term, I received a letter. It was such a special thing to receive a letter in school in those days. A letter was the only physical link with your beloved back home. There were no mobile phones then. My mother would usually write to me in Luganda, our local language, to describe in vivid detail what was going on at home. Her words, like *mwana wange omulungi*—my beloved child— always brought tears to my eyes. But the blue-and-red-flagged airmail envelope I received one day bore nothing of my mother's words. My name was written at the center in black ink.

I moved away from other students to read in privacy. My heart thumped loudly inside my chest. My hands shook as I tore open the envelope and pulled out a piece of pink paper. It was the most beautiful paper I had ever seen. My eyes glided to the end of the letter, and I saw Chris's signature. I sat down to read it. It was full of oval-shaped drawings meant to resemble Chris's ballooned heart, filled with love for me. He said I was his oxygen.

I was so shocked that he felt such deep emotions for me after seeing me only once, but soon his professions of love convinced me, and I accepted him as my boyfriend.

We continued to write to each other and occasionally visited during the holidays. Two years after our first meeting, when I was in senior five, I conceived Chris's child and was expelled from school. My parents were disappointed. For a Catholic, such a pregnancy was frowned upon, but abortion was not permitted. Chris offered to marry me, but my parents wanted me to finish my education first. So after I gave birth to our beautiful daughter, my mother became her guardian, and I packed my books to attend a new boarding school and complete my A levels.

My relationship with Chris continued throughout college, and when I finished my catering course in 1992, I had our second child, a boy. I was still living with my parents, but Chris was a supportive, loving partner.

Four months before the birth of my son, I found out that Chris had a four-month-old baby girl called Maria. I was devastated to discover that Chris had been cheating on me. When I asked him about it, he was defensive, but he continued to be supportive and loving to our young family.

◎◎

Two years later, Maria's mother died, and Chris gained custody of the child. By then, Chris and I were living together, although we had not officially married in church. It was not hard for me to accept Maria, because I had come from a large polygamous family myself. My mother was a source of inspiration because she had not discriminated against her own stepchildren. Maria was like a daughter to me.

However, although my own children were doing very well, Maria's health was poor. I spent a lot of time taking her to the hospital. It was trying. She coughed all the time. She was weak and very skinny, too small for her age. Although it bothered me, I thought that sickness was quite normal for some children.

In 1996—I remember it was the end of April, a Friday—Chris came home from his work as a driver with the United Nations Development Programme, feeling unwell. He had slight diarrhea and a fever. It continued through the weekend.

On Sunday, I called on his parents. When they inquired about Chris, I told them how poorly he was doing. At their home later that day, I overheard a remark that concerned me. My mother-in-law said, "What are we going to tell her?"

I was puzzled but did not give it much thought. When I went back home that evening, Chris was not pleased with me for having gone to his parents' house. I found this rather strange, since he had never objected to my visiting them before. But I assumed he was seeking attention, which always flattered me a little. He still managed to make my heart skip a beat every time he looked at me. The following day, his parents came to take him and Maria to the hospital. They were both treated, but Chris's health did not improve.

The following week, I found Chris unconscious on our bed. I rushed him to Nsambya Hospital, where he was admitted to a ward for critical cases for two weeks. The moods of the health personnel were tense. The ward smelled awful, too, adding to the despair of the patients and their attendants. Many patients had tuberculosis. Some had lost all their hair.

Slowly, I began to realize that Chris could be suffering from HIV /AIDS. My sister, who was a doctor there, encouraged me to take an HIV test. So I decided to leave Chris with a relative and go to the AIDS Information Centre to have the test done. I did so in secret, not wanting Chris to know my plan.

At the center, I joined a group of other people sitting on a bench in the corridor, waiting to see the doctor. They looked apprehensive. I noted throbbing pulses between people's collarbones. I failed to start a conversation with anyone. Any eye contact I attempted to make was uncomfortable. Occasionally, someone would suddenly move out of the line and dash for the exit door, too afraid to take the test. Those who remained watched the door closely, waiting for it to open, in order to read the mood of people who had received their test results. Some people were mopping sweat from their faces despite the cool weather, while others made the sign of the cross repeatedly. I saw blank stares in some faces.

After what seemed like eternity, it was my turn to register with the nurse at the reception desk. I told her my age, my mother's name, and my home village. I was given a pink card with a number on it, which I was to give to the counselor after entering the counseling room.

The next room was well lit, with comfortable bamboo chairs padded with beautiful cushions. There were four other people in the room sitting in a circle. The counselor was a gray-haired woman, who welcomed everyone in a calm, quiet, and motherly voice and thanked us for having taken such a courageous step. She told us the counseling session was meant to encourage us to reflect on the decision we had made to know our HIV status. It would help us to prepare ourselves for the outcome of the test. She passed around an album of people who knew their HIV status and what they were doing to turn their lives around.

The atmosphere in that room was positive in comparison to that in the waiting room. The counselor managed to infuse some hope and energy into us. She led the group on a journey of self-awareness; she suggested that we learn to accept and love ourselves. A question was asked: Whom do you turn to in difficult circumstances? I discovered that I had to have something to hold on to, and that was God. He is the one who gave me the courage to go for the next session.

Each client was given a form that required personal information to be given. They asked many questions, including:

Why have you come?
When was the last time you had sex?
Did you use any protection?
Do you think you are HIV-positive?
What will you do if you find out that you are HIV-positive?
Are you married?
Do you trust your partner?

By the time I was led to the next room to have my blood taken, I was prepared for any outcome. A young nurse tied my upper right arm with a white cotton cloth and inserted a needle into my vein to draw blood. Then she injected the blood into a test tube containing another liquid, labeled it, and passed it across the counter. I was told it would be another hour before the test results were ready. I went back to the counselor's room, where I was encouraged to freely share whatever information I felt was important.

For the first time in my life, I discussed my sex life with someone. The counselor knew how to make me confide in her; she seemed like a good older sister. So I told her that Chris was my husband, the only man I had ever known, and the father of my two children. I explained that we had no reason to use a condom because we trusted each other. I noticed that the counselor spoke very little.

After our discussion, the counselor left me and went to collect my results. When she came back, she still looked me straight in the eye, smiling just as she had before. She told me that she had not read the results yet because we were going to find out together. I faced her, and our heads touched as we deciphered what was written on the card. I recognized it as the same card the nurse at the reception had given me. It read HIV-POSITIVE.

I sighed deeply and thought, So I am HIV-positive! So Chris has AIDS. Is that what killed Maria's mother? Is Maria also suffering from it?

The counselor watched me sympathetically. She drew me to her with empathy and kindness. She consoled me. I counseled myself, thinking, I will live longer if I get treatment. I don't know why I thought that way, because at that time there were no drugs specifically for AIDS. The counselor encouraged me to return to the AIDS Information Centre whenever I wanted help.

I left through the center's gates, quite shaken and bitter, but I managed to return to my husband at the hospital. I did not disclose what I had found out to Chris because he was very ill and I did not want to upset him further. However, I shared the sad news with my sister, who was also shaken but still encouraged me to stay strong. My family was very supportive during this time, bringing food to the hospital and visiting us quite often. I did not have any time to myself, but I knew Chris really needed me.

After two more weeks had passed, Chris still showed very little improvement. The hospital bills were growing bigger by the day, but he was eventually discharged. At home, Chris continued to lose his appetite and became gravely ill. One day, his parents came to see us and suggested that we should put our marriage right before God. They had lost hope that Chris would ever get well; they knew he was dying of AIDS. We both liked the marriage idea and agreed to their request.

The wedding preparations were for a one-day arrangement. Close relatives were summoned, and a priest was booked on short notice. It took place on a Thursday evening. I swept the compound and arranged the chairs for the visitors. My sister and aunts cooked *matooke*, rice, and meat.

The food aromas changed the mood from misery to one of feasting and celebration. My mother-in-law set up the small cakes she had baked the previous evening on stands in the center of the sitting area. Over a hundred people stood up when I emerged from the house dressed in a sparkling white wedding dress. They did not sing the wedding song *"Oluddewo okumpasa,"* which means "I could not wait to get married to you."

I leaned on my father's arm as I marched to join my husband. The maid of honor was my sister. I had two maids and a flower girl. My father gave me away to Chris. When I said my vows, I meant every word. People cried at my wedding. I think they felt sad because, with death lurking around Chris's life, they knew ours was going to be a brief marriage. But the wedding meant so much to me, because we had put our relationship right before God. Today, I know that if my son chooses to be a Catholic priest, no one will stop him, because his parents were properly married.

Chris passed away three months after the wedding. It was Saturday, September 1, 1996. I remember everything so vividly. Chris was feeding the chickens as I prepared lunch. We kept chicken broilers for sale to supplement our income. Chris did not mind helping by giving them water or cleaning their litter. I discouraged him from doing these things on this particular occasion because he was so sick, but he would not hear of it. It was those small things he did around the house that made me so fond of him. He always gave a helping hand.

I had cooked Chris's favorite meal of steamed *matooke*, meat, and vegetables. I knew Chris would love it, but my hopes were dampened when I invited him to eat and he said he had no appetite. He opted to rest instead. Not long after that, I heard footsteps and heavy breathing in the corridor. I rushed there only to find Chris collapsed on the floor. I tried to lift him up, but he was too heavy for me. I struggled and dragged him to the bed. Then I immediately sent for his family. They came shortly after. Chris was in and out of consciousness for the rest of that evening. Later in the night, after I had given him some passion-fruit juice with a spoon because he could not eat by himself, he died.

At first, I could not believe that he was dead. I mechanically attended to his body to make it look decent. I cleaned him, dressed him in his best clothes, and tied a strip of cloth around his head to keep his mouth closed, all without shedding a tear.

The following day, I still carried on strong. I sat and welcomed our guests, guiding relatives as they served tea and maize porridge. Chris's parents looked at me with eyes full of sadness and pity. Later in the day, I went to sit beside Chris's body, chasing away the flies attracted by the smell of death. A slight wind passed through the open door and momentarily lifted the white cotton cloth covering his body. Its movement caught my attention, and I lifted it again. As I did so, my hands brushed his skin. It was so cold, like a cement floor on a chilly morning. It was only then that it hit me—Chris was indeed dead. I screamed and wailed for the first time: *"Kale singa bibadde biseera bino,* Chris *teyandifude kuba edagala welili*—my husband and the father of my children is dead! Chris is dead!" And then I fainted.

Today Chris would not have died, because there is treatment for AIDS.

◎◎

It has been ten years now since Chris died. I describe myself as having climbed mountains of challenges. The naïve, overly optimistic woman in me has had to mature under the weight of responsibility. I have been so ill several times, yet I had to be a normal parent to my three children. It is very difficult to be a single parent, but it is worse when you are also one with a terminal illness.

But my association with the Mildmay Centre has helped me to face these challenges. I became a volunteer in the catering department at the center three years after Chris died. My mother also offered great support during this time. She always looked after Maria when she was admitted to the hospital so that I could stay at home and care for my other children. But one day, my mother died suddenly. Death robbed me of my mother at a time when I needed her most. I lost a friend. Each memory of her brings me pain. Her death came a year after that of my sister Mercy. Everything I held dear was falling apart. I broke down, to the advantage of the HIV virus, which began to manifest itself in my body.

The first sting of the HIV virus for me was a sharp, piercing pain in my upper left arm. I had developed abscesses. Five of them were cut open within a two-week period. The pain was immense during that time. I was admitted to Entebbe Hospital. Months later, I developed many severe skin rashes. My body had turned black like charcoal. With these changes in appearance and ill health, I could not keep my place as a voluntary worker at the Mildmay Centre. I could do nothing but stay at home.

At home, I developed a self-loathing attitude. I hated myself because I looked ugly. My cheeks were hollow; my skin was loose, hanging from my bones; and my hair had fallen out. I was the scarecrow version of my healthy self. I hated other people, too, because of the way they looked at me and the way they treated me. Some people began to abuse my property, taking my things without my permission. I lost faith; I couldn't attend church anymore for fear of others seeing how pathetic I looked. Before long, I had become a recluse, sick and lonely and without a single friend to turn to. It was also a very difficult time for the children. They were disturbed to see me so sick, but I kept telling them that I would be all right.

The Mildmay Centre staff, who were fond of me, had begun to wonder what had happened to me. So my brother got in touch with them to discuss my worrying state of health. They wanted me to go back for treatment and counseling, but I refused. I was too ashamed to show myself in public. I did not want people to stare at me.

After another few weeks passed, the center asked my brother to persuade me to reach out to them for help. One day, pretending to take me to Entebbe Hospital, my brother actually drove me through the gates of the Mildmay Centre. I was furious with him.

In the consultation room, I was warmly welcomed. The doctor spoke to me in the gentlest voice I had ever heard. His kindness and the harsh realities of my life were too contrasted to blend. I cried. I could not believe that anyone could love me in my current situation. Apart from my family, I had experienced a lot of stigma from the people around me.

But this doctor showed me sympathy, empathy, and kindness. He challenged me to accept myself in order to fight the disease. When he told me that Mildmay Centre was there for me, I looked at the strong brick walls in the room and imagined strong pillars supporting my feeble body. I stopped crying and sat up, allowing the doctor to carry out some tests on me.

My CD4 count was very low. It meant I had to start on antiretroviral drugs immediately to boost my immunity. My brother was called in to discuss money issues for the drugs. At that time, they were very expensive. Few people could afford even one month's dose! But as a family, we slowly managed to raise enough money for my first dose.

When we returned home, I resolved to live. I nurtured hope and faith. Only two weeks after I started taking the drugs, I felt much better, and slowly my health improved. The sores from the rash healed and my skin shed some pigment, recovering its original color.

A few months later, I joined the Mildmay International Client Support Association. When I first joined the group, members made me laugh at my habit of wearing a cloth on my head. They said it was suffocating and needed fresh air. After a while, I saw there was no need to tie a scarf on my head because these people accepted me as I was. I never covered my head again.

In this kind of community, where everyone cares about everyone, I no longer felt lonely. I had a sense of belonging. Life began to have meaning. Slowly, things began to go back to normal. After finding out that Maria, my stepchild, was also HIV-positive, I sought ARVs from Mildmay Centre and started her on them without her knowledge. When I first gave her the drugs, I only explained that they would prevent her from falling ill. She already knew how sickly she was, so she agreed to cooperate at first. But after a while, she became defiant. Her siblings did not take any drugs, so it didn't make sense to her to have to swallow drugs every day.

It was confusing when people told her she had AIDS. She asked me to confirm whether this was true. It was hard to give her an answer. I thought she was still too young to understand and was waiting for the right moment to tell her the truth. It came when she was ten years old, on World AIDS Day. On that day, Uganda joined the rest of the world to celebrate and remember its AIDS heroes. A documentary on Philly Bongole Lutaaya was run on Ugandan television. He was one of the first people to tell the world that he had AIDS. His echo of "Today it's me, tomorrow it's someone else" grabbed the children's attention. I saw this as the best opportunity to tell Maria that she too had AIDS and that her mother and father had died of the same disease. I told her that if she continued taking her drugs, she would not die.

Maria's reaction was shock and, later, withdrawal. She asked me where she had contracted AIDS. I tried to explain to her what might have happened. She did not eat for days. She talked to no one. I really identified with her. I left her to do as she wished but ensured that she took her drugs. After only a few days, she came around to accepting her state.

Something happens when one accepts her or his HIV status. You cannot afford to take life for granted anymore. Every minute you live is a great privilege.

With time, Maria and I became closer, sharing our common problem and reminding each other to take the medicine. Maria is a pleasant young girl and very helpful around the house. She is now thirteen years old and acts like a normal teenager. She attends the adolescent group at the Mildmay Centre.

I am independent and work hard to support my family. I struggle to pay fees for my children, who are in senior four and primary six, respectively. I still get offers from men who want to marry me, but I'd rather not. I am too attached to my children to start a new life with another man. At home, we plan family events together. My children know how much I love them. They are proud of me. I wouldn't sacrifice my children's love for anyone.

Looking for Home

BEVERLEY NAMBOZO

Dorcas and I had arranged to meet at the Wampewo polling station just two days after the presidential polls. At our meeting, she recounts the story of her voting experience, which is still fresh in her mind. It is her own way, I suppose, of connecting to the place where we are and also of making me initially aware of her place within these events. I notice she is a keen observer and has what seems to me unexplainable attachments to places.

I am not sure whether she is ready for the interview. But she seems to read my thoughts and tells me that she is ready. I follow her inside the nearby nursery building, and after we both settle into our chairs, she begins.

I glanced upward at the overcast sky, and all I saw were gray clouds. I was standing four places away from the ballot boxes at the Wampewo polling station, silently praying that I would be able to cast my vote before the rain started pouring down. Most afternoons in Uganda are filled with heat and dust. But today, the anticipation of voting for a president is almost tangible, even under the threat of a downpour.

I have lived through twenty years of President Museveni's rule. I was determined to vote that day for someone new, with the hope that my

143

grave would be filled with stories of a different political taste. I wondered what stories my brother and sister were sharing as they lay beneath me, in the splendor of the afterlife. Often I feel they accepted the gift of death too hastily. Hopelessness made them cheat in the race of life. They gave up too soon. I have AIDS complications too, just as they did, but there are so many things yet to be done. That day, for one, I had to vote before the rains began.

My voter's card was tucked safely in my handkerchief. I had left my five-month-old daughter, Winnie, at home. Her constant sickly state worried me a great deal, but I have a household of children who can look after her when I am away.

I inspected my voter's card. Below the distorted picture was written my name and date of birth: Mrs. Dorcas Ndagire, June 28, 1972. The face in the picture was fragmented, giving me the feeling that I was looking at myself through a cracked mirror. It reminded me of how I felt when I discovered I was HIV-positive: cracked and desolate inside and out. I remembered the church shutting me out, how cold and alone I had felt, like I had been thrown out into rain.

I was now second in the voting line. I felt a large drop of rain land on my head scarf like a bullet of coldness. Another drop just missed my breast. *Banange, laba enkuba ezze!* The lame gentleman in front of me hobbled to tick his presidential candidate in the ballot box before skillfully using his cane to maneuver his way to the nearby balcony for shelter from the rain. The electoral officials speedily gathered their equipment. Ignoring my plea to let me vote before the rain worsened, they too scampered to the nearby balcony. All around me people followed suit. The dust turned wet and muddied my legs and skirt. I gathered up my clothes, returned the voter's card to its place in my bra, and sought shelter as well.

The balcony of the nursery school was too small to comfortably accommodate us all. As we crammed together in the tight space, small puddles formed in the children's playground. Rivulets of brown ran down the painted cement walls. The downpour went on, allowing us only a slanted view of the shops and trees in the small trading center.

After what seemed like a lifetime, the rain subsided, and we reconvened to resume voting. Trying to weave my way to my place in the front of the line, I was rudely shoved backward. I tapped the shoulder of one of the officials, but he waved me away as he reorganized the boxes and other equipment. No one was willing to give me my rightful place at the front. Instead, they chatted incessantly above the noise of the rain. Even my neighbor, Mama Rose, picked up her phone and began to mindlessly speak into it when she saw me coming toward her. I couldn't tolerate going to the back of the line when I had been so close to voting only moments before! It was completely unfair, but no one seemed to care. I hugged myself tightly and began moving to the back.

On my way, I pleaded with two more people—two women—to allow me to stand in front of them. One told me she had to rush home to breastfeed her baby. The other told me that she had to hasten back to attend to a sick relative who had been left alone because the maid had gone to the village to vote as well.

And what about me? I felt like crying out. I had two teenagers of my own, a five-month-old baby, two adult nieces, three other teenage nephews and nieces, and a two-and-a-half-year-old nephew. I had to look after all of them.

◎◎

I was born in Mulago Hospital in 1972. As a family, we lived in Kiboga. It was my father, my mother, my twelve siblings, and me. All of us children were born of the same parents, Joyce Nakitende and Onesimus Mwebe. I am the last born. My siblings looked after me very well when we were young. They treated me like the baby I was.

I went to Kiboga Nursery School, where I enjoyed drama and singing. I remember, at one end-of-year concert, I was made to act the part of Mother Mary when other students were acting as angels. I sang a song about having a baby boy called Jesus. The teachers played the piano while some children played the drums. I sang so well, and everyone clapped for me. My parents were there, and after the concert they hugged me. I was given a prize. It was a blue basin and a packet of pencils. The first time I ever used my basin was on Christmas day. After that, I allowed my siblings to use it too.

I lived in Kiboga until 1982 when I was about ten years old. It was the beginning of the Museveni bush war. It was then that soldiers killed my father. It was a very sad time for us. My mother was a subsistence farmer and did not have enough money to look after all of us, even though some of my elder siblings had married and left home. I left home to stay with my sister and her husband in Luweero Triangle, about fifty miles from Kampala.

My sister and her husband were not rich. I stayed there without attending school for one year. All my life I had wanted to be a doctor, but I knew this would never be. Still, I continued to study on my own. When I was not studying, I was looking after my sister's child and working in the garden. I also played a lot with the neighbors' children, and I envied those who went to school. Finally, a year later, my sister and her husband got a little money, and I was able to attend.

The first day of my new term was a very good one. I was in primary four and the subjects were fascinating. In mathematics, we learned about fractions. In English, we read stories and answered questions by filling in the gaps. In social studies, we learned about Kabaka Edward Mutesa II, the first president of Uganda, and about the white explorers who discovered Lake Victoria and Lake Albert. Our teacher used to tell us that the white people were liars because it was the Ugandans who first saw Lake Victoria. She told us that Ugandans had always been there, using the lake for fishing, bathing, swimming, and many other things well before the white people came along to Uganda. The lake was called Nalubaale until the whites changed its name to that of Queen Victoria. That is why we call it Lake Victoria today.

I went to school for three months before the terrible war broke out. It was a war between the president of the time, Dr. Milton Obote, and the current president, Yoweri Kaguta Museveni. The soldiers of these two men fought, but we, the ordinary people, were the ones who suffered. That war disrupted our lives. Some of my siblings moved back to live with us at my sister's house. We were always running from soldiers. I remember many nights when we would stay awake, listening to the incessant shooting. We prayed hard. My elder sister and brother would even make the sign of the cross on each of our foreheads for protection.

One day, a group of us were walking outside the shops—it was advisable to walk in groups—when we saw Obote's soldiers coming toward us. One held his gun up and shot in the air. We got scared and ran for our lives. We ran down the road into a nearby forest. We could hear the soldiers running after us. Then they began shooting. My eldest brother shouted at us to run faster. I was just eleven years old. I had only my slippers on, so the stones were pinching my feet. There were others in the forest who had run when they saw us running; everyone was afraid of the soldiers. We stopped running only when we could no longer hear the gunshots.

We fell down on the grass. My feet were bruised. I had blood on my leg from when a dry tree branch cut me. My sister's dress had a gaping hole in the back. My other sister's dress had thorns stuck in the zipper. My eldest brother had lost one shoe, and his right cheek was swollen. We were all exhausted and thirsty from running so fast. After lying on the grass for several minutes, my eldest brother finally spoke, saying that we should return home. We half walked and half ran back home, each one of us on the lookout for soldiers.

That night, we discussed the hard situation we were living in. I complained that I would never become a doctor and that I was very behind in school. My brothers said that it was hard for them to work and save money to lead a normal life. My sisters wondered if any man would notice them in this war, and they were not prepared to marry soldiers. There was no peace. We had to go in larger groups just to buy basic food supplies for the house. Sugar had become a luxury.

There used to be many raids at night. The worst one I remember happened at our home. We were eating cassava and drinking tea without sugar when we heard the sounds of people screaming and scattering outside. At first, my sisters and I hid under the beds. But when my brother screamed that the house was on fire, I got up to see. Smoke had started to come from under the front door, quickly growing higher and thicker. Terrified, we began shouting for help, but soon I began to cough, and my sister fainted. My brothers tried their best to break the window and to tear through the ventilators using sticks. Finally, they managed to do that, and one by one, we all jumped out of the window. We didn't look back at our burning house until we had run some distance. When we did, my sisters and I wept. I remember wondering how life could be so cruel. With nothing else to do that night, we slept in the forest, along with a number of other people on the run.

The following days were extremely hard. Finding food was a difficult task. President Museveni's soldiers, however, would come to visit us in the forest, and they were fairly kind. But one day they advised us to go to Masulita, where they said they had more control. So we packed our few belongings and went.

Masulita was known as a danger zone in those days, just like Gulu is today, due to the rebel activity. The situation was very harsh, and many people lost their relatives there.

One morning, Obote's soldiers came for mine, too. They pounded on the door of our one-room house and took two of my brothers to be recruited into Obote's army. We cried, knowing that our brothers would be forced to kill many innocent people, or they themselves would be killed. We ran after the soldiers, but they shot at us and did the most terrible thing I have ever seen in my life. They got hold of a woman who was running away with her baby. One soldier snatched the baby from her arms and threw it at a soldier carrying a mortar and pestle. As the woman screamed and the rest of us watched, the soldier put the child in the mortar and used the pestle to kill it. He pounded and pounded the baby until it finally died. That is why even today I still fear soldiers so much.

After we lived in the danger zone for roughly one year, Museveni's soldiers relocated us to Kampala. There the shooting and killing decreased, and I was able to study again, this time at Banda Primary School. Although I was now fourteen years old, I was put in primary five. I was very old for the class, but my English was poor. I had thought that I would be very happy to return to school, but the children called me *Jjajja wa baana*—grandmother of the children—and it made me feel very isolated.

In 1986, the year that President Museveni came to power, I went to live with my older sister in Mengo, Kisenyi, a suburb of Kampala. It was there that I studied catering at Jimmy Sekasi Catering School for a number of years. Jimmy Sekasi was later killed when he went on a trip with his students to the northern part of Uganda.

One day, during the first year of my studies at catering school, I was oiling my hair when the landlady called me. "Dorcas, Dorcas!"

"Yes, I am in my room," I responded.

She entered, and her huge figure blocked the light from the doorway.

"Dorcas, I want to take you for a ride with my brother. You do not have to finish with your hair. Just put on a head scarf."

"I am almost through," I said, hastily oiling the remaining part. I took off my wrapper, attempted to smooth out the creases in my skirt, put on my shoes, and went outside. The landlady was already seated in the passenger side of an old maroon Toyota Corona. The engine was running by the time I reached the back door. A man in the driver's seat, with spiked ears and burn marks on the left side of his face, turned to greet me as I entered.

"How are you, Dorcas?"

"I am fine."

"You can call me Vice. Your landlady is my sister. I am doing some work on my house, and my sister told me that you are very good with your hands. I need some help. We shall pay you for your ideas."

This sounded ideal. I could never say no to a bit more money. I quickly said yes, and we drove away.

Vice looked ugly from behind, and his scar made him look even uglier from the front. How did his wife kiss him with that huge scar on his face? The clock above the radio read half past five. I wondered what time we would be back home. I still had to clean my room and prepare for tomorrow. Vice turned the radio to a gospel station. I allowed myself to drift into a light sleep until the car suddenly stopped.

I awoke and asked, "Where are we?"

The landlady replied, "We are in Mityana. You dozed off and even missed the maize that we ate. You can eat later on. Go into the house with Vice. I am going to check on someone. I shall be back soon."

Mityana? I had never been to this part of the country before. The landlady walked off as I got out of the car. Vice led me into the house. I remember my stomach feeling so empty.

"Dorcas, you can make yourself some tea while you are waiting for my sister to come back. Here is some maize. Let me go upstairs and finish some work."

After he left, I walked around the main floor of the house. It was huge! Looking at the long corridor of doors, I thought it could have been a small hotel. In the sitting room, there were many animal carvings, a picture of Museveni, and paintings of African dancers.

The place looked beautiful. The kitchen was enormous and had three glass cabinets—one was for glasses, another for cups and plates, and the third for dishes and cutlery. It looked expensive. I thought I would be unable to use a stove in this kind of kitchen, but I saw the kettle sitting near the sink. There was even tap water there. I filled the kettle in the sink and plugged it in.

I had never lived in a house with tiles, but I was determined to work hard after gaining my diploma, and I thought that maybe after three years I could rent a house with tiles. Then I could start to look for a man and get married. My mother expressed her concern that I would never find a man who wanted to marry a woman with a lot of money, but I kept telling her that God did not want me to be poor.

The water boiled. I dropped in a teabag—it had a pleasant lemon scent—and began to chew at my maize. I hoped that Vice did not mind me standing while I was eating, because I did not dare eat maize while sitting on one of the expensive chairs in the sitting room. It was past six thirty when I finished eating. As I looked for a rubbish bin outside the house, I wondered when the landlady was coming back. Not finding one, I hesitantly threw the cob over the wall, returned inside to wash my mug, and then sat on the carpet in the sitting room. It was growing dark outside.

Vice came into the room and asked, "Hasn't my sister come back yet? She must have been delayed. Let me show you to a guest room where you can have a bath and rest while you wait for her. There are some albums and magazines for you to look at."

I couldn't believe that I was going to have a hot shower in this mansion! When I reached the room, I was excited and quickly removed my clothes. The water was so wonderfully hot that it nearly burned me. I squealed for joy. Tilting my face upward, I let water enter my mouth and tried singing at the same time. It made a funny gurgling noise and tickled my throat. I turned off the tap. I had never wasted so much water in my life. I marveled at the room full of steam. The water I used for one shower was enough to wash all the bedsheets in my home, with enough left over to mop the floor.

Wiping the steam from the mirror, I looked at my naked body. I was a bit overweight, with big breasts, but that was good because it meant that I was attractive and healthy. I couldn't bear to get back into my dirty clothes, but I put on the skirt and blouse with nothing underneath. After all, I would be returning home soon.

The guest room had a huge double bed with a pink bedspread and pillows. I threw myself onto it. The bed was so comfortable! The wall clock read nine o'clock. Switching off the light, I lay down to sleep.

I dreamed of a long pink wedding gown and a house full of tiles, but a hand on my shoulder woke me up. I sat up quickly. Through the dim light from the open curtains, I could see Vice standing before me with only a towel on. I let out a scream and covered myself with the blanket.

"Don't scream. Let us have sex and then tomorrow I shall take you back home."

My eyes were wide open with fear. I had never been this close to a man. I let out another scream. "Leave me alone. I shall . . . I shall call the police."

He just laughed and dropped his towel. His nakedness shocked me. I tried to get out of the bed before he could grab me, but his hand hit my shoulder and I fell backward. He stripped back the bed covers and stood over me.

"What are you doing?" I shouted.

He covered my mouth with his hand, and before I knew it, my skirt was rolled up, exposing my thighs. He forced them apart with his knees, and I felt his hardness inside me. It was huge, and Vice just kept pushing it in and in. The pain almost reached my ears. I wanted him to stop, but I could not fight. I had lost my strength.

Moments later, he stopped hurting me and quietly left the room.

I looked at his sticky mess between my thighs and my blood on the pink sheets. I felt the pain, and I cried to myself. With the little strength I had, I walked to the bathroom, turned on the tap, and allowed the water to remove layer upon layer of physical pain.

Returning to the guest room, I laid my exhausted body on the floor, not wanting to go near the bed, and eventually I cried myself to sleep. The following morning, Vice found me lying in a heap on the floor. He put three thousand shillings next to me, saying that it should be enough to take me back to Kampala. I knew I was going there with the heaviness and pain of a girl who had been to hell and back. That was the day that I made up my mind to conquer the world, no matter what happened to me.

I felt like I could never put those clothes on again. Searching through the closet, I found a long black skirt and a jacket. It was a bit hot outside, but I didn't care. After changing my clothes, I went out the front door and ran down the road as fast as my hurting body could allow me. I was so scared, and I couldn't mention any of this to the landlady. I didn't even tell my own sister what had happened.

◎◎

I soon moved out and settled into a much smaller house next to a church, the Mengo Church of the Lord. This church, made of papyrus reeds, brought me much joy. It did not matter to me that other believers from mainstream churches referred to it as "one of those *biwempe* churches." I faithfully attended all Sunday services, but I didn't dare discuss my story with anyone at church.

I spent two happy years in that church. As was the common practice with charismatic churches in Uganda, my church found me a husband. This made me a very happy woman. The chosen man was God-fearing, kind, and hardworking, and he came from a respectable family. I fondly remember the introduction ceremony in 1998. It was a simple yet beautiful affair. Three weeks before the wedding, the church started making announcements. It felt good to read my name in the church bulletin and to hear the pastor announce that I was getting married. Every time someone congratulated me, I felt like bursting with joy. I was the happiest woman in the world. I was about to be married to a wonderful man, and I thought nothing could possibly go wrong. But I was mistaken.

One month before the wedding, the pastors suggested that we go for HIV blood tests before we got married. My fiancé agreed, and we both went to Baumann House, an AIDS information center. We took our tests and were told to return after two weeks. When the results came back, my fiancé was negative, and I was positive.

My heart felt heavy when I was told that I was HIV-positive. I wondered how it could have happened. Then I remembered the night when I was eighteen and my landlady's brother forced himself on me. I couldn't believe that he had given me the virus. My fiancé already knew about the incident and tried to comfort me, but I didn't know what to do. Naturally, the wedding was postponed to a later date, but three months later, after another test, he was still negative, and I, still positive.

People at Mengo Church started talking about us. They were saying all kinds of nasty things about me, calling me *malaya*, a prostitute. Suddenly my friends did not want to talk to me anymore. Every time I entered the church, people began to whisper; the church had lost its love for me. The only friend I had was my fiancé. I felt so alone. The most difficult time was when we went to Dr. Mubiru at Mulago Hospital, and he confirmed, for the third time, that I was positive and my fiancé was negative. My husband-to-be and I agreed that we couldn't marry.

I stopped eating and even stopped going to church. I felt like there was nothing left for me to live for. My life, as I knew it, had ended.

I returned to my village in Luweero because I had no job. It was there that I met a Tanzanian man who seemed quite loving. He would sit and talk to me and visit my home very often. Although I told him about my poor health, he continued to show love for me. I liked him and eventually moved with him to Kampala. We had a small introduction ceremony and were traditionally married.

Four years later, after we had two children together, my health began to worsen. My body was covered with sores, and I had lost a lot of weight. I was anemic, and my eyes were sunken. My husband also fell very ill at this time and left for Tanzania. I missed him at first, and the children had no father. It was a very difficult time. It was around then that I heard about TASO and decided to join.

I tried to keep busy with TASO, and my life slowly started to pick up. My children gave me so much joy. I taught them how to act; sometimes I even acted with them. Oh, how we laughed! I had even made many new friends, and they visited me at my home. My sisters and brothers, who were quite wealthy by now, did not want anything to do with me, but my mother came home to help me look after the children.

After I had been involved with TASO for some time, I met another man during one of the TASO conferences. He had noticed me being helpful at the conference and became very interested. He came over to greet me. He was also HIV-positive, and we became good friends. After we were properly acquainted, he persuaded me to have sex, and I agreed.

We did not use a condom, and I became pregnant. I lived with him for a short while before he started falling ill. After about a year, and after the birth of our baby, he went to live in Masaka with his family.

◎◎

At TASO, I have joined Mama Club. The club was founded by Dr. Lydia Mungherera about a year ago and was launched by the Nnabagereka of Buganda on Women's Day in 2005. Dr. Mungherera formed Mama Club after she realized that there was no organization to look after positive mothers. Mama Club looks after the welfare and mental state of mothers who are living with the virus. Many mothers have come out of hiding as a result of the club. Some of these mothers had been kicked out of their homes and faced a lot of hardships and stigma. But at Mama Club they found acceptance and companionship and were encouraged to adopt a positive attitude toward their situation.

We have two anthems, which we composed. And we are going to start a drama club, which I will be a part of because I like drama very much. We laugh a lot every day. These are my sisters. We share a lot and give each other strength. There is always medicine for us when we need it, but it's not the physical medicine that helps, not as much as the spiritual medicine. This is the church and home that I needed from the very beginning. I look forward to going to work in the mornings because I long to share with my sisters about my children. I have learned how to live positively.

My youngest baby is five months old. The father comes from Masaka to visit over the weekends. He doesn't look so happy. When he sees me laughing, I know he wonders where I draw my strength from. I encourage him to live positively and make plans for the future.

I really desire to speak to many people. The worst sickness is not the sickness of the body, but the sickness of the heart. The church stigmatized me, but I have a new refuge now. I found my soul again when I joined TASO and Mama Club. My baby never goes without milk, because my sisters are always there to provide.

But these days, my baby has been falling ill. She has pneumonia and a rash. Her father is not supportive. But I am still a strong woman. Each day brings new hope. It's not always easy. I do fall ill sometimes, but laughing, singing, and my children make my heart smile.

This is what I feel like telling the whole world:

Be firm with your children.

Not all friends are good; the landlady gave me a very bad blow.

Girls who are in school should not have sex for money; they are worth much, much more than that.

And my word to the church is that they should be like hospitals. Many women have been raped and go to the church for solace and help. Instead they are met with hatred and suspicion. The church should welcome all girls and women, whatever their sin or perceived sin. They carry a pain that cannot be carried alone.

I have found my home, and I have found my joy in my children.

In God's Palm

ROSE RWAKASISI

The October sun is burning me mercilessly. Heavy trucks loaded with bunches of matooke and sacks of beans and finger millet raise clouds of dust as they speed past me.

"Damned trucks!" I curse, choking on the dust swirling all around me.

I am on a mission to find the Nyakambu trading center, which is on the border between Sheema, Kashari, and Buhweju counties in western Uganda. Suddenly a boda boda cyclist, with sweat dripping from his oily face, screeches to a stop beside me.

"Where to?" he asks with a big grin on his face.

I tell him my destination, and he assures me that he knows the location and its inhabitants.

"I will take you there, madam; trust me."

I have no alternative, so I agree.

"The word nyakambu means 'small river' or 'pond,'" he explains.

Then he points proudly toward one of Buhweju's gigantic hill ranges. "Behind those hills, there is a place where the rainbow starts and ends. Nyakambu is at the foot of those hills," he adds.

After about an hour, we come to an abrupt stop in front of a house. The impact knocks my forehead against his stone-hard back.

"Oops!" I mutter as I scramble off the carrier.

Before I can venture to ask him whether this is the place, I hear him say, "Here we are, town lady. This is Mulokole's hotel."

Immediately he stops talking as a dark-skinned man steps out the front door of the house and comes toward us. He is tall and slender, with gray teeth and red eyes that look as cunning as a rat's. He has unkempt black hair sprinkled with gray and partially covered with a torn cloth cap that he wears at a rakish angle. The gray jacket he has on has enormous pockets.

"Hello, Boda." He greets the motorcyclist warmly as if they are old friends, then turns to look at me questioningly.

I stare at them silently as the afternoon sun scorches my dark skin. My mouth is so dry that my tongue threatens to clog my throat. I would have given the rest of my life for a sip of the cold yogurt I had left in my fridge.

The two talk at length and exchange gossip before they finally realize I still exist. The motorcyclist moves toward me and says, "Hajji, this lady has come to visit your mulokole!" He explains how he rescued me as I look on awkwardly, trying to keep myself from sinking in the soft ground and my black suede shoes from filling up with soil.

Hajji smiles and extends his hand in a greeting as he maneuvers himself between me and the cyclist.

"Come in, come in, nyabo," he says. "Mulokole has been expecting a visitor, and I think it is you. We've been cleaning this house every day; we even white-washed the inside as if we were expecting a bride!" he adds jokingly.

He leads me inside, and I find Kyosha sitting on a low stool, her knees drawn together and a small child at her side. She stands up with a great welcoming smile on her face and greets me. She looks so small that she could be mistaken for a thirteen-year-old. She might have been pretty once, but her eyes are so intense and penetrating that, when she looks at you, it is as though she can see right into your heart and discover your secrets.

In the middle of the room is a table covered with a clean white tablecloth. A set of shining metallic glasses, two green plastic jugs, and a cluster of ripe bananas are laid out on top. A boy of about ten years and a girl of about five are having lunch. When I approach, they stop laughing and stare at me. I greet them, then turn back to Kyosha and the small girl.

I look at the emaciated child as Kyosha pulls her gently closer and folds her arms around her. The toddler curls up sleepily. Her body is the size of a two-month-old's, but she has an old woman's face, sadly wrinkled and scaly. Her clothes are clean, but her nose is another story. And her right-hand thumb is permanently in her mouth.

Kyosha notices my curiosity and says casually, "She is the daughter of my niece, who passed away about a year ago. She was three years old when her mother died. Children," Kyosha muses with a hint of sadness, "they can surprise you sometimes. Nobody dreamed this one would live even a week after her mother died, but here she is, still!" She looks down at the sleeping child and sighs wearily.

The two-room house serves the dual purpose of a restaurant and a home. Kyosha has partitioned it into two, with a connecting door in the middle. The front room is the restaurant, where she serves food. She tells me that since she became a born-again Christian, she stopped serving supper. She says that the men must have supper with their families. "I provide a service, but I am not a home wrecker. I know how painful it is for a woman to prepare supper and eat it alone, because the husband's stomach is filled with fried food from Kyosha's restaurant. No, I cannot serve supper to my friend's husbands!"

The other room at the back is divided into a sitting room and a bedroom by a blue cotton sheet. Hidden behind the sheet are her bed, suitcases, children's clothing, and bedding.

I have arrived at a busy time. Food is being served under a temporary shed between the main house and the kitchen. As she attends to her customers, I opt for a tour of the place by myself.

As I walk around, I bump into a gray cat chasing the chickens that run all over the compound. After I watch the cat for a few minutes, my attention is drawn back to the chickens. Instead of being chased by the cat, they are now, themselves, chasing a huge white-and-black-spotted cock that is holding a wriggling, nearly meter-long brown snake! Though I am an admirer of nature, I draw the line at snakes. I duck back quickly into the house.

After the number of customers goes down, Kyosha turns her attention to me. We take shelter under a mango tree. She serves me a cup of delicious hot tea with ripe sweet bananas. Her five-year-old comes skipping a rope and tucks her head into Kyosha's skirt. Every so often, she uncovers her face, peeps out at me, then quickly hides again.

Kyosha remembers she has not introduced her children: "This is Serina, the baby! And James, the boy Serina follows, is at school. He is in primary seven and busy preparing for his PLE examinations next month. I expect him to pass well enough to qualify for a good secondary school, such as Ntare. My dilemma is how to raise the school fees. At least, at primary level, the government UPE program covers all fees. But I'm not despairing, because he is always lucky. God gave him the gift of being loved by people, and a number of them have helped me raise him.

"And my firstborn has not been around for many years. When she was in primary seven, my sisters were down with AIDS. Feeding them and buying medicine took all the money my mother and I had saved. I ended up failing to pay her UNEB examination fee. When she turned up ready to sit for the examination, she was chased away because her name was not on the examination register. She was so annoyed and disappointed that she ran away from home and eloped with a man old enough to be her father. She managed to call me on the day my mother died. Believe me or not, it was a big consolation, to hear that my baby was still alive."

"Such men should be dealt with seriously. How dare he ruin the future of a young girl like that!" I exclaim, outraged.

Kyosha cups her mouth with her hand to cover a yawn, then changes the subject. "Yes, you said you came to ask about my life story?"

I say yes, that is the purpose of my visit. She regards me for a while. I see determination written all over her small, hardened face. Then she starts talking in a smooth, steady voice.

"Well, we, my siblings and I, were brought up in a confused home—"

A customer interrupts us, and she leaves to serve him.

In the meantime, the mean-looking cat heads straight for me. It purrs loudly, and I freeze! It rubs its head on my leg. I endure the torture until I see, out the corner of my eye, my savior return, just in the nick of time.

When Kyosha sees the intense fear in my eyes, she says casually, "It won't hurt you," and shoos it away. "Now, where did we stop?" she asks, giving me a big smile that reveals an enchanting gap between her white, evenly spaced upper teeth.

"We were talking about your family," I remind her.

She laughs softly, giving me such a warm look that I feel I have known her a long time. She picks up the thread of her story, saying, "My family wasn't always confused. My elder siblings told me that they were born in a happy and peaceful atmosphere. Problems started with me and will end with me."

She looks away, her eyes fixed upon the Buhweju hills that tower above us.

We are silent for a moment. Then, after she draws a breath and lets it out, she resumes.

*M*y mother used to tell us that Father was not always the rich man he had become. He had neither cows nor goats to pay for my mother's bride-price, so they had to elope. Then he went off to Buganda for long periods of time to work and earn money in order to pay her bride-price. In between the long trips, he used to sneak home to ensure that Mother conceived.

After several of these trips, Father was able to fully pay the bride-price. To put icing on the cake, they registered for a church wedding. It was considered a great honor to marry in church. My mother became the envy of all the womenfolk in the village. She would spend hours bragging to her friends about how fortunate she was to have found such a man. So the next time he left, it was to find money for the wedding feast.

One early Sunday morning, Eva, my eldest sister, rushed in to Mother, who was still in bed, tired from the previous evening's hard work. Eva said excitedly, "Mama, Mama, Taata is back!"

"What are you talking about, Eva? Do you miss your Taata so badly that you resort to lying?" Mother asked.

"Taata has come. He came last night and slept at Grandma's house," Eva insisted.

When Mama went to Grandma's place, she found the old woman seated on a goatskin. Eva was on her lap, curled under her *suuka*. Father was sitting on a stool a few feet from Grandma. A new mat that was always reserved for special guests was spread between them. Mother was not a visitor, so she avoided it.

While Mama and Grandma were talking, Father excused himself and left. He later returned with a woman who was carrying a baby in her fat, brown arms.

"They walked in like a bridal march," Mama used to tell us.

The woman sat on the mat, and there was silence. After clearing his voice several times, Father said to Mama, "Martha, meet your sister, Mary. And Mary, this is the woman I have been telling you about. If either of you don't see me at your house, expect me to be at your sister's place or at the pub."

But that night, instead of hearing the soft knock and gentle call of *Bashemera*, Mama's usual pet name, she heard a thunderous bang, which was followed by the sound of bottles falling to the ground. She was seven and a half months pregnant at the time, and I believe the shock of it all was too much for her to handle, and she delivered a premature baby, me. Thanks to Grandma's care, I survived. Out of the blue, Father denied my paternity. They had long quarrels about me not being his and how Mama had probably given herself to all the men in the village during his absence. All the poor woman could do was protest with tears running down her beautiful face.

Five years after I was born, Father paid my mother a little bit of attention, and their fifth child, Lisa, was born. Soon my stepmother got tired of cooking for Grandma and washing her own clothes, so she convinced Father to bring her to his house, our home. From the day she came to our compound, all hell broke loose. We only existed to make her life easier. We washed, cleaned, and cooked for her. My mother and Eva, the first-born, were in charge of cooking, and I was the nanny to her children. Our stepmother never did any work around the house. And yet she was always complaining about us to Father, who believed her every word.

By the time my stepmother had had her three boys, it had become unbearable for all of us to live under the same roof. She ranted and raved about how my mother was trying to kill her children. Father always took her side, and either Mother or one of us ended up being beaten. Whenever the situation got unbearable, my mother took us to her brother's home, where we sometimes stayed for as long as two years or until my stepmother got tired of housework. But Father would send for us. Mother would then return with a goat for slaughter in order to be forgiven. I never understood why she went back or even why she needed to be forgiven. She would pull the goat all the way from Sheema while carrying Lisa on her back.

Father would welcome us home with the smile of a cunning fox. A few days later, or even the next day, it would be, "You and your brats, there is the door—leave my house. What your brother brought isn't enough atonement."

We would then obediently leave his compound, with our stepmother standing in the doorway, a satisfied look on her heavily painted face, which seemed to say, *I am the woman of this house, understand? And as long as I am here, you won't be.*

We walked from Rubindi to Sheema so many times that I lost count. Meanwhile, Father watched keenly whenever we made our usual roller-coaster trips to and from his house. Eva, the firstborn, was ripening into a beautiful young woman: tall, with smooth skin and a lovely smile. She had turned into a replica of my mother at that age, or so Grandma used to say. The talk in the village was that "when a banana grows and ripens, it should be eaten."

So when her breasts started budding, Father sent for us and demanded a bull as the final atonement! My maternal uncle had one bull, and he willingly gave it so that his sister could get back into a stable home. He couldn't get it to Rubindi fast enough! Uncle led it all the way to Father's compound. Mother carried a fifty-kilogram sack full of millet flour. My father's relatives slaughtered the bull, and we all feasted as if it were Christmas.

Father built us a ramshackle grass-thatched hut, and there he left us to fend for ourselves. The iron-roofed house that my mother had helped to build was my stepmother's and her children's, not ours. Our house leaked during rainstorms, and the wind blew the roof off more times than Father could repair it.

Slowly, the years passed. A policeman spotted my sister, Eva. The man was rich and willing to pay the entire sum of money Father demanded. I envied Eva. But Father ate the entire bride-price alone. Mother got nothing for her struggles. Not even the blanket that is always given to the mother of the bride! Father didn't give Uncle the bull that was due to him either. And Mother sat beside him in that chair, smiling and looking pleased as she watched her husband give his daughter away proudly, as if he had had a hand in her upbringing.

Three months after Eva's wedding, I was bathing my three half brothers when I heard Father roar out, "What is going on in my house?"

My stepmother sniffed and, with her delicate and soft right hand, wiped a tear running down her bleached cheek while pushing him away with her left hand. She turned away from him.

"What's the matter?" he asked her.

"You hardly noticed me at the wedding," she accused him, turning troubled eyes on him. "Go to the wife who has beautiful daughters fit to be companions for princes and presidents."

"Phew!" Father gasped.

I saw an evil grin cross her face. I slipped out stealthily and ran home to alert my mother. When he arrived at our hut later, he was welcomed by dead silence. This time, we trotted back to my uncle's place with nothing.

Uncle, with his family of nine, welcomed us, and we lived together as one huge family. During those days, food was scarce, so Uncle gave us accommodation, but he couldn't afford to give us food, too. He offered us a saucepan and told us to find food and cook it ourselves.

We used to wake up early, before cockcrow, and set off to look for work, Mother with a hoe on her shoulder and a child on her back. We would walk from house to house, stopping outside the door to ask if there was any land that needed to be tilled. And if God was on our side, the people would point at a garden. We would all work from morning till dusk. They would give us a bunch of bananas in payment, which we would carry home to cook and feast on. This was how we got our food, be it famine or harvest time. We moved long distances—sometimes as far as Rweichumi village, ten kilometers away.

And after weeding people's gardens, Mother would go home and plant crops like cassava, millet, and beans. After a year of much suffering, we began to eat food from our own gardens.

◎◎

Mother decided to send James, Lisa, and me to school. Mama and Ruth continued working very hard at tilling other people's gardens, carrying water, and collecting firewood from a snake-infested forest. The strain proved to be too much for Ruth; she eventually agreed to elope with some rich man who had had his eye on her for a long time and had promised to pay our school fees if she married him.

But Mother refused to touch the money. When the man brought her the bride-price converted into money, she would not even offer him a calabash of porridge!

"Ruth has a father. Take the bride-price to him. He is in Rubindi; talk to him, not me," Mother said, as she pointed in the direction from which we had come.

"But your daughter insisted that I give it to you and your brother so that you can use it to pay school fees for her younger siblings," the man explained in an effort to convince her.

But Mother would not touch a coin, in spite of the terrible state we were in. And the man had no option but to take the bride-price to Father, who ate everything alone.

When my grandfather saw that I was no longer at school, he arranged for me to go to Kampala to work for Aunt Claire. Aunt Claire treated me like one of her children. I ate at the same table with them, and she gave me everything except what I craved most, education. I constantly sent the money I earned home for Lisa's education and Mother's needs, but I missed school. I resorted to reading my cousin's old books and doing homework with them. On my visits to the village, I acted as if I were attending school in Kampala.

◎◎

Whenever my cousins broke off for holidays, Aunt Claire would also send me for a break. One fateful day, in the first week of January 1984, I was at the junction of Masheruka and Buhweju roads when I saw Rukundo, a boy I had acted with in a play when I was still at school. He stood towering over me. His height and good looks overwhelmed me. We arranged to meet again, and I talked to him a lot during the days I spent in the village. I unveiled my passionate desire for going back to school. He promised to pay my fees if I agreed to marry him after he completed school. I began to see my dream of going back to school coming true. Rukundo must be a godsend, I thought. But Rukundo had his own devilish agenda.

After the Christmas school holiday, I prepared to return to the city. I told my mother about Rukundo's plans to send me back to school.

"I hope you are not being trapped!" she warned.

A month after I returned to Kampala, I began to feel dizzy and often vomited after waking up in the morning.

Aunt Claire, who had been observing me, came to my room early one morning. "What's happening to you, Kyosha? Are you sick?"

"It's nothing, Aunt. I am just weak," I told her.

She gave me a long look before she finally said, "You must be pregnant, Kyosha!"

"No, that can't be true. It was just once!" I shouted, more as a reflex than a statement of fact. Her suggestion had caught me off guard. I collapsed on my bed, covered my face with a blanket, and began to sob.

After it had been medically established that I was pregnant, Aunt Claire told me to return to the village to give birth—then she told me to come back to work again afterward. Thank God she didn't send me away for good.

As I sat on the bus heading for home, I wondered about the type of reception that awaited me. Should I first go to my mother to break the bad news or to Rukundo to give him the good news, I wondered. I decided to meet dear Rukundo first, my future husband.

I arrived at Nyakambu trading center after dusk, thanks to the old ramshackle minibus, and did not have to face the curious eyes of the villagers. I left my baggage at a relative's shop and began the search for Rukundo.

"He was here a few moments ago, but he left with Agnes," one person said.

"We saw him at five o'clock on a motorcycle—he was carrying Maria," said another.

Finally, around 8:00 PM, I found him in the company of a woman twice his age. He was reluctant to talk to me but finally agreed to do so, and we moved out of his companion's earshot.

After clearing my throat, I began, "Rukundo, I am back."

He just stared at me.

"Aren't you happy to see me?" I went on, "I bring you good news."

"What news can you have for me?" he asked.

"'I am expecting a baby, your baby."

"What? Expecting my baby! Who told you I wanted one?"

"But Rukundo, don't tell me you've forgotten so easily and so quickly!"

"Are you are saying the baby is mine?" His hard gaze swept over me. My heart started beating fast. A muscle in his hard jawbone worked for a moment, as his sleepy brown eyes considered me. He fought for control, and when at last he spoke, his answer was cool. He flung it into my face, and it struck me like a slap.

"Look here, Agnes, or Chacha, or whatever your name is—I told you that one couldn't conceive after the first intercourse. I am always careful when it comes to that business; otherwise I would have a barrack of babies. There is neither girl nor woman in this trading center that I haven't been with."

I tried to plead with him, saying he was my first, but to no avail.

"Was I with you in Kampala? Am I the only man in this village? If you could part your stumpy legs for me, what would stop you from parting them for another man?"

My heart hammered in my chest. I felt my knees buckle. I clung to the wall, staring at him in horror. My breath was shallow. It was hard to keep my voice steady.

"You mean you no longer love me?" I asked him in a whisper.

He just stared at me. I collapsed.

When I came to, I was in a bed. I looked up at soot-covered iron sheets. I was confused and lost consciousness again. When I woke up for the second time, I had improved. My mind raced back to the moment before I fainted. Then I heard Mama's voice. "Your temperature is high. I think you have a fever. I must run and get you some medicine."

"'Mama, it's not fever. I am pregnant," I blurted out.

Life was hard during the first weeks after my return. There was no sugar, no soap, no salt. And the first months of pregnancy were particularly difficult. This, coupled with the embarrassing fact that Rukundo had denied responsibility, made life much more difficult for me. Mother insisted that I try Eva's place, where there was ample food.

When I arrived at Eva's house, the compound was so green and clean that I thought they had spread out a large green carpet there. I hesitated before stepping on it. When the house girl mentioned my name, my sister hurried out to see if it was really me. We hugged, and she led me into a beautifully furnished living room.

Anxiously, Eva looked me over. "So, why are you here?" she asked me.

I did not know whether to tell her yet.

Then her husband walked in, disrupting our conversation. "Who do we have here?" he asked pleasantly. "Don't tell me it is little Kyosha! My, how she has blossomed into a beauty!" he added.

After her husband left us again, Eva turned to me and sharply repeated, "Why are you really here?" Suddenly, the whole story poured out like a faucet turned on full blast.

"What has that to do with me?" Eva asked me. "Don't you see that I have enough of my own problems?"

"I can leave tomorrow, if that is your wish."

"And what story shall I tell David? He will think we are all loose like you!"

That night, Eva and David argued intensely.

"We have a guest room," his voice boomed. "She could help us look after the twins."

The argument went on and on, and I listened until I fell asleep.

Two months after my arrival, the twins got sick and were admitted to the hospital. They were in and out of there for two months. At first they had blisters in their mouths and could not feed properly, but then their private parts became rotten! All the flesh dried on their tiny bones, and they looked like little skeletons.

One night, when Eva was at the hospital, I could not sleep because of worrying about the twins' health. I meandered back to the main house for a drink of cold beer. There in the dark, sitting on the sofa, was David.

"David, what are you doing here in the dark?" I exclaimed.

He let out his hearty laugh. That night, and each night Eva slept at the hospital, I did not sleep in the guest room.

◎◎

Six months after my daughter, Diana, was born, Aunt Claire came for me and my baby. This time, I did not sleep in the main house but was relegated to the servants' quarters. The servants who lived there enjoyed mocking and harassing me because I no longer belonged to the main house but had been reduced to their level. The male servants constantly raped me. But I felt I had no moral authority to report them. Life had turned really sour for me.

One night, as I was running from the night guard, I bumped into Richard. Richard was Aunt Claire's husband's nephew. After I narrated my problems to him, he was kind enough to warn the menservants to leave me alone. At last, some peace returned into my life. But when he returned to school, the watchman resumed raping me, night after night. It was hell.

I left the city and returned to the village. With the little money I had saved from working for Aunt Claire earlier on, I convinced Mother to open a restaurant. The business boomed. Before long, we started employing other people to do the hard work. My job then was to welcome customers and receive cash. Mother started hiring her neighbors to work in the gardens for her! Our business was doing very well.

That was when I met Yusen, a big man with deep, dark eyes. He always came around to buy food. He became a regular visitor. Other men who came showed interest in me too, but I went out with Yusen. He spoke of marriage, but when I told him that I was pregnant, he ordered me to get an abortion immediately. I had learned from my mother, however, that children are special, no matter the circumstances.

"Don't fight with me on this," he warned me. "I don't want this baby."

"But I do," I protested.

"What do you plan to get out of me, huh?" he jeered. "Is your master plan to get more money from me to feed your abandoned daughter?"

To this day, I still remember Yusen's cruel outbursts: "I never wanted a child with you. You bitch, who deceived you that my wife has not given me enough children? Here is one hundred thousand shillings. Go and find a doctor to suck the bastard out and throw it into the latrine."

I delivered a healthy baby boy, whom I named James. This time, it took me seven whole years to take another man into my bed, and when I did, I conceived immediately! I had a daughter, whom I named Serina. This time, I spared myself the agony of telling the father. And you would be surprised to hear of the number of men who claim Serina as their child!

Things seemed to be going well for a while. Even my father's relatives started to frequent our home, and we would send them back heavily loaded with gifts of sugar, salt, and banana pancakes. The situation, however, soon changed.

One evening, one of David's relatives came to tell us that Eva and David were suffering from AIDS. Doctors had told them that there was no treatment, and they sent them home to die. They ended up going to witch doctors, and David died in a shrine not long afterward. After David was buried, his brother took all his money and property and sent Eva, empty-handed, to us. He took their ten-year-old daughter, the only child she had left! Eva died soon after from depression.

Ruth followed in Eva's footsteps. She too had AIDS. We tried to nurse her, but her medical bills dried up the money for our food shop. Our mother went back to digging in order to raise enough money for the shop.

When Serina, my last born, was five years old, we received a letter from the army headquarters. My brother, whom we had not seen for a long time, had been admitted to Mbuya Military Hospital and was about to die of AIDS. I sent Mother to attend to him. She came back with him, and he too soon died.

Meanwhile, my baby sister, Lisa, was growing faster than a weed! At twelve years old, she was already sleeping around. Women were cursing her for stealing their men. It didn't take long before she also contracted AIDS. I spent every penny I had to save her, but I failed. Helplessly, I watched her deteriorate and die.

After my sisters and brother had all been snatched away from me, I remained with only my mother. I relied on her for companionship. The aging woman worked hard in her gardens while I worked in the shop to raise enough money to restock our shelves and feed the orphans left by my sisters.

But alas, Mother also got sick. First her arms became paralyzed, then her legs. She could no longer do any work. The orphans, plus my children, had to learn to stay on their own and fend for themselves as I looked after my mother. She continued to get worse and became blind. I took her to many hospitals, but nobody could determine the cause of her ailments. When all the goods in the shop had run out, I started borrowing money and selling some of our clothes.

And as if that was not enough of a cross to bear, tongues started wagging in the village that Mother was also suffering from AIDS. She was accused of sharing men with us! It took me a long time to find out what

type of disease she had. By the time I knew it was diabetes, it was too late
to help her. We couldn't afford the treatment. Helplessly, I watched my
mother dying, blind and thirsty.

I believe it was God who brought charismatic, born-again Christians
to our village. After my mother's death, I felt wretched and set for desperate measures. One day, I heard a voice inside me telling me, *Get up.
How long are you going to carry all your problems?*

I obeyed the voice. I joined the charismatic church. For the first time
in my life, I felt I had somebody ready to stand by me, somebody all-pow-
erful and very loving. I felt secure. The spirit of peace entered my body
that day. My craving for the love of a father and a husband disappeared!

When I saw my sisters dying, one after the other, and knew I had
shared beds with their husbands, I strongly suspected I might also be
infected with HIV/AIDS. And whenever I heard that somebody had died
of AIDS, panic engulfed me. I lost sleep and my appetite for food. I saw
myself as a dead body in a coffin. I imagined lying on my back with pus
oozing out of my immobile legs. I imagined people coming to see me
when I was sick and alone and had no one to nurse me. I imagined people
laughing at me.

One day I decided to go to the Profam Clinic near our home. I asked
them to test me. They told me I was HIV-positive but that I had not developed AIDS yet. I was determined to fight back, to conquer the virus.

A few weeks later, my resolve weakened. I failed to sleep for a whole
week. I kept asking myself, What is my next step? Where can I go to hide
from these people who know I am Kyosha and have HIV?

Then my mind started lying to me, saying that the Profam machines
were wrong. I started borrowing money to go and get tested again in
Kampala. During that confusion, the same voice that had sent me to the
preacher woman spoke again: *Wherever you go and whatever you do, you
will die according to my plan for you. If my plan is that you die of AIDS, you will
die of it. If it isn't, another disease will be the cause of your death.*

That was the day when all the worries about AIDS flew away from
me! Many people ask me why I go about telling others that I have HIV;
they advise me to keep quiet, but I know what I am doing. I am trying
to save other people through awareness of the disease. A few weeks ago,
two women stood by their husband's coffins and declared to everybody

present that their husbands had died of AIDS. "Declaring" protects widows and would-be lovers. It also enables the widow to live longer if she refrains from sex. After going public, men will fear to approach her. The longer you hide AIDS, the longer it stays in your body and the quicker it kills you. You see, if you hide it, you remain constantly worried and experience no peace. Every time you fall ill, you imagine it is AIDS; if you get a headache or any other ailment, you immediately attribute it to AIDS. When people look at you, you imagine they are seeing symptoms of AIDS on your body. When they talk to each other, you imagine they are talking about you. When they laugh, you imagine they are laughing at you. But when you declare your status, you feel free, and those who want to laugh can laugh, but it doesn't affect you. You know you've done the right thing.

If I hadn't come out in the open, men would have also approached me, and perhaps I would have been tempted to sleep with them. Since I declared my status, no man has ever knocked on my door, asking me to let him in. No man has ever scratched my palm to indicate sexual interest in me. Promiscuity encourages the spread of AIDS. The disease can be controlled if people act responsibly. So going public is, in a way, part of the medicine that can save the rest of humankind.

Counselors tell us to keep our status a secret, but, although I agree with them on other issues, I don't agree with them about keeping silent. For example, if you go to a doctor and he gives you Septrin and Panadol, and the disease you had is healed or cured, wouldn't you tell others to go to the same doctor? So talking has kept men from me, and I will continue to advise fellow sufferers to talk about the AIDS in their bodies. Hopefully it will drain out of our society.

I don't know when I contracted the virus. It could have been from Diana's father or James's father, since both have died of the disease. It could even have been Serina's father, who is still alive. James's father, Yusen, may his soul rest in peace, died thinking he was the one who infected me. But for me, I have never been sure.

I have another man in my life now. You have already met him. His name is Lozio Kenti, the one who carried your bags into my house. It's a long story. In short, he beat up Rukundo when he heard him bragging about how he had infected me. He had to be locked up in jail for ten years. He missed his education and his future all because of me. It's rumored that he got the virus from prison inmates.

I encouraged Kenti to join the Profam AIDS post-testing activities. Now we act out plays, depicting AIDS awareness to our village. I am the main actress, and Kenti is the main actor. Not that we are such good actors, but there are only a few people who are willing to act. We also nurse our members when they fall sick and give them food and clothing. When a member dies, we organize the burial. We cooperate like sisters and brothers. We are all poor and needy, but we share the little we have.

In 2002, I went to the TASO clinic at Masheruka Hospital, near the subcounty headquarters where they first counseled me, and they tested me again. They advised me to take some medication. In early 2005, at my mother's funeral, I met Aunt Claire and told her of my illness. She connected me to the TASO office at Mbarara Hospital. In July, they started me on antiretroviral drugs. I go for checkups and treatment once a month. They are very good to me, and I feel very grateful to them. The last time I went for a checkup, the people from Mbarara AIDS Research Centre gave me a mosquito net, medicine, and a water filter.

When I went to TASO, I was advised to avoid hard work, and I took their advice. But I was so hungry all the time that I started worrying over what to eat. I almost gave up hope for survival. I was thinking that I was going to die of hunger before AIDS killed me, so I resumed working. Now I am digging, and I have enough food. I am strong. You can't know that I'm sick unless I tell you.

If I had continued sexual activity with schoolboys who go to old women like me for money, God would not have spared me. Since I tested positive, I have no new corpses behind me. I believe my sisters died quickly because they went on sleeping around while they were sick. If I hadn't publicly declared my status, perhaps I would have been tempted to do the same.

I worry about my children. What will happen to them when I die? I used to force them to do hard work; it will prepare them to earn their living after my death. They will be able to work in other people's homes. That of course made them very unhappy, but I kept telling them, "You have to work hard. When I am not here, who will work for you?"

One day Diana asked me, "Mama, where are you going?"

I answered, "I want to go very far and not return."

Then she said to me, "I will go with you, Mama."

Diana also had to stand my sick relatives' endless demands. "Diana, bring me this; Diana, bring me that," and so on. I felt sorry for her, but they were my sisters. What could I have done?

I know and believe there is nothing too hard for God, so I pray without ceasing. I'm beginning to see the rewards. Diana's grandfather, who owned a lot of land, died recently and left his property to his grandchildren. Poor man—all his children had been snatched away by AIDS before he died at a ripe age. He left that banana plantation opposite my shop to Diana. I have already dug and planted beans. Within two years I will also be selling bunches of bananas to Kampala traders. Also, a few days ago, the Local Council chairman brought me some forms to file to claim gratuity for my late brother, who served in the army. When I get this money, my children will be able to go to good schools.

I have strong faith in God's mercy and believe that the treatment I'm getting from TASO will help me to stay alive for many years to come. I also believe that in order to check the spread of AIDS, we must be open about it.

III

Farming Ashes

Tales of Agony and Resilience

Today, their thunderous guns rock us to sleep
The burning camps soothe our chopped lips and noses
Crying babies rest their lips on nipple-less breasts.
You still blow on our wounds—
Like a rat and its prey.

—Hilda Twongyeirwe, *"This Time Tomorrow"*

We all say that we hate war, but wars rage all over the world, day in and day out. Wars get declared every day in the name of ending other wars. The war in northern Uganda and the atrocities committed by Joseph Kony and his deadly Lord's Resistance Army have been ongoing for more than two decades. Children have been born and raised in a situation of armed conflict, they have gone through their teenage years and matured in IDP (internally displaced person) camps, and they have courted and married on the run.

While most of the time wars are started and engineered by men, women and children always suffer the most in armed conflict situations. It is unfortunate, however, that the women and children are never given the platform to share their experiences. When it comes to peace negotiations, men sit at the decision-making tables while the women who are most affected are left out.

The dehumanizing experiences of war in northern Uganda have affected women and children in a way that makes one ask only one question: Why? But the women who tell their stories here have moved on despite the ashes. Sometimes they took roads that led nowhere; they talked to the wind and conversed with their shadows. But they did something, and that made a difference. And we can all make a difference if we choose to.

When a pot has a hole, the entire pot is not good, because it can no longer hold water. These stories bring to the attention of Ugandans and the rest of humanity the need to block the opening so the pot can be whole again.

And to the macho men of war: Fire does not put out fire. A world without war is possible if we are all committed to peaceful negotiations.

It took quite some time to get these women to tell their painful stories. But when they finally did, they wanted the world to hear everything. They wanted the stories to get off their backs so they could walk straight again. These are women who have seen it all and endured it all, but they did not endure without action. They tell their stories of courage with a renewed energy and determination.

From the ashes, they will farm. Sometimes out of the ashes grow very beautiful and succulent plants.

VIOLET BARUNGI AND HILDA TWONGYEIRWE

Fathomless Luck

Apophia Agiresaasi

Women speed past me riding bicycles. Children are strapped on their backs. Some women carry jerricans of water; others carry bundles of firewood. They hum different tunes as one pedals on, followed by another, in unison. About a hundred meters away, in Labujje trading center, both young and old men sit on their stools around huge pots of a local brew commonly known as lacoyi. *Each man sips from a straw that connects his soul to the pot of* lacoyi. *Some of them are already drunk; the drowsy look in their eyes betrays them. They are yelling vulgarities at one another and at passersby. Beer has given them that kind of boldness. I hurry past them and head to our meeting place. I do not wait long before Lucky arrives and begins telling me her story.*

*M*y name is Lucky. On January 19, 1988, I was born in Paibwor parish in Labujje subcounty in Kitgum district. I am the product of a monogamous marriage. We were originally ten children. Six of us journeyed to our ancestors in infancy as a result of malaria, meningitis, and measles. Despite that, we remained a relatively happy family. My father used to drink alcohol like other men, but he remained a responsible man and never mistreated our mother.

Our parents would wake up very early every morning at about 6:30 AM and go to the garden to dig. During holidays, they would take us along with them. It is only the very young ones who were exempted from the morning digging. We would return home at about noon, and my mother would prepare lunch for the family while the rest of us shared other household chores. Some would go to fetch water from the well while others went to the bush to collect firewood. In the afternoons our father would go to do carpentry in the trading center near home and then come back in the evening. From their work, our parents were able to provide enough food for home consumption and even pay our school fees. So I grew up a happy child—until the advent of the Lord's Resistance Army and their incursions into our villages. It was in 1996 that I first heard of the Lord's Resistance Army atrocities. Even then it was on Radio Uganda. The journalists had reported that the rebels were mainly in the current districts of Kitgum, Gulu, Lira, and Pader, but Gulu was the epicenter of the rebellion. They also disclosed that the rebels had attacked and burned down people's homes, raped women, cut off people's ears, looted property from homes, and even abducted young children.

Even though my district, Kitgum, had been mentioned as one of those affected by the war, to me it was still a distant possibility, a story, like one of those stories that our paternal grandmother used to tell us when we visited her. I even thought that the affected homes or individuals might have invited what had happened to them or been so sinful that God had decided to punish them that way. It never occurred to me that what had happened to them would one day be my lot.

One day in February 2005, which was a day like any other, I woke up and performed my usual chores of babysitting my young brother, preparing breakfast, and going to the garden. After digging, we decided to go to a nearby bush to collect firewood. I went with three girls from the neighborhood and my mother. I had already collected a substantial amount of firewood, almost enough for a big girl of my age not to be ashamed of carrying after about an hour. If one carried a bundle considered too small for her age, she would be ridiculed and regarded as lazy. I was not a lazy girl—even if I were, I would not bear being ridiculed.

While I was tying my bundle of firewood, I saw three young men moving toward me. At the time I saw them, they were only about two meters away. One of them was in a combat uniform, and the other two wore civilian clothes. Each carried a stick the size of my arm. They looked haggard. They had long, unkempt hair. If one had taken a photo of them, it could be successfully used to launch an appeal for starved youths in Uganda. I wondered where they had come from, although I was not exactly scared of them. I looked around to see where my mother and the other three girls were. It was then that I saw them running away in a different direction. They had perhaps seen the young men before me. It occurred to me then that they could be the so-called rebels that we had been hearing about. I wondered at the selfishness of human nature. My own mother, the woman who brought me into the world, had run for her life without alerting me! My mother had abandoned me to the rebels! I felt angrier with my mother than with the rebels.

Then one of them hit my back with his cane, commanding me to move. They were speaking Langi. I had no alternative but to dance to their tune, since the companions I had come with to collect firewood had deserted me. I just moved in the direction they were leading me without looking back lest they continued to hit me.

Even then, another rebel, the one who was in the army uniform, struck me with a bicycle chain, the kind used for tying luggage onto a bicycle. Ripples of pain coursed through my body.

The rebels told me that if I cried loudly, I would be killed. We moved on very fast. After we had walked for ten miles, my feet began to swell because I was not used to walking long distances. Every time I said that I was tired, I was hit. They would take turns hitting me as if to rid their hands of idleness. Occasionally they hit my back even when I was obeying their every instruction. My body received more than forty strokes throughout the journey. They told me that the reason they were beating me was to make me tough like a soldier. They said that soldiers had to be battle hardened. My back got swollen, and after some time I stopped feeling anything, as if I was paralyzed. It felt like my body did not belong to me anymore.

When we reached the rebel camp, I was taken to the camp commander. He had a hut that served as an office. I later learned that his name was Ojok, although it was forbidden to call him by name. The people in the camp referred to him as Commander. I found him sitting, but as soon as I entered his office, he rose to his full height of about seven feet, perhaps to intimidate me. He was huge too and could not have weighed less than one hundred twenty kilograms. I previously thought I was tall, but standing next to him made me feel like a dwarf.

The commander asked me a number of questions. He asked me where my home village was and where "his boys," as he fondly called them, had found me. I answered all the questions honestly, because I was at his mercy.

He released me, and one of the boys who had captured me came and smeared pounded green leaves on my toes, a ritual, they later explained, performed to prevent me from having "long legs" that could compel me to run away. I was then given green vegetables to eat for supper. The taste was different from any green vegetables I had ever eaten before. They were neither sweet nor sour. I learned later that they were wild leaves. That was all I ate for my supper. It was a terrible night. It was also dark—the darkness was so thick that one could hardly see a few meters ahead. The sky was equally gray and resonated with our somber moods.

That same night, I met two other girls who told me that they had been abducted that day, although not from the same village as mine. The three of us were tied together with sisal ropes, the kind used for tethering goats. We slept bound up that night. We were left on the bare, cold floor without any bedding. The rebel soldiers slept next to us. They said they were watching over us to ensure that we didn't run back home. I will never forget that night. It was the first night in my life that I had spent away from home. I did not sleep. It was cold because there was no covering, but I was more worried about my life than I was about the cold. The atmosphere was tense. I just pretended to be asleep.

I noticed that the other two girls to whom I was tied were also not sleeping. We never exchanged a word, despite the fact that we were awake the whole night. Each one of us was lost in our own thoughts. I was even afraid of turning from one side to the other lest I was suspected of planning to escape and was killed. We did not know what the future had in store for us. We were all scared like rabbits awaiting a slaughter. It was a very long night of discomfort, tension, and uncertainty.

In the morning, the rebel soldiers untied us and ordered us not to move outside the hut in which we had spent the night. We were given a plate of *posho* and beans and told to share it.

After we had been with the rebels for one week, they drew a picture of a large heart on the ground in front of the commander's office and divided it into three sections, because we were three new abductees. They told us to bathe and to remove our blouses and remain bare chested. They told us to bathe there, in front of everyone, and we did. After that, we were told to stand in one of the squares. They dipped an egg in a mixture of white powder and water and drew a heart on our chests and our backs. They also made a sign of the cross on our foreheads and across our lips. Then they poured cold urine on us. If the egg broke, it meant one was possessed with evil spirits and therefore had to be killed.

To my relief, the egg passed the circle without breaking. The commander told us to stay bare chested for three days. He said that what they were doing was written in the Holy Bible. One of the young rebels who had abducted me told us that the humiliating and disgusting ritual was for our protection—it was meant to protect us from the wrath of the gods and from the bullets when we went to war.

The camp commander, Ojok, had scores of wives and children, and his family had the exclusive privilege of eating enough. The entire time I was with the rebels, I was always hungry whether I was involved in the cooking or not. We used to drink dirty water from a well to fill up our stomachs. Sometimes there was no water, since the land is a semidesert. It was not unusual for us to drink each other's urine. Other times we were so dehydrated that we had no urine to pass out.

God is a miracle worker. Somehow we survived. While in that camp I was tasked with babysitting the rebel commander's children, fetching water, and collecting firewood, and I was sometimes called upon to help in the kitchen. By nature I am a loner, and whenever the rebels saw me sitting alone, they would shout at me, asking me why I was thinking about home. On many occasions, they would threaten to kill me if I went on thinking about home. One day, they hit me brutally with a chain and the logs we used for firewood. My back got bruised. When I touched it to relieve the pain, my left arm got severely hit, breaking the bone.

Life in the camp was like a swing; you never knew which direction or with what speed any move would throw you.

Every morning, the rebels would wake us up at 5:00 AM to pray. They believed so much in Joseph Kony and regarded him as their spiritual father. They would say that the Holy Spirit speaks to him. Prayers would be led by the camp commander. The rebel-camp commanders were Kony's representatives in the same way that RDCs are to Museveni, the rebels would tell us.

Sometimes they would pray like Catholics, burning incense and making the sign of the cross. We would even have Holy Communion every Monday—and it would be celebrated the Catholic way. Other times they would pray like Muslims. They would make us kneel, facing east, to pray.

The rebels said they were preparing to overthrow Museveni's government and that Kony would become the new president of Uganda. They said the fight would take place on a day when one of the commanders rose at dawn and saw a hand in the clouds; that would mean there were five days before the fight.

I did not engage in any sexual relations while I was with the rebels. There were commands from Alice Lakwena that commanders and rebels had to refrain from sex. Lakwena was Kony's cousin. Lakwena had disappeared in the waters of River Nile for forty days and reemerged as a prophet, claiming to cure people of all kinds of illnesses. Many rebels truly believed in her magical powers and in her every word. I was not sure what to believe and what not to believe. Sometimes I just got confused.

The rebels always told us that the girls under Museveni's regime were all HIV-positive and that they could not befriend them. As far as they were concerned, we were some of the HIV-positive girls. The rebels would sing to us and drum into our heads almost every day that we were HIV-positive. At some point I even started believing it, although I knew I had never had a sexual encounter before. I even started thinking that maybe there was a means by which HIV/AIDS could be thrown at people through the air. The rebels talked so confidently that I thought that maybe they had managed to do something to infect all the girls in Uganda.

Fortunately I was a *mulokole*, a born-again Christian, before I was abducted, so I knew how to pray. I used to pray against every scheme Satan might have had against my life, and I also prayed for God to help me in everything. If you trust in God, he can see you through any situation. God is faithful. I stayed in that camp for two months before I was taken to live with some old woman who was a rebel collaborator. Her husband was a rebel soldier. I don't know what happened to the other two girls after we separated.

The old lady, whose name I never got to know because we referred to her as Mama, had three children. Her husband was never around. He was always going to war with other LRA soldiers. She was the camp leader. This camp had about twenty people. As soon as I started living with her, the two older children were taken to Gulu to live with her relatives. She remained with only the young one. It was my duty to babysit her. I also used to cook, fetch water, and collect firewood. I lived in the same hut with her and had the luxury of sleeping on a mattress, which was the exclusive preserve of rebel commanders and their wives and children.

When UPDF gunships were sighted, I would carry the old woman's property and run with it. That was my other assignment. I did not quite like it because it slowed me down. On the other hand, this woman was nice and soft-spoken, and I decided to abide by her rules.

One day, I asked her why the rebels were killing mostly our own people, the Acholi. She told me that they did not intend to kill the Acholi but that they were killing them because they were Museveni sympathizers. The LRA rebel movement had zero tolerance for any Musevenists, whether they were Bantu or Acholi or belonged to any other tribe.

I then asked her why they were killing people who attempted to escape from the rebels, and she said that even Jesus did not ask his disciples to come with him; he just commanded them to follow him. But today Ugandans do not follow the Holy Spirit, she said, which is why they are forced or killed.

I tried to reason with her, arguing that if they explained to the people of Uganda about the Holy Spirit Movement without coercing them or committing the atrocities that the LRA rebels were associated with, the people would see reason and follow them willingly. This woman was a very committed rebel. She also said that the rebels would be the first to go to heaven, because they were repenting their sins on a daily basis.

In that camp, there were girls who had previously lived in Joseph Kony's camp. In the night, while we prepared supper, they would tell us what they had seen there. One of them, Grace, used to babysit Kony's children. She had been to one of Kony's huts and seen many strange animals there. She saw huge live snakes of different colors, turtles, and chameleons.

The night she told us, we all feared to sleep alone. The three of us shared a bed because we were afraid that the spirits would come and kill us, but nothing happened. We were a bit surprised to wake up without a scratch.

One evening, as we were going to the well, I suggested to the girls that we should escape. I had been thinking about this for some time, and I knew it was possible. I knew it would be a life-and-death sort of thing, but I hated the life I led out there. I knew I deserved better. But I did not tell the girls all these thoughts.

That evening, only one girl agreed to come with me. Her name was Akim. Akim and I decided to move ahead of the others. But she was still full of fear. She told me that if they caught us, she would report to the rebels that I was the one who initiated the idea of escaping. Then the rebels would kill me and spare her. I ignored her. I did not even get annoyed with her because we were all living in fear for our lives. The well was about five kilometers from the camp where we were living. We had walked about two kilometers and were still arguing when we heard some voices. We stopped to listen and heard them ask each other about who was talking. Then we stopped talking.

Life had taught us not to take anything for granted, so we did not wait to discover who it was. We just ran in different directions. As the rebels pursued us, the people from the camp from which we had escaped followed suit. Perhaps the other girls had returned to the camp and told them that we intended to escape. I mustered all the energy I could and continued running until I came across some long grass, in which I hid. It was green grass that was about one meter high. It was getting dark, and I knew they could not easily locate me in such surroundings.

I sat still and held my breath so as not to give them any clue as to my presence there. They later came and flashed a torch around the spot where I hid for about five minutes, then moved on. I heard them say they had killed my friend, Akim, and if they got me, they were going to kill me too—even more brutally. A pang of guilt sliced my insides.

I stayed in the same spot for about two hours before I crawled into a thick forest nearby. I resumed my escape journey at about four in the morning. It was a dark night, like my first night as an abductee. My feet and legs were scored by scratches from the thorn bushes and tall grass. Nonetheless, they carried me on, oblivious to where I was going. I just walked on, letting my legs decide my direction. I chose to leave everything in God's hands.

Toward morning, I saw a small path leading to a village. I followed it. After walking for about a kilometer, I reached a home with a compound that was littered with mango skins. They looked fresh, as though they had been dropped there the previous night. I thought this might be another dwelling place for the rebels who had eaten the mangoes and scattered the skins in the compound.

Filled with fresh fear, I broke into a run. I ran on and on. When I had run for about two miles, I noticed marks of soldiers' boots on the ground. I decided to follow them in the hope that they might be UPDF soldiers who had come to hunt down the rebels. If they were UPDF soldiers, they would probably rescue me. I followed them slowly until I reached a valley, where the marks disappeared.

I stood around for some time, unsure whether to go on or turn back. I soon decided to turn back. After I had walked for about two hundred meters, I saw another route. I followed it without knowing that I was blissfully walking right into the line of fire.

I heard a voice speaking in Swahili, and I turned to see who it was. I realized it was a UPDF soldier up on a tree branch. He was addressing me, but I did not understand Swahili.

Then I saw many other soldiers up in surrounding trees. They started shooting at me, thinking that I was a rebel and that perhaps there were many other rebels behind me. Machine guns rattled, bullets whistled in the air, and rocket grenades exploded. A bullet whizzed close behind me. I fell down flat in shock. Accidentally, a bullet aimed at me shot one of the soldiers, and he fell from the tree and died. Another soldier in an adjacent tree was injured. One of the soldiers climbed down from the tree and ran to where I had fallen. I panicked as I saw him take up position above me, load the gun, and pull the trigger. He wanted to shoot me at close range.

As he fumbled with his gun, an energy I did not know I possessed ran through my body, and I jumped up, hitting his chest. Both of us fell to the ground. He quickly disentangled himself from me and got onto his feet, but he did not try to shoot at me again. He fixed his eyes upon me, and I wondered what he was thinking. But he must have been thinking about what to do next. His eyes were a mixture of pity and anger.

Sanity returned to me, and I pleaded with him to spare my life. I told him that I had heard him speak Langi and that I was also a Lango and might be a distant relative of his. I said so many things in the space of seconds, perhaps unconnected things too. I also explained to him that I was not a rebel but an abductee who had escaped in order to go back home. That seemed to appeal to his emotions. I was overwhelmed by relief when he led me to where the other soldiers had congregated next to the fallen soldier.

There were about seven soldiers, including the one who had just died. Only two of them were Langi; the rest were Bantu. The soldiers had an argument as to whether they should kill me or not. They argued about it for some time and finally decided that they would not kill me. Some of the Bantu soldiers carried the dead body, and others carried the wounded soldier. The two Langi soldiers walked with me to the main road as the other soldiers walked behind us. They advised me not to run when bullets are flying. They also told me that the Bantu soldiers were full of anger—since it was because of me that their friend had died—and they might kill me in revenge. So the UPDF soldiers too had their little fights, I realized.

As we walked, I told them about what I had been through and how I had escaped from the rebels and how a friend of mine with whom I escaped had been killed. They asked me where I was going, and I told them that I was going to Pader. They also asked me where exactly my home was, and I told them that my home district was Kitgum. They said that they were going to the Pader trading center. I continued walking with them.

When we reached Pader, the commander there ordered that a vehicle be sent to carry the dead body and the wounded soldier. The soldiers congratulated me on having survived. We had become friends, especially the Langi soldiers and me, because we spoke the same language. I thanked God for having put me in the hands of people I could talk to and for having spared my life, at least thus far.

At the Pader barracks, I was handed over to a female UPDF soldier who was in charge of returnees. There I found another girl who had also just escaped from another group of rebels. The two of us spent one night in Pader. In the morning we were taken to Acoopii, one of the rehabilitation centers for rebel abductees.

I stayed in Acoopii for one week and was then transferred to World Vision Pader. At World Vision, there were many other returnees. Life there reminded me of school life. We slept in big halls built like dormitories. There were double-decker beds, and each one of us had a bed to ourselves. The center was fenced, and we had to seek permission before we were allowed to move out.

During the day, we had many sessions; we had counseling sessions where we were taught to open up about what we had seen in the bush and what happened to us. We were also taught how to conduct ourselves when we returned home. The girls were taught tailoring, while the boys were taught bicycle repair and carpentry. We also had time to play, dance, and sing. Our leaders would bring us firewood and food, and we would cook for ourselves. We had a duty roster. Each day, three of us would be assigned to cook. The ratio was often two girls to one boy. The boys' main task in the kitchen was to split the firewood. We ate a balanced diet—beans, greens, meat, *posho*. We would eat at least two platefuls of food each to make up for what we had missed while we were with the rebels in the bush.

A few days after I arrived at the World Vision center, something happened. I saw my paternal uncle. When I told the people who were in charge of us that I had seen someone I knew, they did not believe me at first. But I insisted and asked to go and talk to him. At first they turned down my request, but later they relented, and one of them accompanied me when I went to talk to my uncle.

My uncle was very happy to see me but told me he had not heard from my parents for a long time. He was deployed with the mobile troops and had been transferred to Lukulu, which is close to the Sudanese border.

He said he would tell my sister Teddy. Teddy lives in Lukulu. He said that she would then find my parents and inform them that I was at the World Vision center in Pader.

One week later, while we were attending counseling classes, one of the girls came to call me. I did not know why I was being summoned. I thought that perhaps I had done something wrong and was going to be punished by the authorities. I found out, however, that my parents had come to see me. As soon as they cast their eyes on me, they started weeping. My mother cried, my father cried, and I too cried. We cried tears of joy. We then looked at one another and cried and laughed at the same time. When we were done crying, we started talking. We talked and talked. I asked them about home, and they asked me about what had happened to me since the day I left home. It was a moment of fathomless joy for my parents and me.

After a lot of soul sharing, my father went back home. My mother was allowed to stay with me for one night. We shared the same bed. We talked almost through the night. The following day, she left for home. I was not allowed to go with her because I was doing a course in tailoring. Still, I was happy. Our instructors told me that I would be allowed to go home only after I had mastered the course.

I was later transferred to Kitgum Children and Women's Association. The conditions were the same as the ones at the World Vision center in Pader.

After one month, I was taken home in a Toyota Land Cruiser, accompanied by the matron. I took along a mattress, two liters of cooking oil, one bag of maize, and two kilograms of sugar, which were given to me by the center. All my siblings were so happy to see me that they carried me shoulder high. I let my tears flow freely, mingling with their sweat. I felt complete again.

Shortly after I got home, I started to have terrible dreams. Whenever someone placed an object near me accidentally, I would jump in fear. I was scared of everything, but after some time, this fearfulness ended.

Guilty of Surviving

{emblem}

Rosey Sembatya

The huts that make up Latek-Odong camp can be seen at a distance as a beautiful assembly of dry grass. After miles of thicket, the sight of children carrying small jerricans to the borehole is such a relief from the uniform vegetation one sees as she nears the camp.

Santa tells me her story as we sit by the veranda of the camp leader's office— a relatively small but nice-looking building painted white. Latek-Odong camp is a satellite camp in Amuru district. People are resettled here, close to their original homes, so that they can get the feel of home before they are eventually fully repatriated. Santa's original home is not far from this camp.

Her posture speaks volumes, but I would rather she tell me her story. She slouches and leans her whole self upon her left arm with both legs stretched out in front of her in complete resignation. In front of us is an expanse of land with grass and a sprinkling of short trees. Adjacent to the camp leader's office is another white building that sits uninhabited. Santa tells me it is the health center. In the background is a group of children—some naked, others with torn trousers, and two of them dressed in oversized T-shirts, on one of which is inscribed the word PHILADELPHIA.

Santa's response to my greeting demoralizes me. It's a prolonged "Kooooo-peeeeee"—heavy and carrying tons of grief, as though she is about to faint. Unlike other women I have met who disguise their misery on meeting a stranger, Santa's face is grave, with creases that have permanently sought refuge there.

"I wish I had been abducted" rang throughout my conversation with Santa. When a people's whole existence is eroded by circumstances beyond their control, what is a person to do? That is Santa's story.

Santa is a traditional birth attendant and a dance troupe leader in Latek-Odong camp. The formerly passionate dancer has lost everything. When she first walked toward me, downcast, I couldn't help but watch her barefoot steps laboring to get to the Latek-Odong camp leader's veranda, where I am seated on a three-legged stool.

"Santa, is everything fine?" I ask.

Santa tells me she is recovering from a weeklong malaria attack but will be fine soon. I had all along planned to ask her to do a traditional jig for me, like in the old days, but I change my mind, for, I tell myself, what energy would a recuperating patient have? I instead ask about her passion for dancing.

"My bones are now weak, but even then, who would dance when everyone around is being abducted?" A dance troupe leader among a people robbed of their passion for dancing by the war and its effects, she is burdened by grief. "Orak, Giteke, and Apiti—not anymore, not anymore," she laments.

Having encountered people who mock fate by laughing at their misfortune, I fail to catch a stealthy grin from Santa during the conversation. She has no kind words for this fatal happening—only gloom in heaps.

*L*ife in my home was characterized by laughter and fun. It was a homestead where my husband's family lived. It was a real home, unlike this camp. Traditional social conventions guided everyone at my home. In the mornings, the girls would wake up and do the morning chores without being told or coerced. The boys would also do their own chores like hunting, riding, and mending bicycles. After the chores, the girls would then take a bath, oil themselves liberally, adorn their necks and arms with brightly colored beads, and go to the village arena to dance with their age-mates. The homesteads had hens running around, goats tethered to the trees in the compound, and cows out in the fields grazing. Everything was well organized, and everyone related well with everyone else. The village shared both its joys and its sorrows.

I am now here at Latek-Odong. But I have been to other places before finally settling here. Latek-Odong is close to the home in which I lived before the war stampeded me out. What started out as a search for a safe place for me and my family has instead become a haunting memory. What disturbs the peace of my family and homestead are the abductions and killings that characterize this place. Before we left home, we used to hear about rebel activity in the villages far from ours. So I thought it would take a while before it eventually reached us. I still hoped that the rebels would be intercepted by government soldiers before they reached us. How wrong I was!

It wasn't long before we heard that the rebels had abducted children from the neighboring villages. That was the beginning of our trouble. My children refused to sleep in the house at all. At that time, I had five young people living with me. They preferred the bush because it seemed safer. Every day at about 6:00 PM, we ate the evening meal, and then the children picked up their bedding and hurried away to the bushes. The family routine of sharing fireside stories ceased! It hurt me so much to see children braving the night cold. Children as young as five years old! I knew they were doing this for their own safety, but I didn't like the fact that they were sleeping in the bush. I didn't even know which bushes they went to every night because they did not stay in one area. Each time they left home was a moment of torture, because I had no idea how I would locate them in case something happened. My husband and I were both afraid of staying in the house too, but we stayed because we wanted to encourage the children to come back home.

In the morning, they would trot back, and life would go on as if everything was normal. But each evening, they put on all their clothes for warmth and left home. After some time, my husband and I decided to relocate to Bardege barracks for safety and to save the children from sleeping in the bush. Before we relocated, however, and as the war intensified, we decided to send the other children back to their parents. We stayed with only our little son, Samuel, and my little cousin, because she had lost both her parents.

The decision to leave home for Bardege was not an easy one to make. Survival takes one places, yet home gives you a sense of security that you can't find elsewhere. The allure of the government 4th Division barracks at Bardege was so irresistible, especially since we wanted to ensure protection for our children. We went and settled at Bardege. This was not difficult, because many people had already come to the area. We joined them and built ourselves a small hut in which we stayed with the children. It was only then that we heaved a sigh of relief in the belief that our children's lives would get back to normal.

Ironically, however, it was while living in protected Bardege in 1990 that calamity struck. We didn't even know where the rebels came from or how they came. It was late at night, and we did not see anything or receive any warning. We just heard screams from different huts, and when we looked out, we saw people running for dear life in all directions. Three people were abducted from my family alone that night. That was my husband, my son, and my cousin. More people would have been taken from the camp had it not been for the soldiers at Bardege barracks, who started firing at the rebels. We all dispersed, but the rebels were keen on taking their loot and captives.

All the people who were not abducted were dispersed into the night. Like other camp dwellers, I did not come back until morning. When I returned in the wee hours of the morning, I stealthily walked to my hut amid wailing from those who had realized that their loved ones had been abducted. Other people had already started packing their few belongings for some other unknown destinations. I searched our hut but found no one inside. Perhaps they are still hiding somewhere, I kept thinking.

After over an hour of fruitless searching, I was choking with rage. I walked around the camp asking everyone I met about my family, but none had any information about them. When I had gone around the camp several times and had not seen them, I knew they were gone, so I joined the chorus of wails at Bardege. I cried not just for the abduction of my people but for the guilt I felt. I wished I had held the children's arms as I fled. I wished I had gone in the same direction that they had. I wished I had been abducted too.

Soon after the Bardege incident, I knew I had reached the end of my tether. I was all alone, with a burning guilt about not having protected my family well enough. I kept blaming myself for the abduction of my husband; my son, Samuel; and my cousin. Had I not pressured my husband into relocating to the "protected area," had we stayed in our home and slept in the bushes, my family would not have been abducted, I kept thinking.

I and the other displaced persons started gathering at different locations for the night. We would sleep at Lacor Hospital for a week, Negri School for three days, and Caritas Centre for a week. All this we did because we felt that somehow the rebels were looking for us and could easily get us if we stayed in one location for too long.

As we moved from place to place, the guilt of not having been abducted hit me hard. I felt that it would have been a lot easier if I had been abducted along with my family. As we lived on, oblivious of what the future might bring, we slowly lost touch with reality, passing each day in a zombielike state.

I knew that the abducted people were going through a very difficult time wherever they were, with nothing to eat. I always imagined them dead and surely knew that they would be feasted upon by vultures if they died. I kept asking myself why I had survived while my son was taken. At least I was in a better position to handle the inhumanity of abduction than my baby. As a parent, one must be able to protect one's children, but how could one do that in such a situation? What does a parent do? What was I supposed to do in order to protect my child?

◎◎

Guilt has a way of eating one up slowly. And without a doubt, in the long run, guilt piles up inexorably. My family had just begun to enjoy life together. Samuel, my son, was in primary school. He always came home happy after learning new things at his school. Now, seeing other children of his age group makes life very difficult for me. Every time I see them, I think about Samuel.

After leaving Bardege, the place from which my family was abducted, I found it difficult to settle at any one center. I always felt insecure in one place and would hear voices calling me every night. The strongest of those voices was my son's. It was unmistakably Samuel's. These voices came when I started spending my nights at Lacor. There were many other women and children at this center; they would sprawl on the hospital veranda and the dusty quadrangle. Very few men stayed there. The ones who did were old men; they slept away from the women and children.

My sleeping pattern also changed. I couldn't sleep for long. I kept waking up, especially to the voice of Samuel calling me: "Mamina, Mamina." Whenever Samuel called me, I would not sleep again until the next morning. Then I would wake up very early, fold my mat, and return home. I dreaded the nights! I dreaded the mornings!

Going back to my home was traumatizing. We used to sleep at those safe centers at night and go back to our respective homes early in the morning. And every morning, I dreaded going to Latek-Odong, yet I had no choice about where to go.

Back at home, I would try to stay busy. But all I had to do was clean up a house that was already clean—there was no one to make it dirty. It also took me some time before I could go to the garden. I was still afraid that a rebel could be hiding somewhere and pounce on me. But now I try to survive. I have a small garden that I go to.

My home area has lost its life. Unlike in the past, when one would greet others across the roadside, today it is different. People talk in whispers. Friendliness does not exist anymore. Everyone walks enveloped in her own thoughts. There is no more fun at all. In the olden days, if you had a big chunk of land, friends in the neighborhood would come and help you till it. Things have now changed. Everybody is afraid of being recognized. Nobody wants others to know that they are still alive lest they confide in the rebels. There is utter mistrust among my people.

After my cleaning chores, I used to walk down the road to Lacor past empty homes, dry plantations, and lifeless people. I would leave as early as 3:00 PM. The cackling of the hens was no more. The bleating of the goats was gone. Our lives had become a mess.

At Lacor Hospital, where I spent most of my nights, people would start converging in the stony, dusty yard as early as 2:00 PM. Some had chosen to seek permanent refuge there because their homes were not safe, even during the day. I would get to Lacor and spread my mat on the ground or sometimes on the concrete veranda near the hospital wards. Many times, those concrete places were taken first because they were more comfortable and were shielded from the rain and free of creeping creatures. I would put my mat anywhere I found space, then sit and ponder. Women and men alike would do the same. At that time, it was not considered unmanly to stretch your legs in front of you, lean your head against the wall, and stare at nothing in particular. We all did it, both men and women.

Our gods do not forget. One day, my husband came back home. It was exactly two years after his abduction. He never wants to talk about his experience in the bush. We live together, and we are trying to patch our lives together. We live in Latek-Odong camp. My husband found me on the verge of breaking down. I continued wishing I had been abducted; I was living in torment every day of my life. The situation kept getting more and more helpless by the day. Some girls who had escaped from captivity had brought me the dress in which my cousin had been abducted. This meant only one thing. I didn't have to ask. They didn't have to say anything. Although I failed to accept it, I knew that an uncompassionate batch of people couldn't do much—they thirst for blood. They seek amusement in other people's suffering. My husband's homecoming made life a little more bearable. He found me in this camp. I remember he came in the night and didn't want me to say a word. He said he was tired and wanted some quiet. I made him some porridge, which he gladly drank as I held his hand and looked at him intently. I held his hand tight. I did not want to let go. It was like a dream, and I needed to hold on to it to reassure myself that it was real. I couldn't believe he was back—back to me! I just held his hand all the time. He has never told me the story about how he escaped, but that does not matter. What matters is that I have him with me. My husband rarely talks about what happened in captivity. When he does, he'll say something like, "I used to eat these in the bush," pointing at some leaves by the roadside.

My husband said nothing about Samuel. After their abduction, they had been taken to two different camps under two different commanders. But one day, as we sat home silently, Samuel walked in. This was five years after the fateful evening of his abduction. But Samuel was not the same. My son, who used to be very jolly and so full of life, was now a distant piece of wood. Like his father, Samuel never talked much. But his presence made a difference, and I have let him be. Perhaps I would have understood their new selves better if I, too, had been abducted with them. Although we are a family, we are not quite a family. We've been robbed of the essence of family, which lies in sharing, the sharing of everything.

My people are so deprived that we don't have the simple things, like hens, that characterize a proper homestead. All of that disappeared with Kony's war. We have lost the things that used to define our lives. Nowadays, children don't respect their elders. Their lives are only patches of how it used to be. The only talk on their tongues is about "our rights." They have not been told that rights go with responsibilities. Bathing is not a necessity for them anymore because they are preoccupied with survival in the bush. They are lost children because they are not nurtured. Their parents are either abducted or they sleep in the bushes. All the children who could have continued with the dancing legacy are abducted. Those who live in camps are preoccupied with survival rather than dance.

The White Coat

MARGARET ADUTO

One of the most horrific massacres to shock the world took place on Saturday, February 21, 2004, in Barlonyo village, Ogur subcounty, Lira district. A terrorist group led by Okot Odhiambo, one of the most feared LRA commanders, attacked an Amuka detachment in Barlonyo. Amuka was a militia comprising men from the local communities; it was mobilized alongside the national army to fight Kony. Unfortunately, by that time, an internally displaced people's camp had sprouted up around the detachment that had been established in that otherwise deserted area to monitor the movements of the terrorists. Kony unleashed terror on the soft civilian targets without remorse, and despite the fragile peace that had existed since mid-2006, the wounds of the victims continue festering.

Aketch and I meet at Barlonyo camp in her improvised shack with rattling tins for a roof—a place she now calls home. I can see the steady pain in her eyes even as she signals me to sit on a wooden stool by her side. She starts to narrate her story while firmly gazing into space, as if searching for answers to her endless questions.

*T*hat evening is still fresh in my mind. Unlike other days, when I would wake up haunted by the fact that I wasn't going to school anymore, February 21, 2004, started out well. I remember the day as if it were imprinted on my life. Come to think of it, indeed it was. I have had many nightmares since then—and they may never end—but I hope that as I share my story, it will help me make sense of some of them.

I got out of my papyrus-mat bed looking forward to a new day. For some reason, I felt more aware of my surroundings than usual. The birds sang, and I was struck afresh by the beauty of their voices. The wind blew through the trees, sending a breeze of comfort to the earth. The huge camp that I had lived in for the past seven years seemed more like my home now. All the hatred that I had felt for the war and the Lord's Resistance Army didn't seem to matter that day. It was a beautiful day, and I didn't want to spoil it.

I hurried to the borehole to fetch water. I wanted to get there early before it became too crowded. We didn't have much water in the house, and I knew that when Grandma woke up she would want to make breakfast and take a bath like she always did.

Grandma is a strange woman; most people in the camp don't understand her love for cleanliness. She is one of those people who would wash a cup five times before using it. She is always wiping and cleaning. She is fifty-two years old, but she looks a lot younger than most women in the camp in their early twenties. Most people here claim that the war has robbed them of their youth, which is why they look older than Grandma. Maybe now I understand why Grandma can't stop yearning for the good old days—the days before the war.

When I reached the borehole, Aciro and Akot were already there with six jerricans each. They usually did that, and most people hated fetching water after those two. I smiled at them as I placed my jerricans behind theirs. I was in a good mood and wasn't about to let Aciro and Akot spoil it with their twelve jerricans. I only wished they had delayed a little so that I could have got there before them. I wanted to ask them to let me fill my two jerricans first, but I knew they would just sneer at me. I didn't want them to see the envy in my eyes as the two best friends filled their cans with water before me.

Aciro and Akot had been friends for as long as I could remember, possibly from when they were very young. They did everything together and even seemed to think alike. They had both decided not to get married. Some people said that maybe the two were so much in love with each other that, if it were possible, they would have got married to each other. But we all know that a Langi can't do such things, those things of the *bazungu*.

I have tried to find a friend who would always be there for me and be by my side, but my friendships with most girls never last long. The longest friendship I have ever had was with Apio. I very much wanted Apio and I to become the Akot and Aciro of the camp, but Apio loved to gossip, and her interest in academics was very limited. She wanted a husband and children while I wanted to become a doctor. Ever since I saw Marco, the Italian doctor, walk in the corridors of Lira Hospital in his white coat, I knew that I wanted to be a doctor too. I don't know how many times I dreamed about myself walking in the hospital corridors in a white coat. But these were just dreams. The reality was that seeing Akot and Aciro giggle as if they were young girls made me angry. They are almost twenty; they should act their age, I thought with disgust.

After Akot and Aciro had filled their containers with water, I filled mine too. The handle of the borehole pump is usually very hard for me to lift up and push down, but with the new energy I felt that day, I did this quite easily.

February 21 is a special day, I thought. For some reason I can't put a finger on, I felt I would have a breakthrough with my education. I had sat for my O level and passed in second grade. I wasn't happy with that. I knew that I would have to study harder when I joined high school to study for an HSC—a higher school certificate. My dream school was St. Mary's College, Aboke. If you are a girl and you come from my district, Aboke is the only school you can dream about. All that I could do was dream, dream, and dream. I knew that reality was quite different. I might never live to see the inside of a classroom again. Grandma might never afford to pay my fees. Her vegetable stall in the market could never yield the kind of money required for my school fees.

My mother and father had been burned alive in our home before I moved to the camp. I ran away from home and came to live in Barlonyo with my grandmother. When she saw me, she simply said, "They have killed them, haven't they?" It was more of a statement than a question. The reality of it all was written on my tear-stained face. I nodded, and that was enough for her to understand what had happened. She gave me food to eat and never asked another question.

I know that someday, when the time is right, I will tell her that I watched from a distance as Mama and Papa and my siblings were dragged into the house. I will tell her that the one who set the house on fire was a boy not much older than me. Virtually all LRA recruits are abducted children who are brainwashed through fear and forced to commit atrocities, such as shooting, hacking, and burning people—men, women, and children—alive. The abducted male children are often made to join the LRA ranks as fighters, while the girls are turned into sex slaves. But I will not tell her how my bowels gave way as I watched the house burn to ashes. I will not tell her how I helplessly heard the screams of my people from inside the burning house. I know she knows a lot, because on several occasions she has heard me scream in my sleep. Several times I have woken up to find her seated on my bed, telling me that all will be well. But I know deep down in my heart that nothing will ever be the same again. We have to live each day one at a time.

I was still at the market when evening fell. I was waiting to see the beauty of the sunset. I had gone a long time without watching the sunset. Many people were still going about their daily chores. Young mothers had their babies strapped to their backs, buying *boo* vegetables so that their children would not go to bed hungry. Men were drinking *kongo ting* brew.

The market was so small that I knew almost every person who came there. It was a place that brought together those who had something to sell and those who wanted to buy. I personally frequented it because I always found something to sell, be it secondhand clothes, food, anything that I could lay my hands on. When I had nothing to sell, I would go to the swamp to look for wild vegetables, and I would sell those.

I watched the sun setting and lingered for a while. As the evening grew darker, there was a sudden loud noise that took everybody unaware. Immediately we knew it was gunshots. First I thought it was the government soldiers doing their evening patrols, but as the gunmen approached, talking loudly, the urgency in their voices and the varying ages of most of them made me realize these could not be soldiers on their routine patrols. They were strange. They were Kony rebels! These were the very people who had destroyed my family! I knew my turn had come, and there was no escape. Fate had indeed caught up with me.

"All of you come here!" one of them shouted. He held his gun pointed toward the sky, perhaps to show us that if we delayed he would point it at us. He was just a boy. His oversized uniform hung shapelessly on his body.

By then I had already learned to follow orders. Many of the stories I had heard from people had made me realize that it is always wise to do exactly what the rebels wanted. Child commanders were reputed to be especially merciless, maybe owing to what they went through themselves. The fighting had worsened the brutality of the young abductees who had been made to lose all reason. How else could one explain the senseless killings that cost a once-vibrant region a substantial number of its population? How else could the executions, the amputations, the mutilations, and the violations be explained?

When all the people in the market had gathered together, the rebels told some of the men to disappear, because they were contaminating them with their alcoholic blood. The men quickly disappeared between the huts. Many more rebels appeared from nowhere and tied the remaining men into groups of four, each with ropes knotted at their backs. They were led away, and only the females were left behind. The rebels then picked out the elderly women and women with babies strapped to their backs and ordered them to go back to the camp. They warned the women against saying anything to the soldiers; otherwise all the girls would be killed. How I wished I had borrowed a child earlier or was at least carrying someone's baby when the rebels attacked!

After what seemed like a sorting exercise, there was a group of rebels that was given the responsibility to loot while the rest watched over us just in case we were tempted to escape. They kept on picking and bringing out whatever they could lay their hands on, especially the foodstuffs. It never even occurred to me that we would have to carry those heavy loads. At one point, I even nursed the hope that they would tell us girls to go.

I scanned the girls to see if I could recognize any; Aciro sat next to Akot. I also saw Apio seated alone. I was glad that at least the girls I knew were here. Perhaps later we could plan our escape together—and maybe I would become Aciro and Akot's friend. I managed to count how many we were; we were thirty-five girls all together. We watched as the rebels packed their loot. They never asked any of us to help them.

When they were finished with looting, we were shocked to see one of them pull out one of the girls, push her down, and then lie wriggling on top of her. The rest of the rebels started doing the same to the rest of us. I watched everything as if it were a horror movie unfolding right before my eyes. I had never imagined that something like that could happen to me, not in such a public place as a market. I had escaped getting burned with my whole family only to end up like this. I watched through my mind's eye as my body landed on the ground with a thud. I saw my beautiful dress roughened and my white panties pulled off my womanhood. The greatest betrayal was that this act was neither swift nor painless. Each move was calculated to ensure that the pictures would be imprinted on your mind and would haunt you for life. I was glad that the sun had disappeared and was not witnessing what was going on.

I don't know what exactly happened later, but I know I suddenly found myself carrying this huge piece of luggage. Perhaps after all the girls had been raped and the rebels were satisfied, they wanted to take us with them. I swear I don't think I heard anyone talk until we were on our way.

We started walking away from the camp. We were made to carry heavy loads of foodstuffs and to walk for a very long distance. Those who got tired were automatically helped by those who were still strong. We were gripped by fear, and many of us pleaded with our creator to take us home, for the pain was unbearable. The torture, the trauma, the humiliation—it was more than one could bear.

At such a time, even the sound of gunshots was welcome in the desolate hope that it could be government soldiers trying to rescue us. But there was no sound except that of crickets in their holes and frogs in the swamp.

We walked through forests that I had only heard about before. I was not sure what would happen next. We walked on and on. I prayed and hoped that the government soldiers would follow us. I knew that if the soldiers followed us, some people would get killed during the rescue operation, but as much as I was afraid that I might be one of those who would die, at least I wouldn't have died at the hands of those who had killed my whole family.

We continued walking with the heavy loads on our heads. I could see that the distance between the camp and us had become huge. I thought of escaping, but the many stories that I had heard about the rebels hacking to death those who tried to escape stopped me from giving it a second thought. I also prayed that none of the abductees would attempt to escape, which would make the commander order one of us to kill her.

The rebels stopped in the middle of a dense, thorny thicket, where we spent the night. I didn't know where we were or where we were headed. I was glad that we could at least rest, but I knew that it wouldn't be easy to carry the luggage on my head again and walk some more without breaking down.

The rebels checked what we were carrying, cooked some food in less than twenty minutes, and ate it. We were not given any. I was hungry, but I guessed that it would be a while before we ate anything.

The night was very long. My feet hurt so badly because of the bruises that I got on the way. I held my body tightly and hoped that I wouldn't feel cold. It was a warm night, and I was glad that there was no sign of rain. I knew that God wanted us to survive that night and perhaps many more to come. Yet we—the abductees—all failed to sleep properly as a result of hunger, isolation, and fear.

I was suddenly jerked awake. I don't know what happened; perhaps I had a nightmare, or maybe it was my God alerting me to what was about to happen. I saw the rebels who had gathered us return from a bush situated a distance from where we were. One of them had a scar running down his chin. His eyes were as red as *lakwal* seeds.

To the rebels, the break of day meant we had served our purpose. With their machetes, they started cutting the girls who were still sleeping. First was Aciro, then Akot, Apio, then the next, and the next, and the next. I tried to run, but they had blocked our exit. The knowledge that the end was at hand paralyzed many. There was nowhere to run; it appeared that our captors were everywhere.

I noticed the circle that the rebels had formed. It seemed impossible that any of us could get away. I was deeply afraid of the fate that awaited me. I imagined that perhaps this was the kind of helplessness that my family had felt when our house was set on fire. I tried to pray, but no words came from my mouth.

I kept saying, "Jesus, Jesus." I couldn't make any sentence. I knew that there was no way I was going to escape being killed. I tried to numb myself, tried to pretend that I was already dead, but it didn't work. I had to wait for my fate. I imagined myself being hit by the machete; I imagined the pain and what it meant to be dead. Each time the rebels pulled an innocent girl and slashed her to death, the shrieks of another ebbing life shredded the air, as body and soul separated in anguish. One by one, the girls became silent; blood covered the earth. It might have been the end of the world.

I died the death of each of those girls. When the machete finally hit me, the cries of the other girls were still reverberating in the air. The rebels grabbed me and dumped me on the heap of dead bodies. I was battered with clubs and left on that mangled heap. Our blood mingled as it seeped into the ground. I could hardly tell the difference between day and night. My face was damaged, and my eyelids could no longer support my eyes. I had become practically blind, even to my very own existence. The brutes had done the one thing that breaks any human being: they had killed my hope. It's a miracle that I survived at all.

I don't know how long I stayed there. Up to this day, I can't tell whether I died and was resurrected or not. I can't remember. Maybe one day I will—I will remember how long I stayed on top of the corpses. For now, I only know what they tell me.

I was told that three days later, while on routine patrol, a UPDF unit was welcomed by a stench and a heavy swarm of flies that led them to a pile of already decomposing bodies. What they found was most disturbing. They searched the heap with the butts of their guns and their mouths covered with dirty handkerchiefs to see if there were any still alive. They found me still clinging to life, perhaps still dreaming of walking in the hospital corridors in a white coat.

I am told that the soldiers carried me to safety using a stretcher made with tree branches. I was taken to their base and later transferred to Lira Main Hospital, where I was admitted. I don't know how long I stayed in the hospital or what transpired after my discovery, but I know from

Grandma that the doctors almost gave up on me. They didn't see the reason why I still breathed when all the girls I was abducted with were dead. They told Grandma to take me home and wait, as I was sure to slip away in my sleep. Grandma said she never gave up on me; she prayed that the God who had brought me back to her would keep me going. She said that I had come back to her twice, and this time I would live as well.

God must have heard Grandma's prayers, because I am still alive. Of course I am. I remember the stupid question I asked a teacher once when he told us that a huge snake had bitten him. I asked him if he had died. I guess if he were to ask me the same question now, I wouldn't have an answer for him.

Many people have advised me that I should test for HIV/AIDS because different girls' blood may have entered my open wounds and also because of the rape, but I think that's not important. I survived when thirty-four girls were hacked to death; nothing can be worse than that. I have cheated death a number of times! The God who saved me will determine my tomorrow.

For now, I live each day as it comes, because I know that I survived for a reason. I see the beauty in everything. I used to be scared of birds singing in the morning, because I thought they were warning me that the rebels were coming back for me, but now I have overcome that. I think the birds will continue to sing long after I'm gone. I'm twenty years old now, and I still hope that I will go to school and that one day I will wear the white coat and walk in the corridors of Lira Hospital. I may have been dreaming my dream, but I'm sure one day my dream will become a reality.

Bitter Escape

APOPHIA AGIRESAASI

John, the Local Council chairman of Pagen parish, offered to take me around the camp as I waited for my appointment with Pamela. The compound at the sub-county headquarters was swept spotlessly clean, but as we walked around the camp I discovered that some details revealed its poor sanitation. For instance, it was evident that some children either did not know how to use toilets or did not have toilets. When John noticed my discomfort, he disclosed that camp dwellers used mobile toilets. Each toilet, he said, was shared by about five homes, and in some homes there were about twenty people, most of whom were children. He further explained that the Lord's Resistance Army rebel attacks that had lasted over two decades had left many children orphaned, as some of their parents were killed and others abducted by the rebels. This left many children unattended.

Determined to make me understand why too many children was a main feature of camp life, he explained that many people were idle because they could not go to the fields to dig for fear of rebels. He also said that since they lacked varied entertainment, most people resorted to sex as the main leisure activity at their disposal. This resulted in the births of several unplanned-for children. This analysis was substantiated by the number of women carrying children. Every

woman we met in the reproductive age group was either carrying a child in her
belly or on her back or both.

"The HIV prevalence rate resulting from the rapes, polygamy, and the break-
down in the health system has also claimed many adult lives. It is much higher
than the national average. HIV/AIDS here kills more people than the bullet does.
This is because the school dropout rates are high, leading adolescents to seek
pleasure in premarital sex. Condom use in the camp is low due to lack of educa-
tion, and almost every man in the camp has more than one legitimate wife," he
added.

Coincidentally, we met Pamela, who was coming from a meeting. Pamela
is about four and a half feet tall. She was wearing a faded black T-shirt, and
a green-and-red-striped lesu *was wrapped around her waist. The bulge in her*
lower abdomen indicated that she was pregnant.

We walked together to her home. She offered me a wooden dining chair, on
which I parked my tired bones. She then brought a mat for herself and sat next
to me. She smiled at me, revealing her black gums and a set of milk-white teeth.
Hers was a story to tell, a story to listen to.

*M*y name is Hakim Pamela. My home district is Gulu. I am the firstborn in a family of nine children. I have three brothers and five
sisters, and both my parents are still alive.

I was abducted in 1996 from Sacred Heart Secondary School. The
rebels came to our school at about eight at night, entered our dormitory,
which was still open, and ordered us to follow them. All of us in that dormitory followed them. We were about fifty-five senior ones and senior
fours who used to sleep in that dormitory. I was in senior one myself.
Other students in the school survived the abduction because their dormitories were closed.

The Lord's Resistance Army soldiers who abducted us were all armed
with grenades. "Move fast," they ordered us.

We moved quickly, with others running toward the school gate. They
then made us walk to Sir Samuel Baker Secondary School in Gulu, but
when we reached the gate they stopped us there, and about five of them
took positions to guard us. We remained at the school gate while other
soldiers went in to abduct more students from that school. As we waited

at the gate and knew what was about to happen to Sir Samuel Baker, we felt so sorry that we could not alert them.

A few minutes later, the soldiers joined us with about fifty students of Sir Samuel Baker Secondary School. Some daring boys managed to run and jump over the school fence and escape. The rebels were not yet done that night. We then moved to St. Mary's, Aboke. Again they left us outside the gate and entered the school. Some minutes later, they joined us again with more girls. We were more than one hundred fifty students who started the long journey with the LRA rebels that night.

The rebels did not tell us where we were going. We walked long distances through bushes. Many of the students were killed because they could not walk any further. They were stabbed with bayonets in their chests and heads. The rebels would first pray over their souls, then kill them. Sometimes they would do the killing themselves, but most of the time they ordered us to do it. They would tell about five of us to hit them with clubs until they breathed their last. Then we would leave their bodies lying in the bush. It was so horrible; I felt that I was going crazy. I felt dizzy, and my head was spinning most of the time. Those who got tired or whose feet got swollen were also killed. Some of them had their feet chopped off with machetes when they failed to walk. They would then be left to bleed to death. Then the rebels would tell us that the chopping of our friends' feet was to train the rest of us to walk faster and properly. Indeed, this worked, because after our friends had been chopped and killed, we tried as much as we could to walk faster in order not to get killed.

We walked on for several days till we reached Sudan. In Sudan, we were taken to the Nan Kamdule Brigade headed by Vincent Otti, who was then deputy to LRA rebel leader Joseph Kony. In that camp, there were about seventeen hundred people. Like all newcomers, they said we had to be anointed so as to be blessed by the "Holy Spirit." We were anointed with oil from the shea tree. The rebels then smeared a sign of the cross on our foreheads, our shoulders, and our chests.

"You are soldiers of the Movement. You can now eat with us," they told us.

The camp was being supplied with food by Sudanese Muslims. They would supply the food twice a month, on the fifteenth and on the thirtieth of each month. They seemed to have an agreement with either Kony or Vincent Otti. The supplies would include sorghum, cowpeas, and other small, flat seeds grown in Sudan.

The day after we arrived in Nan Kamdule, each of us was assigned a husband. The camp commander first chose the girls he wanted, and then the rest of us were distributed to other men. The men were told to place their shirts in a line, and we were ordered to go and pick a shirt each. We were then told that the owners of the shirts we had picked would be our husbands. Those men came and picked their shirts from us, and we followed them to their huts, where our womanhood journey started.

None of us could refuse any of these newly acquired husbands. It was a must to submit to them. If one refused, one would be killed. Refusal was a sign that you were in love with the UPDF soldiers. We had been warned beforehand.

The man I was given to already had twenty-five wives. I was the twenty-sixth. I felt just like another pair of underwear added to his toilet bag—taken because I was available. As wives, we had a timetable. Each one of us had a day on which we would spend a night in his hut. The nights I spent in his hut were the worst nights of my captivity. I hated him with a passion that only I could understand. If love were to be measured in sacks or kilos, I would not even raise a grain of love for him. Whatever took place in that hut whenever my turn came was just a ritual I had to perform in order to survive. I was lucky I did not bear any child with that monster. I got pregnant once, then had a spontaneous miscarriage, perhaps because of the hard labor we were subjected to. Maybe it was God's plan not to bless the hateful situation with a child.

We were expected to remain faithful to our husbands, even if you were in Juba and they were deployed in Uganda. Our feelings did not matter at all. If your husband died, the camp commander would give you to another man, or any other man who was interested in you would take over. There was no one who was single in my camp except those very young girls and boys who were below twelve years.

The young girls worked as babysitters, but even then they had assigned husbands who would take them up later. The boys were treated as slaves. They were first trained to raid homes and steal food and abduct fellow children, and later on they were trained to go to war. The boys would go to the villages, abduct young girls, and bring them to the commanders, who would give them wives after they considered them grown up enough. All marriage unions were polygamous. Marriage was like a sport to them.

The wives never harassed each other, because we all understood that we were victims of the same fate. The rebel soldiers would even threaten us, saying that if we quarreled they would kill us. We would eat together, sleep together, and share our challenges. Our fate bound us together.

We would cut grass from the bush and pile it together, and then the rebel leaders would give us long black polyethylene bags that we would place on top to make mattresses. It was not so bad; each one of us had a bedsheet.

Each day in captivity was its own story. One time, for example, I participated in killing a person. A student with whom we had been abducted tried to escape and was caught. We were ordered to kill her with a pestle used for pounding. The rebel soldiers pointed their guns at us and ordered us to kill her. We stood in a line, and the first person went and hit her hard on the back and gave the piece of wood to the next person, who also did the same. The rest of us followed suit—silent, tearless. When my turn came, I was shivering, and I felt my legs trembling. The idea of hitting her repelled me, but I still hit her. By the time the last person hit her, she seemed dead already, but her body was still shaking. She had died a senseless death, and I had taken part in it. I knew it would take me long to forgive myself. I knew I would never forget.

That night, I had terrible dreams. I saw the spirit of the dead girl asking me why I had killed her. I also got wounded by a bullet while in the bush. We were armed and sent to fight the Dinka so as to steal food and property from them. The Dinka are a people who live mainly in South Sudan, and they are the lot that have mainly suffered in the South Sudan war. As we struck at them to steal, they opened fire at us, and one bullet hit me in my left leg while another hit my back. I collapsed.

My colleagues carried me back to the camp and treated my wounds with hot water. Every morning and evening, they would fill a twenty-liter jerrican with hot water and press it to my rotting back and leg. They also got short sticks, which they tied on my leg to keep the broken leg in position. They kept doing that until I healed. I went through a lot of pain as they pressed the heavy jerrican of hot water on my leg and back, but I had to bear the pain because there was no medicine, no painkiller; there was no other treatment. Some people died of their wounds. I was so lucky I healed.

I lived with the Lord's Resistance Army rebels for six years. It was believed that Joseph Kony was a spiritual leader and had supernatural powers that could easily detect those who wanted to escape. Whenever he addressed a gathering, someone would record his speech because it was believed that he himself did not know what he was saying. It was believed it was the spirit speaking through him. This could have been true. Whenever the Ugandan government was planning to attack the LRA rebels, his spirit would warn him, and he would take precautions. Kony himself was tall, dark, and handsome.

One time, my group was sent to Aweno Oluoluyi to ambush vehicles. We came back at around noon and found Kony addressing a gathering. According to the LRA rebel rules, no one was supposed to go near Kony with a gun. So since we were still carrying our guns, we kept our distance and instead listened to the radio.

We were listening to a program in which a former LRA commander, known as Onekomon Kozor, was addressing people on MEGA FM, a popular radio station in Gulu. He was talking about his escape and encouraging rebels and other abductees to come back home. As we were listening to Kozor's speech on the radio, we did not know that our colleagues—the rebels—were spying on us. In a few seconds, they had us surrounded.

They immediately ordered us to remove our clothes and descended on us with canes and logs. They hit us everywhere and anywhere, as if they were hitting an already dead python to ensure it remained dead! They beat and kicked us viciously and jumped on top of us with gumboots. I curled myself up, trying to avert the blows with my hands and arms. Once in a while some people would cry out and plead, but all this died down and was replaced with silence. After a while, one victim after another breathed their last. When the soldiers were sure that we were all dead, they left. I too thought I was dead.

I regained consciousness at around four in the morning. My head was spinning, and my feet had become numb. But I was sure of one thing:

God had given me another opportunity to live. This gave me the determination to escape. I hated the idea of dying in the bush, my bullet-riddled body left on the battlefield as a prey for the vultures, like my colleagues were.

When I got up to start my journey, I never looked about me. I just looked ahead and started moving, hoping and praying that I was heading for Uganda. Eventually I realized that the group of survivors was actually big. Of the twenty who had been clobbered—ten men and ten women—four of us had survived. I was the only female who survived. The rest were male.

We walked together from Juba in Sudan to Uganda. Some of us who were too weak collapsed and died on the way. Whenever one got tired, some would rest, and others would move on. We had long ago learned that everyone had his or her own destiny. It was painful to leave their bodies on the road and walk on toward our freedom and our prison of guilt.

After some time, I realized I was walking alone. I had lost everybody again. I just walked on without knowing where I was going. When I reached the main road, I saw a vehicle coming toward me. It was a double-cabin Toyota pickup with the words PADER MISSION inscribed on its body. When I saw the vehicle, I made to dive into the bush again, but I noticed that the driver had already seen me. I moved backward slowly. At about ten meters away, I stopped. The vehicle also stopped. I first stood rooted in one spot before I noticed that the driver had a white collar and a large rosary around his neck. There was silence as we both stared at each other. Then he spoke, asking me whether I had just escaped from the LRA rebels. He sounded confident, as if he did not need an answer, as if the identity of an escaping abductee were unmistakable.

Slowly I walked toward the vehicle and responded positively. He asked me where my home was, and I told him that it was in Gulu. Then he offered me a lift.

I hastily grabbed the opportunity like one stranded on an island would with a rescue team. Of course I had no idea where he was going to take me. But I was sure it was not back to the ruthless arms of Kony! He drove to the Padibe mission hospital, where I was immediately admitted for treatment. Remember, I had been beaten and left for dead.

I had no idea what a sorry state I was in till I reached Padibe, where I saw more human beings. My body was covered with sores from the beatings, and my feet were swollen because of trekking the long distance. I had not eaten for about three days. I survived on wild leaves and raw cassava that I uprooted from people's gardens throughout my journey from Sudan to Kitgum. I was so thin that a gust of wind could easily have blown me down. I was just skin and bones, and my eyes were popping out of their sockets. Mine was indeed a narrow escape.

Today I am OK. I have put on weight. I am much better now. If that man who picked me up had not been a religious and humble person, he wouldn't have allowed me to enter his vehicle. I was quite a sight.

As soon as I arrived at the hospital, I was given a new dress and relieved of my lice-infested rags. I had not had my monthly periods for about six months, and I was worried that I could be pregnant. I confided in an elderly female nurse, who advised me to take a pregnancy test. I was very glad when it turned out to be negative. She explained to me that stress and long periods of starvation had caused a halt in my periods. I also took HIV and syphilis tests. The HIV test was negative, but the syphilis test was positive. I was given medication to treat it.

The Reverend Father who had picked me up kept on coming to check on me until I got well. He would bring me new clothes, sweets, tinned milk, sugar, fruits, and many other food items. When I recovered fully, I was transferred to World Vision Gulu, where I stayed for seven months.

While at the World Vision rehabilitation center in Gulu, we were counseled and told how to resettle in our communities. We were also encouraged to open up about what we saw and what happened to us while with the rebels. They told us that sharing our experiences would help us recover from the trauma much faster. But I could not bring myself to open up to anybody. I did not trust anybody. Each one of us had a counselor assigned to us.

I found it hard to tell my counselor what I had gone through. She then told me to draw pictures of what I had seen. She assured me that whatever I told her was going to remain a secret between us, and if she ever disclosed it to anyone, I had the right to report her to higher authorities. That was when I started trusting her. By the time I left the rehabilitation center, we were good friends, and I could share with her many things. I felt human again.

We were also encouraged to play. We used to play volleyball, netball, skipping, hide-and-seek, and all sorts of other games.

When it was time for me to go back home to my people, I was taken in a pickup truck. The matron at the center accompanied me. I was given a mattress, a blanket, and shoes. World Vision also gave me seeds for planting.

Everyone at home was glad to see me. My parents and siblings screamed when they realized it was me. They surrounded me as the things were being offloaded from the vehicle. No one seemed to notice the matron. I later introduced her to them as one who was caring for us escapees at the Gulu World Vision center. She greeted them and left shortly afterward. My siblings were very excited about having me back. For about a month, my young sisters took turns sleeping next to me.

After some time, some of my friends, who were also returnees, wanted to go back to school and were taken back. At the time, I was not interested in going back to school. I went back to school much later, because my parents insisted that education was the only way to a prosperous future. I went back to senior one. When I got to senior three, I got pregnant. I decided to get married to my boyfriend. He was a fellow student. That is why I am now staying in Kitgum. It is my husband's home district. I am expecting our first child.

I am still interested in continuing school, but I no longer have support from home. If I go back to ask for help from my parents, they will say that they cannot pay school fees for a married woman. But I hope to manage and go back somehow. I hope to cross that bridge when I get there.

Thinking about the peace talks in Garamba, I highly doubt that Kony will turn up to sign the peace deal, because he has been elusive since time immemorial. People in the camp are still living in crowded conditions. They do not feel safe enough to go back to the villages to dig, save for a few brave ones. So they depend on handouts from the World Food Programme and other NGOs. They are willing to go back home, but as long as Kony is still at large, they feel threatened.

But someday, I strongly believe that God will rescue northern Uganda. Someday, we shall be whole again.

Pages of My Life

Rosey Sembatya

I have searched for this story like a nomad searches for green pasture. I wanted something new, something untold, a story of a woman's experiences of armed conflict. Amuru district is my destination. Amuru neighbors Gulu district, and much of what is now Amuru is a camp surrounded by trees, shrubs, and thickets. On the many murram roads I ride, I can't help getting nostalgic about my own village—the quiet, unadulterated land with a few men riding their bicycles and women carrying baskets on their heads.

With no itinerary in mind, I chance on Lii camp, a relatively small satellite camp with more than forty grass-thatched huts. Surrounded by small gardens of maize and beans and overgrown sorghum crops, two hens while away the mid-morning pecking at the ground. Looking through the neatly swept compound, I see a group of seven-year-old girls huddled together, concentrating on some cans that one of them is holding. In front of the camp is a big, tall tree that stares straight into the huts that make up Lii. Under the tree sits a goat, bleating like it is taking part in a competition of sorts—on and on and on.

Gong, gong, gong, echoes the tire rim that is used as a bell. From different corners of the camp, the residents file in the direction of the gong. There is a village meeting. In twos and threes, women slouch to the meeting venue, which is under the tree opposite the goat. They call each other from their gardens, but a lone woman remains standing in hers. No other woman goes out to call her. This intrigues me. The lone figure does not come back to the camp until the meeting is over. But before it starts, I ask the two women next to me why they have not called her and why, after she saw others gather, she did not join them. Their response tickles me.

"She kills all her men," one of the women says.

I meet Susan in the late December heat that burns bare feet to the sinews. Its fiery shine makes my eyes ache. Susan approaches with a bundle of millet balanced on her head. Putting down her burden, she extends her hand in greeting.

"Afooyo," she says.

"Afooya ba," I respond, taking her hand in mine.

Susan and I sit by the tree at the far end of the camp. The wind blows in earnest, but the pain in her eyes is so strong that the wind does not trigger a response to counter the heaviness there. She folds her arms across her chest and looks at me intently.

In response to my question as to why nobody called her for the meeting, she says, "I have no female friends." She then looks across at the array of grass-thatched roofs.

"They are afraid of me. They say that I have a chest that kills men."

Before I can find my tongue, she looks at me piercingly, perhaps asking for my response. Her arms fall to her sides, and I pick up on that cue and sigh.

*M*y first husband and I met in Palenga. I was about fourteen years old. I fell in love with him and wanted to get married to him and start a family. He too was interested, and our families knew each other because we stayed in the same area. He used to go to the forest with his friends, cut down trees, and burn them for charcoal. He would then take the charcoal to Gulu town and sell it. My mother and I were involved in farming, so I was very skilled at tending gardens. I knew that we would manage to be a happy family through my supplementing his business with my farming abilities.

My mother liked the young man and didn't mind my getting married to him, because I was ready. My husband-to-be went ahead to visit my family and express his desire to marry me. My family agreed, and he paid the traditional bride-price to my mother for my hand in marriage. Then we started living together.

After he paid bride-price, we started a family. Then I lost him in a flash. Although I hate being reminded of it, I would rather I get it off my chest.

One evening, the Kony rebels attacked our village camp in Palenga. We never knew they were coming; it was a complete surprise. Wielding machetes and guns and wearing mean faces, they abducted many of us. During abductions, it is survival of the fittest, so each person has to run to save his or her life. At that time, my husband and I already had three children. During the abduction, my children were at my mother's hut but in the same camp—Palenga. My husband and I separated at the time of the attack. I was fleeing to safety, or so I thought, when I found myself in the hands of the rebels. I have no idea how they guessed that the tall shadow running across the grassland was not one of their own but one who should be abducted. I was thus made to join those who had been captured. At this point, I didn't even know where my husband or my children were. With machete-wielding rebels, there is very little that one can do but to accept one's fate.

Rebel attacks set off wails of helplessness. After the abduction, I, together with other women, was made to carry the rebels' loot from our huts. We carried many things, including mats and beans. As we traipsed to our places of suffering, another fierce encounter occurred with the government soldiers, and everyone had to flee once again. I had never before encountered such a deafening spate of bullets. We had only walked for about five hundred meters from Palenga when the government soldiers struck. The rebel who was leading us told us to lie down to avoid bullets, but everybody just ran in different directions. In my mind, I said that I would rather be shot running to safety than lie down with rebels.

At that time, I was not thinking about my husband. The only thought on my mind was about my children because, apart from knowing that they were supposed to be with my mother, I didn't know whether they were alive or dead.

As torrents of gunshots echoed throughout the area, I abandoned my luggage—a saucepan of beans covered with an old piece of cloth. I didn't even know where I was running to, but I just ran on, hoping to find a hiding place. A few meters away, without even knowing whether that was safe enough, I fell down under a nearby tree and covered my ears with my hands.

I stayed in this place patiently, but I feared that any moment might bring a gumbooted foot down on my head. After a long time of hiding, with my heart pounding wildly all the while, I found other escapees, and we retraced our footsteps to Palenga. We all ran to our compounds to look for our kin. A few government soldiers were still around patrolling the camp. Thoughts about my husband and children concurrently crossed my mind with each step I took.

We got to Palenga as wails of loss enveloped the area, each survivor fervently searching for her relations. My eyes were smarting with apprehension, tears threatening to break free, but I had to remain strong and look for my people. I half walked and half ran to my mother's hut. It showed no sign of life, apart from abandoned bits of cloth. Everyone else kept turning things about in their huts to find out what had been left of them. As I approached my own hut, two bodies lay sprawled on the ground, and a few people stood around. I could see from a distance that they were men because they were wearing trousers.

As I got closer to the small crowd, they all turned their eyes on me, then quickly looked away. I knew my household had been touched. I knew that I had lost him. But I kept hoping it was somebody else, at least some old man who had already seen more of life. I hoped it was someone else I knew as an acquaintance or a distant relation or a neighbor. I had somehow hoped that my husband would live. When I finally realized that it was indeed him, I was at first too angry to cry. I was angry with him for having left me, angry with the government soldiers for failing to save him, and angry with myself for having run away without him. As seconds ticked by, tears broke loose and streamed down my face uncontrollably.

Many others, upon finding their own dead, wailed uncontrollably. It is a very trying moment, because, upon finding one's own, one loses all strength. Then one painfully accepts that they are gone and moves on to the next source of hope.

My next step was to search for my children. My husband's body meant that anything could have happened to my children as well! I had no strength to continue with the search, but I had to. I kept asking everyone I bumped into if they had seen my children. Either nobody knew anything about their fate or they were too engrossed in their own miseries to pay me any attention. I walked back to my mother's hut, and this time I found her there.

"Mamina, where are the children?" I asked.

She looked at me intently and led me into her hut, where I found them snug and in a deep sleep. We didn't get into details of where they had hidden or how they had escaped from the attack. I just uncovered my children and touched them to make sure that they were still alive. Upon confirming that, I let them sleep and turned back to the painful reality of the loss of my husband. He was gone, and I had to fend for our three young children alone.

@@

A few months passed as I pondered my next move. I wanted to get another man to help me bring up the children and also to help me ease my misery. I met Jacob some months after losing my first husband. The circumstances under which I met him were quite normal, if one is to be sincere. It was difficult to live alone. Living in these war times, one needs to heal and find some solace in something. I couldn't find solace in my digging or in my mother or in my children. Granted, each of these occupied a special part inside me, but I needed a man in my life. I needed someone to talk to in the night, someone to hold and comfort me when I was in the grip of nightmares. From the time of the attack, I had never been able to sleep peacefully. A recurrence of vivid memories of my first husband—shirtless, lifeless, and surrounded by a crowd—disturbed me. Other times, I imagined someone trying to kill me, Mamina, and my children.

Jacob had lost his relatives but had never had a wife. He was lonely too and afraid of living alone in his hut. He pitied me, and I think I also pitied him. After some time, Jacob started wooing me. He wooed me for about one month, then suggested that we start living together. I didn't hesitate even one bit, because I really wanted to live with someone—my hut was so empty. My heart was empty too. But I think it would have been a little easier if Jacob and I had decided to relocate to another area. A widow living in the same area with another man is considered very disrespectful to the soul of her late husband.

It started with my mother, who didn't agree that Jacob and I should be living together. Her reason was that I was a widow. In my opinion, that wasn't a strong-enough reason to keep me away from Jacob or even stop us from living together. I explained the aching loneliness I felt to my mother. She still insisted that it was very wrong. My mother was a little understanding, but everyone else in the village accused me of robbing Jacob of his youth. They kept saying that through being a widow, I was too contaminated for a young man who had never had a wife, and too old at that. I was told to stay home and raise my first husband's children. But I did not see the point in that, because I could look after them just about anywhere.

I was supposed to leave Jacob's hut and go to my late husband's hut, but I adamantly refused. In the midst of a raging war, a culture can't retain its purity, and a bit of stubbornness makes everyone leave you alone. I refused to go back to my late husband's hut because I had found a good man in Jacob and wanted to keep him. I found all I desired in Jacob, and he understood what I had gone through so well. I did not feel any guilt because I had not seduced him. He had wooed and taken me to his hut. So what was their problem? And come to think of it, when men lose their wives, don't they remarry when they feel like it?

From the day we started staying together, everyone seemed to avoid me, but Jacob knew about my late husband and accepted me—and that was all that mattered. I lived with Jacob very happily. We even had one child together. Jacob, like my first husband, was a charcoal seller. From Palenga, he would travel all the way to Lii to burn trees and sell charcoal. He maintained us on the profits from his charcoal business.

One fateful day, he awoke like he always did, only this time earlier than usual. I never made him any breakfast on other days, but on that day I did because he was leaving home very early and I insisted that he take something. So I warmed some *posho* for him and made a cup of tea using the fireplace in the hut. He had to go to Lii with three other friends. The three friends were already at our door, so he had to do everything in a hurry.

The area where Lii camp is located is very far from any community and not inhabited at all. It was also said to be a haven for rebels. There, one was exposed to rebel attacks. On the other hand, however, it was famous for its trees, so many charcoal sellers would flock to the area because of this. On this day, none of the four friends came back to tell us the story. We just heard that the four charcoal burners had been abducted and butchered. When Jacob and his friends did not return at the expected time, we did not need to say much or ask any questions.

It was a pity that Jacob, who had risked his life to be able to maintain us, was butchered as he tried to look for a livelihood. And even more unfortunate is the fact that we could not bury him. All that remains of him are memories, fond memories of him. That was my second misfortune. I had been so optimistic that we would stay together and raise our children jointly. It was so sad; we had been married for barely five years. And we loved each other.

This bad luck that has enveloped me like a plague must have been passed on by association. When two people get married and start living together, their closeness robs them of their individuality, merging them into one. Maybe this misfortune came from my first husband. His family was characterized by tragic deaths—many of them were brutal.

My first husband's mother had been murdered by rebels, and soon after that, many of his family members followed suit. I don't blame them for my misfortunes, but neither do I blame myself for getting married to my first husband, because he was a good man. But I must have caught this curse from him. I remember my third husband's mother was brought to my house one morning. She was ill with a terrible cough, back and neck pain, and an ache in her legs. These are common ailments, and there was nothing to be worried about. She wasn't so bad off, because she had started showing signs of recovery. She had started taking her meals regularly and was even able to bathe herself. But that very day, after having her evening meal, she passed away in my home. It has been a life of one misfortune after another ever since.

I met Charles, my third husband, a month after the death of Jacob. I was distraught, with no one to talk to. No one wanted to associate with me, because everyone thought I had a spell or some sort of bad luck on my head. Right from the beginning, Charles knew about me, since he had lived in Palenga. Maybe it was my misfortunes that attracted him to me. When he expressed his interest in me, I left my children to come to Lii camp to live with him. Right from the time I met him, we have never discussed my past. We live as if it doesn't exist.

Leaving Palenga for Lii camp was like a hide-and-seek game between my children and me. I just escaped from them. I escaped when they were asleep very early one morning. Charles had left Palenga a few days before to prepare our new home. When the morning came, I escaped from my children. I had no choice—something indescribable was gnawing at my very being. I had to go.

Charles has made it easier for me, because he actually ignores my past. Unfortunately, however, this includes my children as well. He does not want my four children from my previous marriages to live with us or even visit us. They live with my mother in Palenga. I think he doesn't want to accept that I had a past and therefore shuts it completely out of our lives. He has chosen to give me a fresh beginning, but I miss my children, and that is a barrier between us, because I am not ready to forget them.

I have no child with him, and I plan to stay with him only temporarily. He didn't even pay any bride-price to my mother. I have no obligation to stay with a man whose aim is to separate me from my children so as to block out my past. My past is part of me. I keep lying to my children about what I am doing in Lii camp. I keep telling them that I farm here because there isn't much farmland in Palenga. With each passing day, I feel so guilty. Charles does not even want me to go and see them in Palenga, and neither does he allow me to let them visit us. When I want to see them, I pretend that I am going to the field or somewhere else. I also don't want them to know that apart from doing some digging in Lii, I have another man. How will I be able to explain these lies to them? I take them some food once in a while without my husband's knowledge.

Fortunately, my children have no relatives to visit them who would have told them the truth. Apart from the school to which they go, Palenga is the only place they know. All the relations I knew have died in the war. My children are now mine. My heritage is their heritage.

I think Charles loves me because he has never beaten me, and he always tries to provide for me as much as he can. He is trying to give me a fresh start, but there can never be a fresh start that does not include children from my previous marriages. Charles has completely refused to accept them into our lives. For me, the only new beginning can be with my children. I will go home to my children soon.

The Family of Three

Beatrice Lamwaka

It did not take me long to find a child-headed household in Laguri camp in Pader district. Pader district has been at the front of the war between the Lord's Resistance Army rebels and the Ugandan government in northern Uganda since 1986. It is the scene where people have been boiled in pots, where bodies have been mutilated, and where massive abductions have occurred. The rebels used the district as their exit point from Uganda into southern Sudan; in addition, the traditional Karamojong cattle raids continued to affect the people living there. As a result of increased rebel activity and the growing number of deaths from HIV/AIDS, there are many families that are headed by children. I went out with the intention of giving such children a voice.

Laguri camp looks like a forest of mushrooms from a distance. I am not sure an aerial view would be different. Huts are built on both sides of the main road that leads to either Gulu or Kitgum town, depending on which end of the road you are looking from. The huts are built close to each other, so that if one hut is set on fire, virtually the whole camp can burn down with ease. The newspaper accounts that I have read about such fires attest to this. Children in tattered clothes play with one another. Men sit in circles drinking lacoyi beer, using straws dipped in pots of the beverage.

I am told by a young girl to look for the camp commander before I speak to anyone. I find him eating his breakfast. He tells me his name is Komakec. I tell him I want to talk to a member of a child-headed family. He calls one of his children and tells him to go around the camp and tell some of the girls that they will have a visitor soon and should get prepared. I don't know what he means when he says they should get prepared, but I don't ask. I had not imagined that I would be assisted this fast. I wonder whether I should give him something in appreciation. I place my hand on my bag as I ponder my next move, but then I remember what I have been told by people who work for the organizations that deal with them on a daily basis: "Do not give them money, because they will begin to demand money for whatever they do, and we can't allow that."

"Let's go," Komakec says as he leads the way. "We'll start with Amito, who lives close by."

For close to an hour, I move from one hut to another. I am glad that the huts are not far from one another. I speak to a number of girls who fail to say anything except their names. I begin to think that perhaps their stories are too traumatizing for them to want to relate, making them unwilling to say much. I respect their silence and refrain from asking further questions. Komakec realizes my dilemma, but he leads me on to the next home and the next. In one of the huts, Laker tells me that she is attending a UNICEF-sponsored primary school. She says that no particular level has been allotted to her class, that it has people of all ages, and that it is only after they have passed tests that they are promoted to primary four. Maybe they are all in primary three then. That is all she says.

"Let's go to the next home," Komakec says.

"I want to speak to someone who can tell her story," I explain to him.

"Don't worry, we will find you one," he says.

We walk past more huts. They seem unending. People seated in front of their homes watch us as we go by. They mumble greetings, and Komakec responds warmly.

We walk further into the camp. Komakec slows down as we approach a certain hut. I know that this family has been told about my arrival. He tells me this is a family of three children: Latua, thirteen; Layet, ten; and the youngest, Okeny, eight years old. I know they don't have to tell me their stories, but I hope they will be able to talk to me so that I can relay their stories to others. Then people will know what the children are going through in northern Uganda, and something can be done to help them.

Latua's compound is about six meters square and is freshly swept. Her small grass-thatched hut stands in the middle of the camp like a dry weed in a forest. Some of the grass from the roof has been plucked away, probably to light fires for cooking. She stands with an otok broom in her hands. When the children who have been playing in front of their hut see us, they scatter like millet spilling from a winnowing tray. Her younger brother and sister come forward, leaving the other children behind. I recognize them immediately from their close resemblance; they are dark and tall, with big, bright eyes.

They stand close together as if they are positioning themselves for a picture. I take out my digital camera from my bag. Latua and her siblings smile as I take their picture. Komakec joins them, and I take more pictures. They stand close to each other, but none of them touches the others.

When I am done taking their pictures, I look around. Firewood has been neatly placed in the compound, a sign that Latua has just returned from collecting it in the forest.

"Let's get into the house," Komakec says.

I follow Komakec as he bends and enters the hut. I find a mat on the floor. I sit at the far end. Komakec finds himself a stool. The three children—Latua, Layet, and Okeny—follow each other like red ants. They sit opposite Komakec and me. Latua is in the middle, with Layet and Okeny on either side. Komakec knows his way around. This is his village.

Latua has rearranged the hut that has seen her mother and her grandmother breathe their last, she would later tell me. Her sister and brother stay close to her as if to guard her.

Latua's hut is small, with a grass roof and a wall like all the huts in camps in northern Uganda. I don't see anything luxurious inside. It is a very small hut for Latua and her siblings. I think about my small bedroom, which I think is triple the size of their hut. I glance at the dirty and torn mosquito net hanging on a string in the center of the hut. I know that it has been provided by an NGO. I wonder whether they will share it in the night or if only Latua uses it. The fireplace looks like it has been abandoned; perhaps they haven't cooked in days. Huge saucepans blackened by smoke are arranged near the fireplace. I scan the hut to see if there is any food stored anywhere. Dry cassava tubers that have almost turned yellow lie on an aged winnower. The cassava looks almost inedible. I wonder if Latua will cook that for her family after I have left. I don't see any other food. I can sense that perhaps Latua and her siblings have not eaten *in days and may not be eating their next meal soon. I know that whatever is in the hut is all they have.*

My name is Sunday Latua. I study in Laguri Primary School. I'm in primary three. I was born in Laguri camp. I hear that the camp has more than ten thousand people. My mother, before she died, told me that I was born on December 26, 1994. She studied up to primary six. She was one of the most educated in her family. She used to write and read letters for the villagers. I have not seen my birth certificate. I believe I have to remember my siblings' birthdays so that I can tell them in future. My sister, Layet, was born on January 12, 1997, and my brother, Okeny, in 1999. Ma couldn't remember the date and month because the disease that killed her had already started eating away at her brain.

I hear women say behind my back that Ma was killed by slim; that's why she was very thin when she died. They say that the three of us may have the disease. I feel all right. I hardly ever fall sick, so I don't know what the women are talking about. I know that she was sick for such a long time. She had a cough, a very bad cough. She always complained that she felt very cold most of the time.

We never took her to the hospital. She stayed in this house until she died. On the night that she passed away, the three of us were sleeping. She called out to me to cover her. I gathered the blankets that she had thrown off and covered her. She later called out to me again and said that she was cold. I looked around for something else to cover her with. We hardly had anything else, so I covered her with the blanket that I shared with Okeny and Layet. She later called out to me yet again to cover her. This time I had nothing, and I ignored her further calls. I somehow slept, because I didn't hear her call my name again. When I woke up, I went to tell Komakec that Ma's condition had worsened. He came over and checked her. He told my siblings to get out of the house. That is when I knew that she had died. She was buried on that very day, I guess, because we wouldn't have had any room to sleep.

Ma was buried at our real home. So were many of the members of my family. That's the home that I will move back to when we leave the camp. We have already been told to go home and start farming our land. I'm afraid to go there though. The houses were burned down many years ago by the rebels when they killed most of my family. Some people say that our home has got to be cleansed because my people were killed there in such a terrible way. I wouldn't know what to do. And they said that the cleansing needs cows, goats, and chickens, which we don't have. I'm also afraid that the rebels will come back and then we will have to run to the camp again. So it's useless going back now.

I know that maybe our neighbors are already farming back home. I hope that they won't encroach on our land. I don't even know where the boundary stones are located. The Local Council said that they would assist me in getting the portion of the land that belongs to us. I'm relying on their help. I can't do much by myself.

One day, Okeny was very hot but complained that he was cold. I took him to Laguri Medical Centre, but the nurses told me to go back home and get my parents. I told them my parents were both dead. The nurse said she wasn't joking. She insisted that I needed to get my parents to provide more information about Okeny's history. I told them I had all the information they needed. I was told to leave anyway. I had hoped to see someone who knew my family so that they could help, but nobody came to my rescue. We came back home and Okeny got well somehow. Sometimes I worry that he may become as sick as Ma was and die.

Many people tell me that my sister, Layet, has a mental illness. I don't know what that means, because the mad people I see in the camp walk about naked talking to themselves. Layet doesn't do that; she is like any normal child I know. Layet goes to school and is learning how to read and write just like I am. I know that sometimes she watches movies through the cracks in the shelters, but most children do that. Is this madness? What can I do to stop people from saying such things? How can I stop my sister from acting like a mad person? She is all I have.

At school, the teachers never ask me to bring my parents like they ask other pupils. I wish I had someone to come over to school to check our performance. One time, I asked my English teacher why the parents of other pupils come to school. We have cultural days at school, and parents come to watch their children perform. I always remind Layet and Okeny that we have each other. I'm their mother as much as they are my father. We always stick together, but sometimes Layet doesn't listen. She wants to play with the other children instead of doing her chores.

She knows very well that we have to go to school and we have to do our chores and also be able to find food. But sometimes she is stubborn.

The World Food Programme gives us food. We belong to the category called the vulnerable. This group consists of the elderly, those suffering from HIV/AIDS, and the orphans. The food is never enough. That is why I have to dig for other people in order to get more food. The food that the World Food Programme gives us is usually *posho*, cooking oil, and beans. We can't eat that all the time. So I have to work to supplement this food.

My little brother, Okeny, is eight years old. He always asks me when Ma is coming back. I don't know how to tell him that Ma will never come back. I don't know what to say or how to explain to him that Ma died. I wish I could understand the world more so that I could teach and protect my brother and sister.

I worry all the time that the war may intensify again. How will I protect Layet and Okeny? What if they get abducted? Will I be able to cleanse them with *opobo*?

When I was about eight years old and Ma was very ill and we didn't have enough food to eat, Ma sat me down and told me, "We don't have food anymore, and you are now the head of this family." I thought she was going to tell me that she was about to die. I heard some women whisper behind my back that my mother was going to die soon and I would have to take care of my siblings.

"You are a strong girl. Go back home and get the vegetables you find growing in the ruins," Ma instructed.

I picked up the basket that Ma usually used when she went out to look for food.

"Make sure nobody sees you," she shouted weakly as I left.

I didn't know exactly what that meant, since she usually told me not to go to places where there were no people. But in the camp there is no single place that doesn't have people at any one time.

I hurried to a home that I didn't know much about. All I knew was that Baba and Ma had lived here before the war and that this was the place where Baba was buried and where Ma would also be buried when she died. All the houses in the compound had been burned down by either the rebels or the government soldiers, and the grass had grown over almost everywhere. *Akeyo* and *obuga* vegetables had grown where the rubbish dump might have been.

The vegetables looked really good, and I wanted to get as many as I could. We had spent many days without eating proper food—only millet porridge. I was so excited—you should have seen me. I plucked the vegetables like an expert and put them in the basket. The basket was almost full when suddenly I heard someone walking toward me. I froze. It was too late to duck and hide. I waited for whoever it was to come up. I hoped that it was one of the villagers looking for food.

I saw a girl not much older than me approaching. She wore oversized army fatigues. I knew she was a rebel. She had a gun slung over her shoulder. The stories I had heard came back to my mind. I remembered Ma's story about how some members of my family had been boiled in pots because the rebels accused them of betraying them.

"Leave whatever you are doing and follow me," the girl ordered.

I dropped the *obuga* I had in my hands and followed her like a dog. Many years of war had taught me to follow orders without question. So I just followed her. We reached another ruined home and found people of all ages seated there. They were being guarded by rebels. The girl pushed me down into a sitting position without saying a word.

I heard one of the rebels say, "She's very young, but we can't let her go right now. You know how these children are; she will run straight to the UPDF barracks."

A lot of things were brought. I heard people walking all over the place, but I remained still, not looking at the rebels. I feared that if they saw me looking at them, they might attack me with their machetes.

"Young girl, leave now," I heard, feeling a hand poking at me. "Run and don't look back. If you do, I will shoot you. And don't say anything about what you've seen," the man warned sternly.

I jumped up and ran without looking back. I don't even know if the rebels pointed their guns at me. I ran till I got to the camp.

When I entered the house, looking exhausted from running, Ma looked at me and asked quietly, "They found you?" I nodded my head.

Later I heard that the older men who had been captured were hacked to death and the girls and boys abducted. I can't explain my luck, but I was glad I was spared so that I was able to take care of Ma, Layet, and Okeny.

IV

Beyond the Dance

The Torture and Trauma of Female Genital Mutilation

I cried and wailed until I could cry no more.
My voice grew hoarse, and the cries could not come out,
I wriggled as the excruciating pain ate into my tender flesh.
Hold her down! cried the cursed cutter . . .
Then she ordered the women to pour hot sand on my cut genitals.
My precious blood gushed out and foamed. . . .

—Maryam Sheikh Abdi, "The Cut"

It is incredible that, in Africa and elsewhere in the world, a protracted form of violence continues to be committed against women in the name of tradition. This criminal act is female genital mutilation (FGM), which violates women's human rights and denies them their God-given gift of womanhood. This gender-based violence not only denies the rights of a woman or a girl-child but subjects the victims to many health hazards, including HIV/AIDS, incapacitation, fistula, and even death. Many victims of FGM cannot enjoy a sexual relationship with their partner because of the untold physical and emotional pain, and husbands often abandon wives who fail to fulfill their marital obligation to their husband's satisfaction—never mind that being circumcised is a prerequisite to finding a husband.

Since 1996, NGOs like Reproductive, Educative and Community Health (REACH) have been trying to teach communities about the serious health effects of the practice and advocating for its elimination. They have set up counseling centers for FGM victims and support for those who wish to rehabilitate their lives by going back to school. They also encourage women circumcisers to give up the business and find an alternative source of income.

Tradition shrouds the practice in mystery and superstition in order to make women more compliant and subservient to archaic and irrelevant societal norms that don't take their welfare into consideration. The good news is that FGM is now a topic of public debate, with activists and all right-thinking people advocating for its worldwide eradication. Many countries have outlawed FGM, including Uganda, which passed a law in 2010. However, because the abuse is still accepted as a cultural tradition by many, even in countries where it is banned, the practice still goes on.

VIOLET BARUNGI

Saina's Story

CATHERINE ANITE

Cherotich Saina is a seventy-year-old illiterate Muslim widow who lost her husband and two children in 1993. Her husband was a lot older than she, although she did not know by how many years. In her interview, Saina, a one-time circumciser and mentor in circumcision matters, reveals a great deal of information surrounding all the myths and stories about female circumcision.

It is widely believed that female circumcision in Kapchorwa is associated with witchcraft and evil spirits. Before I went for the interview, I had been told that Sabiny culture contends that after a woman who has been circumcised has healed, she is taken to the jungle where she fights with a leopard that scratches her arms and makes four marks. The women who have short scratches are stronger than the women with long scratches, because they are thought to have overpowered the leopard before it could make long scratches on them. Indeed, most Sabiny women have scratches of different sizes. Of course, others say that it is the mentors and circumcisers who scratch the timid girls in the dark jungles.

I had wanted Saina to tell me the truth about it, but as Saina talks, I begin to get anxious about my mission of finding out the secrets that are the driving force behind the knife. I ask her to comment on the marks on her arm, but she keeps silent on the matter. "That, too, is taboo to reveal," she says.

Culture normally involves music and other forms of drama, and it is evident that the Sabiny are passionate about their culture and express it through song. During the time of preparing for mutilation, all the candidates are taught traditional songs and dances, which they must learn before they can be initiated into adulthood. The songs sound vulgar, and the dances are quite seductive. One of the songs Saina gives me is a factual song that explains the pain of the practice and the transformative effect it has on the candidate, saying mutilation turns you from a child into an adult, and in the process you are recognized in the community as somebody of high standing.

> If you have accepted, you accept until the very end.
> If you can't manage please go away because it is a painful
>   experience.
> So you have to endure.
> Killing you by an arrow is even better and less painful than
>   circumcision.
> So if you feel you prefer an arrow and want to remain a girl
>   please go away.
> You still have a long clitoris.
> You are just a girl.
> If you get a short a one, you will become a real Sabiny
>   woman.

After this very long and interesting conversation, I realized that the Sabiny culture is still deep rooted, and trying to eradicate it is like chasing a mirage in the Kalahari Desert. We only hope and pray that one day all the mist and smoke will be cleared from everyone's eyes, and they will see clearly and understand that the girl-child in society is as important as the male child and that some cultural practices, especially female genital mutilation, cause more harm than good. The sun will surely shine very bright the day all the blunt knives and sharp razors are destroyed and peace is returned to the soul of the girl-child.

Hope, don't die!

In our days, a long time ago, the elders glorified the practice of circumcision, and by the time I reached the age of sixteen, I already had the courage to go for it. Together with my age-mates, we encouraged each other and prepared for it. Our parents paid the circumcision fee, and for about four months, beginning in August, we trained each other in dancing styles specifically designed for the ritual. We danced on the rocky paths as we waited for the month of December, when the date of circumcision would be communicated to us.

When the day came, our parents brewed local beer, and there was a lot of drinking and celebrating. We danced all night with the mentors as the circumcisers sharpened their knives. At dawn the following day, we were taken to a river to clean and cleanse our genitals in preparation for the cutting. When we were done, we were taken to the circumcision grounds while singing songs of cultural glorification. When we reached the grounds, the circumcisers were already waiting for us under a shelter constructed specifically for the occasion.

The circumcision takes place at dawn because the circumcisers need enough light to clearly see the area to be cut. At the grounds, a ram was slaughtered, and all the firstborn daughters were smeared with sheep chyme. After that ritual was completed, we were then ordered to lie down on a mat, where, one by one, the surgeon cut out the labia and clitoris in a matter of seconds. Thus, we were initiated into womanhood and became adult role models in our community.

After being circumcised, I felt that I had become a heroine and deserved the respect that all circumcised women in the community got. Shortly after circumcision, my parents found me a man to marry. Before a year elapsed, we were married and had started living as husband and wife. We bore children, and I must confess that the gods showered their favor upon me because, unlike other women, I did not experience any complications while giving birth. Even during sexual intercourse with my husband, I did not feel any pain and lived a normal life. The only pain I felt was immediately after I was cut, but it disappeared after a few days.

I had a happy family of two sons and a loving husband who, I must confess, was way older than me. Unfortunately, they have all passed away, and now I am all alone. I lost my husband in 1993, and ever since I have felt so lonely and completely deserted, since there is no one to look after me in my old age.

Before I became a circumciser, I was attacked by spirits. As a result, I became mad and started wandering and running around without cause and direction. It all started in the year 1957, when I started getting weird dreams, and then I menstruated for the whole year without stopping. When the bleeding persisted, my people decided to go and visit a diviner, who revealed to them that the spirits of my grandparents had returned and had chosen me to engage in the circumcision of Sabiny girls. You know, these days, witch doctors are not truthful like they used to be. Those days, it was easy to discern truth from falsehood.

I come from a line of circumcisers. I must have inherited it from my father's lineage, because my father's aunt was a circumciser. Unfortunately, this did not stop with me. The spirits disturbed my younger sister Amina as well, because they also wanted her to become a circumciser. They would take her to the river, to bushes, and to caves, and we would look for her and eventually find her in those obscure areas.

I started circumcising in 1957 and continued until 1960, when I retired. It is interesting how I was inaugurated into the world of circumcision. I was given circumcision tools and other cultural items. The elders organized a ceremony and performed cultural rituals linking me to the gods as I received the tools. They prepared local brew and spat it on my face and all over my body. During such rituals, the drink is either sprinkled on you with a broom after it has been dipped in a pot or spat all over your body, as they did in my case. While the drink was being spat on me, the elders handed over the tools to me. These included the knife for cutting and a whetstone for sharpening the knife. You see, you do not sharpen the circumcision knife on just any stone. Everything is special.

During the period when I was a circumciser, I circumcised many girls. It is hard for me to calculate the number, although my estimate is at least twenty girls per day each December. Sometimes some families were not ready and didn't have the means to organize feasts. Some parents could not afford to buy meat and drinks for the people, so it was a hindrance. This meant that some girls dropped out and had to wait for another season. It is strenuous, but each family tries as much as possible to have their daughters circumcised, because it is believed that circumcision is a prerequisite for marriage, and here women are largely dependent on men economically.

In addition, a girl who is not circumcised is generally considered a coward and a weakling and therefore not worth marrying. A girl who does not have her clitoris removed is considered ultimately fatal to a man; she is a great challenge in terms of sexual appetite.

I can't explain some of these things to you, but, for personal reasons, these days I no longer circumcise girls. But, as much as it is being fought, I want you to know that circumcision is still going on secretly. Girls sneak into the deep forests of Kapchorwa to be circumcised there.

When I used to circumcise, I would never sterilize or even use different knives, because at that time AIDS was still a myth to most of us. But when it started spreading, all circumcisers were advised and cautioned against using the same knife. The health authorities advised them to at least sterilize their knives in hot water if they could not afford to use different knives.

As a circumciser, I enjoyed a number of benefits. Each circumcision candidate would pay me a fee and also bring me chickens and good food. These things kept me very healthy and gave me more energy to cut and keep the culture alive and strong. The candidates benefited too in the course of visiting their kin, when they would be given gifts of chickens, goats, and sometimes cows.

During circumcision, the girls are made to lie down with their legs wide open. Unlike men, who are supposed to face up when they are being circumcised, the girls are instructed to turn their heads to the right as the surgeon gets ready to cut. The surgeon then gets some roughly ground millet flour and sprinkles it on the labia and clitoris to stop the area from being slippery. This helps to make it easy to hold and cut.

If a girl screams in pain during the cutting, she is considered to be a very weak woman. Such weaklings are left for married men who are looking for second wives, or they are given to disabled and mentally impaired men in the community who have failed to marry. Able-bodied men are not permitted to marry such weak women, because they are a big embarrassment and a disgrace to society.

I used to spend the whole night sharpening my knife with the other circumcisers. Since the other circumcisers would drink and smoke, they had an added advantage because they kept themselves busy. As a Muslim, I am not permitted to do any of those things. On the other hand, most of the circumcisers are not attached to their religions because they are possessed by spirits that instruct them on cultural issues. But currently people are refusing to listen to the spirits because they are so engrossed in religion.

While sharpening our knives, we talked little. We would occasionally talk to the mentors, since they were our apprentices. They helped us to carry our tools and other material.

I was committed to my work as a circumciser, which made me fast and popular. In a short time, I would go through twenty candidates, and then, within the same dawn, I would quickly proceed to another village to circumcise more girls. The speed went hand in hand with the craft. I should also add that no candidate of mine ever got any complications after being cut, because I was pretty skilled at my job. This shows how committed I was to it.

Sometimes the circumcisers would not cut out the labia completely; in that case, they would have to do the cutting again. The mentors closely monitored the girls until they healed completely. They also imparted to them cultural values and the postcircumcision secrets. Therefore, it was the mentor who ensured that the required amount of cutting had been done. And if she realized that some parts had not been cut properly, then she would call back the circumciser to trim it down to the required level. But if the circumciser was out of reach, the mentor would complete the job. At that stage, the pain is worse than the pain at the first instance.

It is the duty of the mentor to collect all the parts of the participants after they have been circumcised. It is a cultural norm that these girls— now women—are not allowed to bathe for three days after being cut. When the three days have passed, the body parts are then thrown or buried in an undisclosed place. That is our secret.

Now I will tell you a bit about the circumcision of twins. There are some rituals that have to be carried out before twins are circumcised. These are very different and more complicated than those of ordinary children. In a scenario where a twin had lost the mother or father or the child that followed her or him, the elders, who included the mentors and circumcisers, would go to the grave of the deceased and remove the deceased's bones. These bones would then be placed in a basket and taken in a procession of elders, the twin, and all other candidates awaiting circumcision. Every person would dance and sing cultural songs as the whole procession moved along.

But these days, it is different. In case any of the above died, the elders would just go to the place where they hid the mother of the twins after childbirth. In Sabiny culture, when a woman produces twins, she is hidden in a house for some time before she is brought out and unveiled to society. That is the place where the twins are taken in preparation for circumcision. Soil is dug out of this house, a goat is killed, its blood is mixed with the soil, and the mixture is smeared on the twins, after which they go for circumcision.

In Sabiny culture, immediately after twins are born, a hole is dug, and a green tree is planted in it. Leaves from this tree, called *takamuda*, are then mixed with the offal of a sheep that has been slaughtered for the ritual. The mixture is then used to smear the parents of the twins. The rest of the carcass is buried. The mother of the twins is hidden in the house for some time, and after other subsequent rituals have been performed, she is set free to mingle with others.

After all the rituals have been performed, the green tree is watered and well taken care of. The house is also held sacred. When the twins come of age, soil is dug from around the base of the tree and used to smear the heads of the twins before they are taken to a cave. After the twins have returned from the cave, they are taken back to the house where the tree was planted. The green tree is then uprooted. After that, a cowhide is laid down and the stem of the tree is put on top of the hide. The twins are then asked to stand on the hide. This is believed to prevent them from bleeding and going into shock when they are circumcised.

The rules for circumcising twins are so numerous and the standards so high. A twin cannot get circumcised if her mother has never been circumcised. If it is a non-Sabiny woman married to a Sabiny man, there is absolutely no problem with that, but if it is an uncircumcised Sabiny woman who produced the twins, they have to first circumcise her before recognizing her as a mother of twins.

There is no way you can dodge circumcision after producing twins because, shortly after their birth, the twins and their mother are hidden in the house. Before they are brought out, the mother must be circumcised.

However, sometimes a mother of twins dies after giving birth when she is not circumcised. When this happens, her body is not passed through the main entrance; the back of the house is broken into and her body is passed through the backyard! This is to show other women who dodge the practice that even in death they will be regarded as social outcasts and carried to their graves in humiliation.

In Sabiny culture, it is a taboo not to circumcise both twins, but there are cases where an exemption can be made. For instance, if one of them is too sickly and it is well-known that she might not survive the pain of circumcision, she will be exempted, but only on the condition that she stands by the side of the other twin who is to be cut. There is really no way the other twin can get circumcised when her sister is not around and not standing by her side, unless she is dead. In that case, her grave will be dug up and her bones scooped out and brought to the circumcision grounds.

After circumcision, twins are treated the same way as the other girls. The elders believe that to heal quickly, the girls have to urinate on themselves. In my time, there was no treatment after circumcision. The treatment was urine. The girls were forced to urinate regularly, and while doing so they had to cross and close their legs tightly. This would go on for two weeks, and by the third week they would have healed. Any girl found to be holding her urine would be flogged.

The girls are not allowed to use water for bathing. They are only allowed to use sap squeezed out of banana stems into a calabash or pot. And the first bath they are allowed to have will be three days after they are cut.

◎◎

I surrendered my circumcision duties to my younger sister, Amina, but I volunteered to help her in mentoring the girls.

One of my duties as a mentor was to administer local herbs to the girls during circumcision. The rationale was to change the childish attitude of the girl into a sense of maturity so that she would become a strong and respectable woman in society. On the eve of circumcision, the girls are made to dance as they visit their kin and friends. Then they are given food and drinks, and after that they are taken to a room where cultural secrets are revealed to them with a strong caution not to tell any of the secrets to anyone. They are also given a small portion of a certain herb to strengthen them during the actual cutting. The night before the candidates are cut, they go through certain cultural drills, and the pain they encounter is equal to that of the actual cutting.

Another role I assumed as a mentor was to take the girls through the oath of secrecy. There are several cultural secrets that we Sabiny treasure, and the girls know that it is taboo to reveal these secrets to any person, including their very own blood relations, especially those who have not gone through the initiation process. When you reveal those secrets, you get cursed.

Because of the restrictions surrounding such revelations, I am not in a position to reveal them to you, even if you threatened me with a knife or a gun. I would rather die than let my people down. As soon as anyone reveals these secrets, the person who did it either runs mad or is struck dead.

I must confess that I actually do not know anyone in my village who has run mad or even died, but I have heard so many stories of women in other villages who have run mad and even died because they violated the oath of secrecy. Cultural beliefs should not be taken lightly. I have been asked before whether as a circumciser I was involved in the cursing since I was a cultural goddess, but that is one question I cannot answer. Even if I was involved, I cannot tell you anything concerning witchcraft because it is against my cultural norms. We keep all our secrets.

I would not wish to become a circumciser again because the government has now criminalized the practice, and I fear being hunted by the long arm of the law. Besides, my successor, Amina, also left the practice, so why would I go back to it?

On the other hand, I am indecisive on the whole issue of circumcision. Those people trying to stop the practice should see to it that they provide for the women circumcisers whom they are stopping from continuing with the practice, because that is how they earn a living. If they do not provide any assistance, then I am ready to go back to the practice even if they have criminalized it. Currently, some people have turned to thievery to escape from poverty, and this year I am willing to circumcise secretly just to earn a little money.

I used to sell fruits and vegetables, but now I have become very sickly and weak. Because of that, I cannot work. Old age is also an encumbrance to me, and to make matters worse, the assistance REACH gives

me is too little to sustain me. Therefore, I will not repent at all for having earned my living from circumcision, but I can only pretend to adjust
to modernity. How about those people who slaughter animals? Do they
feel sorry after killing the animals, or do they become happy that they
are going to eat meat? If government had not made it a criminal offense,
I would continue encouraging the circumcision of girls.

Do Not Count on Me

❈❈

BETTY KITUYI

Amina Atare Buraimu is a tall woman and looks sixty-something, with a stoop and a wrinkled face that seem to cover her past. She abandoned her culturally revered role as a circumciser of girls in 1996 when the REACH program identified her as the most dangerous person in the district and talked her out of it. As the most experienced circumciser in the Kapchorwa district, she was as swift as Moses Kipsiro, the Kapchorwa-born athlete, scampering from village to village and from hill to hill in her red circumcision uniform as if possessed, cutting an average of one hundred girls per village. According to the rumors circulating around the villages, if circumcision is harmful, then she was the one who harmed the largest number of girls.

"When Kuka or Chokomondosi—the ministers, our own women from the Sipi—stand up to speak against the cutting, who is Amina to continue doing it? They must be right when they say it is wrong, because they have watched it all their lives," she says.

They told her that the traditional cutting of girls before they are considered fully women is no longer acceptable or considered honorable. She was told that times have changed, and with them a lot of the things once considered culturally

243

important. *New diseases like slim are killing the young before the old. The knife no longer makes the girls clean but frequently transfers the AIDS virus from one girl to the next, if one girl in the line has it and the girls share one knife.*

In her time, the girls were virgins when they were cut. Today, modern habits and practices lead them into having sex before marriage. It was uncommon then to circumcise married women, but now it is the trend. This is very risky, because in Kapchorwa the infection rates for sexually transmitted diseases are higher among married couples than among unmarried people, since many married people are not faithful to each other. The young women no longer keep the tribal secrets. Some circumcised ones are saying they feel pain when they have sex with their husbands. When Amina was still a thin girl with a flat chest and her mother was breast-feeding her younger siblings, it was taboo to reveal what was going on in the bedroom. But now that people are talking, she says, it could be true that circumcision of girls is harmful.

Yet Amina relished those days when she was the most skillful and powerful woman cutter in the land. She had a lot of money to spend and was able to afford almost anything she wanted. Mutilating girls earned her a lot of money and gifts from the girls' families. From a single circumcision season, she would collect close to ten million shillings as payment for her services.

Her current circumstances give no glimpse of her former riches. As she talks, her sunken eyes and dry, cracking lips confirm her ill health, which she blames on the poverty that attacked her, like locusts do a cassava garden, ever since she stopped excising girls. She tells me that she cannot afford any medicine and that her granaries have long been out of maize and millet, since she is too weak to tend the gardens and is too poor to hire people to lend her a hand in tending them.

"*A*re you one of those government officials who always come to ask me about my experience?" Amina asks, patting my hand lightly. "Over the past few years, strange people from the government have come here, driving their big vehicles, condemning the circumcision of girls. They have convinced me and my other four colleagues to stop it. But only two of us have stopped. Others still do it deep in the villages, like Bukwa. They are still doing it for the money especially. You look at me; I have nothing now! Those government people make promises they never fulfill. Some people visited my home two years ago and promised to give me some money to start a chicken-rearing project and build me a *mabati* house, but they have not honored their promise. Yet I told them that I did not have any other means of livelihood."

As if poverty has choked out any rational thought in her, her sentiments seem to contradict the reasons she has earlier given for stopping the circumcision of girls. She sounds like she was forced to stop the practice and that if she does not get any other means of livelihood, she can very easily slip back into the practice of cutting girls.

"We do not like being held up in Paradise during the circumcision period," she says, explaining that Paradise is a hotel where people from the REACH program make the circumcisers stay for a whole week in order to stop them from going out to cut the girls. "They tell us to relax and not to think about circumcision. They promise to give us money to start projects, but they do not fulfill their promises."

Like the hovering clouds in the Kapchorwa skies, Amina's moods shift and seem to brighten when she tells me how she became a circumciser. It turns out that she never wanted to become one after all. As a young girl, she had heard stories of some girls who bled to death when they were badly cut. She did not want to shoulder any blame should such an accident happen to her. She resisted being a circumciser for twenty years before she gave in to the sickness that tortured her, which was sent by the circumcision spirits.

"In those days," she says, "one became a circumciser under a special calling by Ayuik, the circumcision spirits. The gift to circumcise ran in families from one generation to the next; a grandmother who was a circumciser could pass on the tools of circumcision to her granddaughter if Ayuik identified her and gave her the knowledge of the knife. When Ayuik identified a suitable candidate, it possessed her, took over her mind, and made her act with supernatural powers, doing unbelievable things like walking on the edge of a cliff without falling or being able to sense danger. The one chosen by the spirits could even sleep in the deep caves, sharing them with wild animals and coming out unharmed."

For Amina, one thing led to another. By nature she was a sickly child. At fourteen, when no traditional herbs or white man's medicine could cure her of the ailments that ate the flesh off her bones and left her as thin as a cassava stem from her mother's garden, the elders suspected her to be suffering from circumcision spirits and decided to circumcise her. When a young girl suffered from some mysterious sickness and became thin, circumcision was often resorted to as a possible treatment for the sickness.

"I was circumcised by a very old woman who came to the inner room where I lay. She was being carried on a man's back. When he put her down, I saw that she could not stand without support. Because I was too ill, I did not sing or dance with the other girls."

Amina pats her brow as if to smooth away a headache before she tells me more. "I fainted and slipped into a coma and woke up five days later to the deep murmurs of a witch doctor who had been summoned from the Kalenjin tribe in Kenya to treat me. With deep groans and a shrieking, scary voice, the witch doctor prophesied that I had special powers and that I would circumcise many girls when the right time came."

Since she was destined to be a custodian of the special Sabiny knowledge and believed to have the special powers of a circumciser, Amina's health improved. She even put some weight on her bony frame. With these special powers, she was no ordinary young woman, and that made her more attractive to many men, who sought to marry her.

As was expected of the newly cut woman, and one of her caliber, she was carried off one day on her way to the well by a man who became her husband in the mountains.

"I was balancing a big water pot on my head and walking without a care toward our home when suddenly I heard heavy footsteps behind me. I saw a man I had never seen before. He grabbed my pot and put it down carefully. He then carried me on his shoulders like a banana stem. I tried to scream, but he covered my mouth with his hand and ordered me to keep quiet, because he was now my husband. After we had moved a good distance from our home, he put me down and held my hand firmly and led me to his hut. That is how I became his wife. My parents never looked for me, but they got to know through rumors. Eventually, he went and told them of his intention to marry me. He paid the bride-price, and I became his wife officially."

Five years of marriage brought her some health but no children. She believes that her childless condition aggravated another health condition. Her husband and mother-in-law caused her sleepless nights for failing to bear them children. She slipped into a depression, and soon she was in the world of spirits. What was left of her private parts began itching. When that happened, her grandmother told her that she was being attacked by female spirits. This was another confirmation that she could become a circumciser.

"Later," she narrates, "I heard three women's voices within me. They were saying that they would kill me if I did not want to circumcise the girls. I heard them whenever I put my head down on a mat to sleep. I hid in the forest to flee from them. But when it became dark and the owls began crying *two-whee-two-whee* in the foliage above me, I knew I was a dead woman, and I ran back home. There is a legend around the crying of owls; when they cry in the village in daylight, someone dies.

"One day, I heard the women's voices in my head in broad daylight. Their voices were louder than the village gramophone. They were saying, *Hold the knife of your grandmother.* My head became so hot I had a strong urge to stand under a waterfall to soothe it and drown out the spirits' voices with the falling of the water. When I began running at breakneck speed toward the falls of the Cheptui River, my husband ran after me and tried to stop me. I ran as fast as an antelope fleeing a hungry lion. I went to the deep end where the falls pour into a hole several meters deep, and I plunged into it. When I did not come up, my husband thought I was dead, and he called for help.

"I don't remember anything that took place while I was under the water, but I remember that I was brought to the surface of the water by my husband and panic-stricken villagers. To everyone's amazement, I had jingles on my ankles and wrists when I came out of the water. This was surprising because I did not have the jingles when I entered the water. Suddenly I felt well as I was being led home by my husband, the jingles on me making a hunting dog's sound, attracting people to pop out of their houses like white ants emerging after a light evening rain."

As Amina talks, I ask more questions, but she is not willing to be diverted from her version of the story. Begrudgingly I listen, with a lot of reservations.

"My husband took me to my parents' home in Kibanda village in Kwoti subcounty on the northern slope of Mount Elgon. To my parents and elders, the jingles were confirmation that I was destined to be a circumciser. They decided immediately to summon my old grand-mother, who was also a circumciser, to hand me the tools so that I could begin cutting the girls. The tool-giving ceremony was an interesting ritual in which a goat was slaughtered for a feast. The tools my grand-mother passed on included two new knives made from nails that were hammered flat, which they tied to both of my hands; a *lutetyo*, a whet-stone made out of cement for sharpening the knife; millet for rubbing in the private parts of a girl to make it rough and easy to grip; and a short-sleeved red gown marked with a danger sign painted in white. A special alcoholic drink of *komeka baka* and *komeka teshonik* was spat on my face by my grandmother, who then declared me a circumciser."

Amina Buraimu did not begin to circumcise immediately because she was still scared. One day before the circumcision season, some spirits called her by name in a dream.

Amina, Amina, they said, *why do you refuse to circumcise the girls?*

They promised to stand with her, make her brave, and teach her. They would give her the knowledge. They also threatened that if she refused, they would kill her.

"The following morning," she recounts, "I heard whistles outside my father's mud hut, and by the time I came out, three girls were danc-ing vigorously in the yard, accompanied by an excited crowd of women, young and old. When they saw me, they bowed and fell on their knees and, in song, told me that they had come to fetch my knife, as they had chosen me to circumcise them. By custom, that is how it is done. The girls fetch the knife from the circumciser a day before they are to be cut, and when she gives it to them, they take it as a sign of commitment and return home to prepare for the rest of the ceremony.

"I remember the first girl I cut quite vividly, because I was very frightened. It was in 1978, and I was thirty years old. I first prayed to the women spirits for wisdom and strength. Immediately afterward, I swiftly cut off the girl's clitoris. Then I fled and hid in the bushes because I thought I had not done it properly. It is the mentors who picked up my knife and the remains of the clitoris and threw them in the pit latrine as the practice demands."

But, true to their word, the circumcision spirits guided her and took over whenever she carried out subsequent circumcisions. She became very competent with the knife. All the girls she has cut regard her as a godmother, and she is often called on to give advice to them and their families.

I asked Amina whether she had passed on her special powers to anybody, and she said that she believed it was not within her powers to do it, and no one in her line had shown signs like those that she had prior to being initiated into the practice. Amina sees her abandonment of her role as circumciser as an inspiration to the others, and her wish is to be rewarded for leading others out of the practice, though some of them were persuaded by REACH to abandon it through the gift of cows.

Amina has been married for thirty years but never did have children. She left her husband and now lives alone. Her husband married a second woman, who bore him children. I asked whether her being unable to bear children was associated with FGM, but she dismissed the question, saying that that would take us into another story that she did not want to tell. She had learned that FGM could be the cause, but it was too late to help matters.

"In the past," she states, "such information was not available, because no one complained and no one found out. But with the anti-FGM campaigns that condemn the practice, the people now know the truth."

But one cannot help wondering why the spirits that started her cutting in the first place did not object to her quitting.

Her final words about FGM underscore her belief that only education can wipe it out and empower the girls to be conscious and ask questions about their lives. She appeals to the government to assist her to start some income-generating activities so that she can have a new means of livelihood. To all those girls intending to get circumcised, she says, "Do not wriggle your waists counting on me, because I am no longer a circumciser."

Petals for the Wind

SHARON LAMWAKA AND HILDA TWONGYEIRWE

It is Saturday morning. As we approach Hanifa, she does not acknowledge our presence. She sits quietly at the gate of the offices of the African Centre for Treatment and Rehabilitation of Torture Victims, a nongovernmental organization that provides medical treatment to torture victims in Uganda and the neighboring countries in the Great Lakes region. The organization also advocates against torture in an effort to prevent its occurrence.

Hanifa is a very striking young woman. Locks of shiny dark hair dangle by her ears, escaping from the black-and-white scarf around her head and neck. She looks at us very briefly, then looks away again. We are not quite sure how to start our interview on this prickly topic.

When we greet Hanifa, she responds cheerfully, although her eyes do not quite meet ours. But we are encouraged by the warmth in her voice. We then invite her to the FEMRITE offices in Kamwokya, Kampala, and she gets into the vehicle with us. During the drive, we chitchat about nothing in particular.

At FEMRITE we offer her a cup of tea, but she does not readily accept it. Nevertheless, we set the tea in front of us and sip from our own cups. We are still not sure how to begin, but, as if she is reading our minds, she clears her throat and breaks into a smile.

"Faith says you would like to talk to me about female circumcision." Faith is the person who arranged our meeting with Hanifa.

"Yes, yes," we respond enthusiastically.

"That is not a problem, but I will tell you my story on one condition."

We are suspicious of her condition. We are taken by surprise at her confidence and strength. "One condition?" we ask.

"Yes, or maybe two."

"Let's hear them, then." We smile and encourage her to speak.

"I will share my story on condition that you will avail it to the rest of the world so that it can eventually help other women not to undergo the pain that I went through and still go through. Second, I would like to keep my identity undisclosed, because circumcision is such a demeaning experience that no woman would want people to know that she is circumcised."

With our eyes we make a silent agreement, and Hanifa proceeds to tell us her story. She had believed her mutilation bestowed "virginity" on her, but through violence and heinous abuse, she discovered FGM had taken away the essence of her womanhood and turned her into a sex slave. When the petals of a flower are blown into the wind, the flower is no longer a flower but something else.

I was born in Ethiopia, in a town called Mega. My father is Ethiopian; my mother is Somali. I have no idea where the two of them met, but they are husband and wife. I have six sisters and five brothers, and all of us were born in Mega town in Ethiopia. I am the third born in the family. It is very unfortunate, however, that I do not remember anything about my childhood with my parents and my siblings.

At an age that I do not know, my mother's sister came to our home and requested that my mother give her a child that would become her daughter. My aunt had had six sons, and she desperately wanted a daughter who would help her, especially around the house with domestic chores. Because my mother had several daughters already, she agreed to donate one, and the donation was me. I have not found the heart to forgive my parents for entering into such an arrangement. My mother says that it is a common arrangement in Somalia for families to share children, while my father says that he agreed to it because he did not want to antagonize my mother. I find neither reason convincing.

My father is from the Oromo tribe, one of the smallest tribes in Ethiopia. The Oromo traditions are not very different from the Somali ones on issues of women. In most Ethiopian customs, just like in Somalia, women do not have rights equal to those of men. For example, in the Oromo culture, men dictate how women should behave and sometimes how they dress. Men eat first while women wait upon them. A woman does not openly talk about the man she has fallen in love with, because it is the brothers or fathers who approve and recommend husbands. Arranged marriages are still very common in Ethiopia and indeed in Somalia. But Ethiopians respect women more than Somalis do. In the Oromo tribe, women are not circumcised.

Due to instability in Ethiopia and Somalia, many people have relocated to countries all over the world. It is for the same reason that my aunt, with her Somali husband, relocated to Kenya—Mweyale village at the border with Ethiopia. This is where my aunt took me, and that is where I grew up believing that the family in Mweyale was my biological family. My aunt was my mother, and her husband was my father. They had six boys who were my cousins but also my brothers. And there was not a single day when any of them made me doubt I belonged there. But at one point in my early childhood I got burned, and my aunt-mother made a very cruel remark, and I thought she was just a cruel mother. It never crossed my mind that she might not really be my mother.

In Mweyale, I was taken to Mweyale Primary School, where my cousins-brothers also studied. Life was normal until sometime in primary three. I don't remember which holiday it was, but I vaguely remember that I was in primary three and it was holiday time. One morning my aunt called me and told me to bathe and be very clean. She said that she wanted to go with me to visit her friend in a nearby village. She gave me my best clothes, and I was very happy. I always enjoyed visiting with her, because it made me feel important, especially if we left the boys behind.

We set off very early in the morning. We walked a short distance, and I was surprised that I did not know the homestead at which our journey ended. This dampened my excitement a bit, but I was happy to find two other girls also with their mothers. But before we could talk and get to know each other, we were taken straight into an empty hut in the homestead.

All the mothers stayed outside, and we were accompanied by three other women into the bare room. I found this a bit strange, but I never suspected what they were going to do to us. I believed that since my mother had brought me there, nothing harmful was going to happen to us. But one of the girls was older than us. She was grumbling all through, but she did not talk openly. She just looked at everyone suspiciously, her eyes moving from one woman to the other. As for us, we giggled and wondered why she was being difficult and disrespectful.

When we got into the room, the women first sat us down and told us that we were now being prepared for chastity.

"From today onward, you should never sleep with any man until your wedding night. If you do it, we shall know, and all your people will know, because your virginity will be broken," the women told us.

As they talked to us, I remembered that my aunt-mother had also mentioned to me something to do with not sleeping with men until my marriage.

"What we are about to do today is going to protect you and keep you chaste," one of the women continued.

I had vaguely heard about virginity, and so I thought that these women were going to give us virginity. I thought that this big girl who was grumbling was scared of getting her virginity from these women. I thought that perhaps she was not a good girl and knew she would not protect hers till marriage. But of course I never said anything. For me, I was not willing to shame my parents and brothers; I was eager to receive my virginity and protect it till my marriage. But I must admit that all these concepts were very vague in my mind. It was much, much later in life when I realized this girl must have known what they were going to do to us.

The preparation talk took a couple of minutes, and then we were told to sit on the floor. I do not quite remember what happened after that, but suddenly the three women pounced on me. One mountain of a woman quickly sat behind me and thrust her legs between mine, forcing mine wide apart. She also held my arms tightly against my stomach. The second woman quickly blindfolded me. Suddenly I felt an awkward shuffle between my legs and a sharp pain that felt like hot chili in a wound. The blindfold was removed as fast as it had been put on. The mountain woman let go of my arms and legs.

When I looked around, I did not see anyone. The two girls were still there. The women were there. But I saw none of them—all I could see was the pool of blood that surrounded me. There was so much that the women were scooping it with cupped hands and pouring it in basins. I screamed, not because of the pain but because of the shock of seeing the blood that threatened to form a lake around my body. For a moment, it was as if I were going to drown in my own blood. I even remember that my aunt-mother appeared at the door, and she too let out a scream.

"My God, what have you done to my daughter? That is too much blood. That is not normal," she said. But they shushed her into silence.

I must have been the first one to be cut, but I do not remember seeing the other girls being cut. I was too shocked to think about the others, too shocked to look beyond my own blood! In addition, everything happened so fast that I did not get the time to reflect on anything.

The women then poured a reddish, gummy herb on the cut area to stick the wound in place. Then they tied my legs together, one rope around my ankles and another around my thighs. I heard them say that the ropes would keep the legs in position. As the shock wore off and the women held me up and started to pour tepid water on me to wash the blood off my legs and groin, I realized that the other two girls were also being held up and being washed. They too were in ropes. A sorry sight we were, if you ask me.

We were all finished within minutes. Incidentally, I don't remember seeing many razor blades. I vaguely remember seeing one woman with one. The room was cleaned spotless, and clean mattresses were spread for us on the floor. For three weeks we stayed in that room, and our legs remained tied together for the entire period.

Every single day of each week, the big girl complained. She quarreled with the women all the time. In the evening, our mothers would attend to us, sleeping in our newly acquired room in turns.

Whenever the mother of the big girl came, the big girl quarreled with her and even refused to eat the food she brought. It was funny that she never talked to us about why she was complaining. She just looked at us as if we did not exist. I was very sure that I wanted to grumble like her because of the pain I was going through, but at the same time I was grateful to these women for having given me virginity.

When it was time to urinate, we would just stand and let the urine run down our legs, holding our breaths and shivering with the unbearable pain.

All I wanted now was to keep the damn virginity in order to win the respect of my husband-to-be and give my family the pride they deserved. I had no idea that I was already a virgin before these women did what they did with my budding femininity.

I know that the big girl already understood issues of sexuality. She was so disturbed that she left our house of seclusion as soon as we were untied after the three weeks. I and the other girl stayed for a few more days, during which we were taught how to walk and sit with our legs tightly closed. The warning was always the same: "If you open your legs wide, your womanhood will open, and that will affect your virginity!"

We did not stay long after the big girl left. Our mothers came for us and took us back home. They bought me new clothes and a bigger mattress. I don't remember being excited the way I used to be whenever I got new things. This time my feelings were blunt, as blunt as they wanted me to be. My aunt-mother never asked me anything to do with what had taken place. She never referred to the days I was away. I felt bad that she behaved as if nothing had happened. But of course she did not forget to remind me that if I ever slept with boys, I'd lose my virginity.

◎◎

I was happy when school resumed and I went back to my friends. I lived with my aunt-mother until I was in primary five in Mweyale Primary School.

Before I completed that class, my aunt-mother passed away. They did not tell me what had killed her, but one day I returned from school only to find mourners at home. All my brothers were older; I was the youngest child in the home. Everybody sympathized with me, and my uncle-father was especially sad about me. Most of my brothers were already away in schools, and the others were away looking for jobs. So most of the time, I was alone with my uncle-father.

That same year, 2004, I was at home one day when a strange woman came to visit. I wondered who she was, but I noticed that my uncle-father was very happy to see her. They sat and talked for a long time. When it was time for this woman to go back to wherever she had come from, my uncle called me aside and told me to pack my clothes. At that age, you only have a few clothes and nothing else.

"You are going with her," he told me.

"What do you mean, 'going with her,' Father?"

"You are going to live with her."

"To live with her?"

"Yes, my dear daughter."

"But who is she?"

"You are going to live with your people. She is your mother," he said, not quite looking at me. "You are going home, my child."

"Father . . ." But my questions had run out. I honestly wondered why he was sending me away with a strange woman. If it were today, the days of child trafficking and child sacrifice, I would have thought that she was going to sell me as a slave or to be sacrificed.

"I am taking you home, my daughter. I am your mother," the strange woman said.

When most people talk about shock, they have no idea what it means to be shocked. I was too shocked and did not believe what I was being told. Then they talked to me for some time, and indeed I realized that my father was not my father, my mother was not my mother, and my brothers were not my brothers.

My feeling then was, and still is, that I had been duped all my life. Although I was still in primary five, I was already a big girl. I had started school late and sometimes missed exams, so I never got promoted to the next class. I was more of a domestic worker. My aunt did not think that my education was a priority. I also suspect that relocation played a role in my slow schooling.

As I tried to figure out the saga of family and belonging, I remembered that incident when I felt that my aunt-mother was a cruel mother. I thought that as a mother she did not have a big-enough heart for me as her daughter, especially her only daughter. That was the time when I accidentally burned my leg and foot. The burns were quite deep and painful. I cried so much, and I desperately needed both her help and her attention. I was shocked when she said that I had caused the burns myself and so should suffer the consequences. She totally ignored me.

For several days, she left me on my own and did not even take me to get any medical attention. I was very hurt, and I spent many days hiding and crying. I was in so much pain and felt so alone. It was not until the wound started rotting and stinking with pus that she took me to the hospital.

As I thought about who I really was, I connected the burn incident to the time the woman I called my mother led me to the women who made me bleed so much. But I am naturally a reserved person and never showed her what I felt or the anger I carried in my heart toward her. I silently felt very unfortunate that I had a mother like that. On the other hand, I had an excellent relationship with my brothers. They liked me a lot, and I lived among them like a princess.

To discover that I had another family was shocking beyond measure and raised many questions that I dared not ask anyone. My uncle-father told me that he loved me very much but that he could not continue to raise a girl on his own.

When I asked my mother why they had never showed up to check on me, she told me that it was done on purpose to cut our ties and help me fit in with the new family. It was very ironic that the ties I now needed were those to connect me back to my original family.

When I finally agreed to go with my mother, it was not because I was convinced and excited about finding my family but because my uncle-father could not keep me. I had no choice.

◎◎

Life in Ethiopia was too inauspicious for me. My sisters and brothers had no dreams beyond grazing cows. And so I joined the gang and never went back to school. My parents' life was pastoral—looking after cows and looking for pasture. They had relocated to another area, away from Mega town where we were born. But they kept their house and land there. By 2007, I had become very restless about leading a pastoralist's life, and I was sure all everybody was thinking about was finding me a man. Already a few sons of other pastoralists had started frequenting our home after my arrival. I did not want to get married to any of them. I asked my parents to let me go and live in Mega town. While in Mweyale I had learned to cook well. I therefore decided that I could start a restaurant in Mega in my parents' house. My parents granted me permission and even gave me two cows for milk.

I relocated to Mega in March 2007, and I set up Hanifa's Restaurant. People liked my food, and my business boomed. I could make very tasty naan that men came looking for all the time.

Four months later, I was at the restaurant when government soldiers entered without warning and accused me of hiding rebels. At first I took it as a joke. I had no idea about the whereabouts of rebels. And I thought that it was obvious to them that I, Hanifa, would not have anything to do with rebels. Of course I had heard about OLF rebels, but all I knew was that they existed. Where they were was not any concern of mine.

"Show us where they are," they insisted, and I could see their anger rise with each word they uttered. I told them to search the whole house.

"You house them. You hide them. You feed them in this restaurant," they shouted.

I was in shock.

"Where is your family? Why do you live alone here? See, your family is away helping rebels."

All my family was interested in was their cows and pasture, and I, my restaurant.

I denied all their accusations, but before I knew it, the soldiers were shooting in the air and at people. Everybody ran in disarray. Within seconds, two bodies lay on the floor in pools of blood. The blood motif was becoming very much part of my life, and that made me so sad. I was arrested with a few other people who did not manage to escape.

The soldiers took us to their camp, where they imprisoned us in small, dark rooms. I was locked up in my own room, and for three days I did not see anyone. On the fourth day, they let me out in the evening and gave me a heap of their clothes to wash. After the washing, they took me back inside, and I felt slightly relieved that I had gone outside. I was drifting into sleep when I heard the door open again. It was dark, and so I did not see who was entering, but I could tell there were three or four people.

I waited for them to speak, but that was not what had brought them. Without saying a word, they descended on me. One pinned my arms to the ground while another held my legs apart. The third raped me. He entered me again and again, and every time it was like a sharp knife cutting right through my heart and my brains. There were quick shuffles, and another was on top, and then another, until I lay still and closed my mind to who I was or what was happening. Every time I remember that experience, I get a splitting headache.

From that day on, soldiers would enter my room and rape me repeatedly. It was not possible to tell who was who. It was the most painful experience of my life, not even comparable to the circumcision I had gone through. Every night three, four, or five soldiers desecrated my body. I could only tell that it was not the same man by the different sizes that tore into me. Every night was a nightmare, and that is when I came to understand the essence of circumcision, because as the men raped me repeatedly, they talked.

"This girl is a miracle come to us. The secret behind her tightness is beyond what we have ever experienced in this camp. She opens for us every night and closes after we leave. Every night we are eating a virgin, the secret of circumcision," they would say, and they would laugh in a very vulgar manner.

That was when I understood that I was different. That I was not like other women. That it was no longer a case of virginity, but a war on my womanhood.

The soldiers would tear into me every night. Every encounter was a new opening, a new breaking of virginity—their new pleasure, my new pangs of pain. Every night I begged these men to kill me. I begged them not to leave me alive, but they laughed at me, their voices resounding against the dark room as they left me for dead. Sometimes I passed out and woke up hours later with pain that only I could understand.

A few days after the repeated rapes began, I started itching in my private parts. From then on, every time they entered me, I would get a sharp pain as if they were thrusting very sharp nails deep into my uterus. It was painful, very, very painful. The pain almost drove me mad.

After they left the room, the pain would persist the whole night long and throughout the day. I could not sleep, could not sit, and could not stand. I would spend the whole night shifting, trying to find a less painful position. I would squat one minute and kneel down the next, thinking I was going to die. The beasts did not care about my pain, because every evening they fetched me from the lockup and asked me either to cook for them or to wash their clothes. I would limp and do the work. I did not need to know which of them had been in my lockup in the night. I hated them all with a passion!

When a war is in the open, it is easy to know what is going on and to get help from the outside world. The war in Ethiopia is silent and deadly. The world will never know exactly what goes on there.

On August 10, 2007, a fight broke out in the camp. I don't even know who was fighting whom, but there was a lot of commotion involving soldiers. That evening, I was outside with an old man. I don't quite remember what he was doing. When the soldiers who were guarding us ran in the direction of the fight, the old man quickly walked over to me and told me to run away.

"Pick some clothes from that heap and put them on. No one will notice. They are too busy now trying to save their own skin. Just run. By the time they come looking for you, you will be out of sight. I will do whatever I can to divert their attention."

"Let's go together, Father—let's escape together," I said.

"No, I am old and wasted. I will stay. But you, my daughter, you have your whole life before you. Let's not waste time. Go!" He showed me the direction to take. "Don't look back. Just keep walking, my daughter. If they are to kill you, let them do so while you are on the road to your freedom."

Quickly I picked a jacket from the heap of clothes and limped away. There were no good-byes, and I was soon out of the camp. I was surprised to find other people running, and I joined them. We ran for a long distance and then saw a truck and stopped it. The driver told us that he was heading for Mweyale. The mention of Mweyale, my former home, made me feel as if I was already there. I was so excited when he agreed to take us on top of his truck. He told us to lie flat and not to raise our heads. We jumped onto his truck, and he drove off.

When he finally stopped and called us to disembark, we were in Mweyale, Ethiopia, on the border with Mweyale, Kenya, where I had spent my childhood! I jumped off the truck, leaving the stolen jacket there. I then walked smartly, greeting a few people I recognized in that part of town. I behaved as if I had not been gone for years, as if I had just crossed the border to buy a needle or bread. This was something we usually did when I lived in Mweyale, Kenya, and so I knew a number of people in the shops and the tricks of crossing to and fro.

I don't know where the people I came with on the truck went, but as for me, I mingled with the locals and walked straight home. I was very delighted to find my uncle-father there. For the three years I had been away, I had never been in contact with him. I think our people are strange. We just keep away from one another without feeling guilty. But of course the conditions do not favor constant communication.

When I told him my story, his face turned cloudy.

"They will follow you here," he said. "Those people are very danger-ous." He told me how they had been following people and killing them in Mweyale and other surrounding villages. "No, my daughter, you can't stay here."

"But where can I go?"

"Somewhere far from here—go to Uganda."

"How can I go to Uganda?"

"You have no choice, my daughter."

"Please, Father, let me stay."

"No, I am sorry. When you get to Uganda, ask for any Ethiopian or Somali, and they will help you. There are many Ethiopians and Somalis in Uganda."

My life had become one of no choices. Uncle-father gave me some money, and I traveled with his friend to Nairobi on a fuel tanker. It was a very long journey. Somewhere along the way, the man left me on the tanker and went away, maybe to his home, which I later learned was Masabiti village. He was away for about five days, and I stayed on the tanker alone. But his people brought me food every day.

We later moved on to Nairobi, and I was directed to Akamba bus sta-tion, where I caught a bus to Uganda. It was a very long journey too. I used all the money my uncle had given me to pay for the bus ticket. I did not have any money left. By the time I arrived in Kampala, I was hun-gry, I was spent, and I knew no one in Uganda. But I had one wish—to survive it all.

I did not get off the bus in a hurry. I waited for everyone to disembark, then followed. I had been warned that some people could take advantage of me if they noticed I was a stranger. So I took a bit of time and located the friendly young face of a woman seated on a bench at the station.

This girl had Ethiopian neighbors! Can you imagine? I felt as if she had said that my family lived just across the road and all I had to do was walk over and say, "Hello there!" This girl took me to her neighbors straightaway. I later learned this was Nsambya village and the good Samaritan was called Juliet.

It was a family of Ethiopian girls. And they also lived with their mother in different houses in the same compound. The girls welcomed me very warmly, and they gave me a room to share with them. They were very friendly too. I was a bit surprised when they told me that I could join them in their business so that together we could make some money to survive on. I was happy and agreed to join them. They said that I would like the business and that it was lucrative. They did not even wait for me to settle in before they asked me to join them in their work.

When they finally brought me clothes and told me to dress so we could go, I was taken aback—their business was prostitution on the Kampala streets. I was not ready for anything that involved sex, and I told them so.

"How do you think you will survive?" They tortured me with endless, rude questions, but how could I tell them that I was not like them? I just told them that I was not able to join them, and I instead begged them to let me be their housemaid. But one day they tormented me very much, and I decided that enough was enough. As they dressed for work at their business, I walked out and returned with a packet of quinine tablets from a drug shop. I had heard that quinine could kill if you took an overdose of it.

As soon as they left the house, I swallowed all the tablets and went to bed. I wanted to die in bed. I was very sure that this was the end of the road for me. I was tired of trying to run away from myself. For hours I waited for the tablets to work and to start sweating. I waited to start vomiting and dying, but I instead drifted into a sweet, deep slumber. I woke up in the morning feeling completely OK, as if I had taken a sedative or a painkiller. That was when I decided I was going to live and live!

The following day I asked Juliet to help me, and she took me to the Old Kampala Police Station, where I started the process of registration as a refugee. In my journey to seek refugee status, I met some new people who came to change my life. I met a refugee woman operating a small restaurant in Kisenyi. Because I had experience in restaurants, I asked her for a job, and she agreed to hire me. I also started my side business of making *mandazi* and chapati, as customers had been asking for them but she did not have them. I left the girls in Nsambya, and the restaurant became my new home. I would wait for all the customers to leave in the evening; then I would make my bed there and sleep.

At the restaurant, a middle-aged man got very interested in my *mandazi*. He ate them for breakfast and supper, but in the end it was clear that it was not the *mandazi* but the *mandazi* maker he was interested in. I liked him too, and we talked quite a lot whenever the restaurant was not very busy. Eventually he proposed marriage. Much as I liked him, when he proposed, my heart sank with grief. I had enjoyed his chats and even flirted with him a little, but that is where I wanted it to end. I knew I would never want to have any other sexual encounters.

When he insisted on the issue, one day I plucked up the courage to tell him that it was not possible. I told him about my body and my sexual experiences. I told him that I was not a woman like other women. He was sympathetic, and he convinced me that it must have been because of rape that it hurt. He promised to help me out if I accepted him.

It took me time to accept, but when I finally did, it was the same pain all over again. Gentle as he was, he still tore into me, and I still felt the sharp pains, even long after the sexual act. He apologized and said he was going to ensure that I got help somehow.

A few weeks after our blessing from the mosque, I got my full refugee status, and I was forced to go to Nakivale camp for refugees. Even though we had already been to the mosque and were husband and wife, the law did not recognize that, and so I left him. But we remained in touch, via the telephone especially, and sometimes he came over and visited.

Camp life is very interesting. The government just packs you off to one. You don't know anyone there, there is no house for you, there is no one to receive you, and there is no system for newcomers to follow; no one tells you what to do upon arrival. But when I got there, I was fortunate to quickly find an Ethiopian family of the Oromo Borana tribe. It was a very loving family, and I stayed with them. But the pains of circumcision in Mweyale and of rape in the Ethiopian prison had followed me across borders. I still itched, and now it was really acute. I still got sharp on-and-off pains tearing into my lower abdomen.

One day I decided to go to the health center at the camp. While I was waiting to see the doctor, a mother walked in carrying a small girl whose dress was all soaked in blood. Blood again. They went straight into the doctor's room. Within a few minutes, everyone at the hospital was whispering about the girl. She was eight years old, and she had just been sexually molested by a thirty-year-old man. People were describing the girl so that everybody who had seen her could recall who she was. I felt angry at them all and thought that they were being unfair to the little girl. Telling everyone what had happened to her was very wrong. And mind you, no one was describing the man. The poor girl was now being stigmatized.

When I saw all that, I knew that if I entered the doctor's room for the examination, by the time I came out, everyone at the camp would know what my problems were. I had intended to tell the doctor everything and even show him everything in order for him to give me the best help, but the girl's story made me change my mind, and I carried my troubles back to my Borana family.

I called my husband and told him about my pains, and he advised me to get a letter allowing me to leave the camp and go for treatment in Kampala. With his advice, we eventually contacted people at the Refugee Law Project, and they connected me to the African Centre for Treatment and Rehabilitation of Torture Victims. At ACTV, I was counseled, and for the first time in a long, long time, I got proper medical attention. The ACTV doctors referred me to Bugolobi Nursing Home, where I underwent a three-hour corrective surgery on my private parts. Through it all, my husband was there for me. I took about one month to heal from the surgery wounds. That was toward the end of 2008.

The wicked circumcisers had sealed me off! They had left only a little hole. I was surprised when, after the operation, I could hear the sound of my urine when urinating. Before the operation, it had been drop by drop. During menstruation, I would push out clots as if pushing out a child. As a result, the cramps of my menstruation periods were always excruciating.

To be honest, I cannot understand why a normal, straight-thinking person would subject his daughter to such ugly and unbearable pain. I feel sad for women from Ethiopian and Somali tribes that circumcise and other women of the world who undergo circumcision.

At the same time, I am very conscious of my linkages to the Somali people. If by any chance I got daughters, I would protect and defend them against this dehumanizing ritual. Even from my grave, my spirit would still protect my children, their children, and the children of their children. I ask Allah to grant my spirit that power! Unfortunately, since the prison rapes, I have never had any periods. The doctors said that I contracted a sexually transmitted infection that, coupled with the rape, may have affected my reproductive system. I am grateful for one thing— that maybe if this had not happened, I would have got pregnant by those scoundrels. What would I tell the offspring?

Recently I was shown a Somali woman in Kisenyi, Kampala, who circumcises Somali girls in Uganda. I went and attacked her. I told her that I was going to report her to the police if she continued. She then said that if I dared to do so, she would make me walk naked on the streets. Maybe she feels that she has special powers, but I know she does not. Those people only create fear in society. If I saw her doing it to any girl, I would attack her and maybe get killed, but I would rescue the girl.

I would like the government of Uganda and the concerned women's NGOs to know that circumcision is going on right under their noses in the Somali refugee communities. These girls need help. Some may need to be operated on and reconstructed like I was, while others need to be protected from the ritual. And because of the assumption that the girls are still virgins by the time of circumcision, the circumcisers do not take precautions against HIV transmission during the ritual. I strongly believe, for example, that the razor blade that cut me was the same one that cut the other girls I was circumcised with.

After the operation, I now feel like a woman. I enjoy sex with my husband. But of course sometimes I am apprehensive about it, especially in the dark. But at least when he touches me these days, my blood warms in anticipation. Before the operation, I was like a piece of wood. Now I want to have children of my own. Those days I was scared that if I dared get pregnant I would die in labor. So many circumcised women die during childbirth. But my husband has taught me to trust again. I think he is a loving man, and he is playing a big role in my reconstruction. But he tells me that sometimes I scream in the night and also talk a lot in my sleep. But I believe all that will go with time.

I am still interested in a restaurant and might set up another Hanifa's Restaurant in the future. I have had to do a lot of self-education; I watch TV programs and learn a few things.

I have no idea how my family in Ethiopia is. But I do not really miss them. I instead miss Mweyale; I miss my brothers and my uncle-father. Maybe someday I will look them up. But a refugee's life is a prison of its own. My prayer is that Ethiopia heals from its wounds so that we can go back home. Unfortunately the wounds are festering from underneath. But for now, life has to continue, and I am a part of it.

The Woman in Me

BANANUKA JOCELYN EKOCHU

Eight kilometers before Kapchorwa town, along the Kapchorwa-Mbale Road, in a makeshift kitchen that cannot accommodate the fireplace and the cook at the same time, a woman is busy preparing lunch for her family. Judith is forty-seven years old but could easily be mistaken for sixty. About two and a half meters from the kitchen is a small grass-thatched mud-and-wattle hut. This is the family home. A peek inside the hut reveals a smooth floor of mud and cow dung, nothing else. A wall separates the sitting area from what must be the bedroom.

The place is just a few kilometers from the famous Sipi Falls, the tourist attraction found on both sides of the road. It has just rained, making Judith's compound soggy. She sits at the entrance of the kitchen, which spits out smoke that mercilessly attacks her eyes. Every now and then she wipes away a tear with the back of her hand. Her head, wrapped in a scarf of undefined color, is covered by ash, courtesy of the stubborn fire, which, owing to the weather, is not easy to keep lit. Judith has to keep blowing at it to make sure that it continues burning.

On the higher side of the hut, scattered in the grass, are utensils—plastic plates and cups and saucepans blackened by soot, waiting to be washed. An eight-year-old girl approaches to do just that. She is the daughter of Judith's sister, who came to help with domestic chores. But, now that her mother is dead, she has to continue living with Judith's family.

"She is now mine, and she helps me with the work when she comes back from school," Judith says.

Judith feels guilty. She feels that she should be the one doing all the work as the woman of the house, but she cannot. Her niece is very young and should not be working, but there is simply nothing that can be done about it.

On the lower side of the hut near the door, an old woman is helping by shelling fresh beans. They make a beautiful mix of colors as she casually tosses them into a wide basket. Some are pink and some are white, but most of them are maroon. The old woman is Judith's friend, and once in a while she comes to help her with any kind of work that needs to be done.

On seeing us, she gets up with an agility that makes one wonder about her age. Her face reads seventy or above; her swiftness points to fifty. Her face is wreathed in a smile as she greets us and starts speaking very rapidly in her language. She must be a very jolly soul, we think. After a short while, she seemingly loses interest in us and goes back to her beans.

Across the road, a lone cow is feeding from a wooden trough. Next to it, a young man is busy cutting a banana stem into pieces. He cuts with the speed of an angry butcher while the cow, as if trying to slow him down, feeds with the grace of a satisfied zebra. He sprinkles salt onto the pieces and adds them to the ones in the trough. The cow continues to feed, not allowing him to break its rhythm.

"You are welcome," Judith says shyly as we approach.

Her son, about twenty-two years old, gets us seats in a show of hospitality: one wooden folding chair, a piece of flattened wood, and a metallic chair with plastic strings, half of them lost to old age. He places a seat in front of each one of us, shaking them a bit to make sure that they are firm on the ground. It is not until we have made ourselves as comfortable as we can that he opens his mouth to talk.

"You are welcome," he echoes his mother's greeting, hovering around her in an impressively protective manner. He finally finds himself a comfortable spot on the veranda of the hut to squat. He then fixes his eyes on us, his heavy lenses giving him a fierce look. His manner clearly says, "You upset my mother and you will have me to contend with." Many strangers, as it turns out, have been coming to listen to Judith's story. It is not a story that she enjoys telling, and sometimes she gets upset.

An official from REACH explains the purpose of our visit, first convincing her son that we are harmless, then persuading Judith to tell her story.

"My English is bad," she says shyly. "I stopped in primary six." Actually, I think her English is quite impressive, considering the time she has spent out of school and her living in a village where English is not always spoken.

Eight-year-old Miracle, the youngest of her five children—all of them boys—plants himself at her side. He looks at us suspiciously but does not say anything. His first smile appears when his mother explains the reason for his name. It is when he smiles that one realizes how handsome he is. As if realizing that all eyes are on him, he turns shyly and faces the other way.

"His birth was a miracle," Judith explains. "Nobody thought I would ever be pregnant again, and when it happened, nobody believed I would carry the pregnancy to full term, let alone deliver the baby." She has a reflective look on her face as if she is thinking, The woman in me died at the hands of the circumciser.

Her husband, a quiet, healthy-looking, dark-skinned man, doesn't say a word. He just moves around with a few freshly picked coffee beans in a transparent polyethylene bag. One has to remember that Judith is only forty-seven years old in order not to mistake him for one of her five sons. Finally he enters the hut, comes out with a camera slung on his shoulder, and disappears down the road. He has to saunter around the village in search of people who may want to have their pictures taken. He is a small-time photographer.

Judith is one of thousands of victims of female genital mutilation. Together with her cousin Monica and their friend Betty, she was subjected to the knife in 1976, at the age of sixteen.

"I didn't think much about it, but my family felt I should and pressured me into having it done," Judith says. "And of course at the time, I also wanted to get married. During our time, unless a woman was circumcised, she would not get married. She was treated as a child but without the love that is usually accorded children. She would be subjected to all sorts of ridicule, and finally she would be circumcised by force. Circumcision was not something a woman chose to do; it was what she had to do."

Judith craved the respect given to circumcised women and never thought about the consequences of the practice. She was led to believe that the pain was the same as that of childbirth, which passes and is quickly replaced by the joy of the baby. She believed that joy would come in the form of marriage. She would have a husband, children, and a home of her own.

On that fateful day in December 1976, sixteen-year-old Judith and nineteen-year-old Monica were collected from their homes under guard by their relatives and other members of the community to have them circumcised. Their friend Betty, who was employed as a nurse at Kapchorwa Hospital at the time, was on night duty. When she discovered the plan to circumcise her by force, she tried to hide. Unfortunately, when her relatives came for her, her fellow staff members and the patients revealed her hiding place. She was pulled out, tied up, and dragged to where her two friends were.

"We were made to dance the whole night. Some people kept insulting us. At one time, we were taken inside a hut and trained to become witches," Judith says in her soft voice, shaking her head as if wondering how she could have gone through with it. "They taught us how to bewitch any woman who misbehaved."

However, she cannot tell anybody, not even her closest relatives, any details of the training. Whatever they were told to do to become witches cannot be revealed.

"They told us that if we revealed the details they would also reveal us, and then we would be punished severely, probably by death. I can't tell you."

At dawn the following morning, they were taken to a kraal in Kapchorwa town, seized, and held down as the "surgeon" took their womanhood away. Monica was the first one to be cut because her father was the oldest. She was followed by Betty, and Judith came last.

There were no painkillers. A woman was expected to look after herself and not to complain about a petty thing like pain. The exercise seemingly went as planned, as there were no immediate complications. The girls walked four kilometers to their traditional nursing home, where a lot of rituals were performed. Most of these they are not allowed to disclose, but there is a belief that a leopard makes four marks on their right hands, a sign for all circumcised girls.

The nursing home was a one-room grass-thatched hut where the girls spent a week. There were no mattresses, not even mats. Nobody was allowed to sleep on a mattress until she bathed and was clean. However, nobody was allowed to bathe until the bleeding stopped. The girls were therefore made to sleep on a hard floor covered with leaves for one week.

"The mentors were supposed to help with washing the wound, but in most cases they would not. They just took the severed parts with them, which they would use to bewitch whoever did not pay them. If they bewitched you using your private parts, you would neither get married nor have children. That is how they made sure that everybody paid," Judith narrates.

The mentors never monitored the girls' healing, but they often checked on them to see if there was any part that remained. If one did, they would call the circumcisers to complete the job.

Even though they were not completely healed, after one week they left the traditional nursing place and went home to prepare for their pass-out ceremony known as *yotunetap cemerik*. Many rituals were performed during the pass-out ceremony.

Judith's wound healed, but her legs started to feel numb once in a while. It did not seem like a serious problem at the time, so it did not bother her much. After all, she was now a complete woman and not a girl anymore. She was fit to be a wife. As a young girl, she used to look forward to the day she would get married and have children and a home of her own.

She realized her dream one year after circumcision, in 1977, when she found herself a husband. When she got pregnant and gave birth to a baby boy, her joy was complete. She consented to sex out of a sense of duty to her husband, but she never enjoyed it at all. Not even once! But there was some strangely agreeable feeling that came out of the pain she had to endure every time she gave in to him.

"And I was very happy when I had my first child, and everything was OK. But the numbness in my legs was becoming more frequent than before," she says. That was the beginning of her suffering.

◎◎

Meanwhile, the two friends with whom she had faced the knife were going through the same experience. They experienced unexplained sensations in their legs that progressed into numbness. Three years later, they all complained of pain in the knees and waist, especially after walking long distances. After heavy work, they would suffer general body pains.

Eleven years after their circumcision, in 1987, the three women could no longer walk without help. They had to use crutches or walking sticks or lean on another person for support.

"After I had my third child, my legs became very weak. Every time I tried to walk I would fall," Judith explains.

She visited many clinics and saw many doctors, but nobody could diagnose her illness. Her friends also visited numerous doctors but received no help. No cure could be prescribed.

"Every doctor I saw told me that there was nothing wrong with me. I even went to Mulago and Nsambya, where I had my fourth child. But they could not find anything." The puzzled look on her face says it all. She could not understand what was wrong with her.

Betty had a brother who was working in Kenya at the time. In 1987 he arranged for her to be taken to Kenyatta Hospital in Nairobi, where there were better facilities. This was a time when Uganda was just recovering from the effects of a five-year civil war and had poor medical services. But even the best doctors with the best facilities could not give a clear diagnosis. All they could give her were painkillers.

In 1992 Monica developed numbness in her legs, and by 1997 she was totally paralyzed. She had visited several health centers and private clinics to no avail. The mysterious sickness simply progressed. As is always the case in rural areas, any sickness that cannot be explained by doctors is attributed to witchcraft. Judith and her friends were therefore advised to seek the intervention of a witch doctor.

"Every witch doctor we visited told us that we were bewitched by the circumciser. We did not understand why she did this to us, since we paid her in full," Judith says, her gaze shifting to a donkey weighed down by a load of cabbages as it carries them up the road.

The women then decided to confront the circumciser. "She did not deny the allegations. She just said that we should pay her more to remove the curse. Although we did not know why she had cursed us, we went ahead and paid her. We gave her whatever she asked for, including a cow. We only wanted to be healed." They were willing to do anything to be able to walk again.

After they paid their tormentor, they sat and waited for her to remove the curse. They fully expected to be healed and to return to their normal lives. After all, the person whom they believed had caused their suffering was willing to undo the damage. But this did not happen.

"She did not remove the curse," Judith says sadly. "We heard that the mentors advised her not to remove it. They told her that if she removed it she would be admitting that she had bewitched us in the first place, and our families would kill her because we had suffered so much already."

Now Judith believes that it was all hogwash. "I think she did not do her job properly. She must have damaged something as she circumcised us. Maybe she cut the wrong place."

They continued looking for a medical solution to their strange sickness. At the beginning of 2000, all the three women developed a skin rash all over their bodies that worsened during the wet season. The rash would respond to medication and generally disappear when the dry season started.

Later the rash intensified and developed into wounds affecting the lower parts of the body, from the waist down to the toes. Monica, who had been the first to be cut, had the most severe rash, followed by Betty. For Judith, who was the last to be cut, the rash was mild. No one knows why it was so. It appears that whatever caused the rash had something to do with the knife that was used to cut the three women.

By December 2005 Monica was bedridden and suffering from bedsores. She was admitted to Kapchorwa Hospital on January 8, 2006, complaining of abdominal pains, vomiting, and diarrhea. She was very weak, and her body was generally wasted. A number of tests were done on her, including blood film, a hemoglobin test to establish whether she had enough blood in her body, an erythrocyte sedimentation rate test to establish the volume of her blood cells and see if there were any abnormalities, an HIV test, and stool and urine analysis to see if there was any kind of infection. Interestingly, except for some pus cells that were found in her urine, all findings were normal. Monica was treated with antibiotics, analgesics, and other forms of supportive therapy.

But then, as a result of her persistent ill health and poor appetite, Monica's HGB levels became dangerously low. She had to be given blood transfusions on several occasions. Her bedsores were extensive and severe despite the treatment she was receiving. They had to be surgically debrided, which meant the dead cells had to be scraped away.

On February 8, 2006, Monica was admitted to Mbale Hospital. Her health had deteriorated further, and her bedsores had become septic. The wounds had to be dressed two to three times a day, and they were very painful. Later she suffered a pathological fracture of the femur with necrosis.

Monica was diagnosed with malaria on April 18, 2006, and she started treatment immediately. She was also given more blood transfusions to boost her low blood count. The only change in her condition, though, was downhill. By this time, her immunity was very low, and her body had been weakened by her prolonged sickness.

On April 30, 2006, Monica lost the fight and passed away after battling her sickness for close to thirty years. She was fifty years old. According to an unsigned document from Kapchorwa Hospital, Monica's death was caused by septicemic cutaneous ulcers (body sores) and paraplegia (nervous system disorders).

◎◎

Betty had gone through pretty much the same experience as her friend Monica. She had suffered paralysis, skin rashes, wounds, and bedsores. In addition, she developed high blood pressure and needed continuous treatment. Betty was a staunch Christian of the Anglican faith. When she became disabled, a friend introduced her to the Perfection Church Ministries, which started supporting her financially. She lived by faith and was hopeful about a bright future. After the death of her friend, she began praying and fasting, seeking God's intervention in a fight that she no longer understood.

She started fasting on May 8, 2006. Three days later, she complained of severe epigastric pain and a mild headache. She was admitted to

Kapchorwa Hospital and diagnosed with severe cystitis, an inflammation of the bladder. Soon after her hospitalization, Betty suffered a stroke and had respiratory distress. The medical team did all they could, but it was becoming increasingly clear that her condition needed more advanced facilities. She was then referred to Mulago Hospital in Kampala. An ambulance was provided for her transportation.

On May 13, 2006, a few kilometers before she reached Mulago, Betty breathed her last. She was fifty-three years of age when she died. Her death was reportedly caused by complications due to low blood sugar.

◎◎

According to REACH, the cause of the three women's crippling and the deaths of Monica and Betty cannot be medically explained. But the women and their relatives firmly believe that their ill health has to do with the genital mutilation that they went through.

The locals also talk. It is rumored that when it was time for the circumcision dues to be paid, one of the parents was drunk, and he poured hot water on the mutilator and the child she was carrying on her back. This annoyed and humiliated her so much that she cursed the girls she had cut. Others said that there was competition between two groups who were supposed to perform the initiation ceremony for the three girls. The group that was left out is believed to have cursed the operation because they lost their business deal. Another possibility is that some veins and nerves were damaged during the cutting.

REACH officials have called for further medical research into the sickness of these women, because that kind of thing had never before happened in the Sabiny community. They said that cases of overbleeding and shock, sometimes leading to death, had been reported, but that kind of prolonged sickness—the kind that led to disability and death—had never been witnessed.

Judith, the only surviving member of the trio, is permanently crippled and fears that she, too, might soon follow her friend and her cousin. She has a wheelchair, but her disability is such that she finds using it at home inconvenient. She cannot, for example, do her cooking comfortably in a wheelchair, because she would be perched too high above her cooking area. If she tried it, she would risk toppling over and falling into the fire. She therefore uses two small pieces of wood to move around. She sits on one and pushes the other in front of her. With the support of her hands, she hauls herself forward and sits on the front piece. Then she reaches behind her and picks up the rear piece, pushes it forward, and repeats the exercise until she gets to her destination.

When it became evident that nothing could be done to reverse the damage that had crippled Judith, her husband packed his bags and left. He had no use for a crippled wife, and he wanted out. It did not matter that she had given him the best of her life, including four children.

Judith and her friends' story has traveled far and wide. People have come from all over the country and beyond to listen to their story. When her husband abandoned her because of her disability, REACH gave her one million shillings. With this money she started a small business. She opened a small shop by the roadside. Her stock included soap, salt, paraffin, and other essential commodities.

One day as she sat waiting for customers, a shadow fell over her. She raised her eyes, expecting to see a customer. Lo and behold, there was her husband, larger than life, looking pleased with himself. He had come home. Shortly after this, Judith became pregnant and had Miracle. Nobody had expected this to happen, given the state of her health and her severe disability.

◎◎

As we prepare to leave, Judith, in a show of generosity, instructs her son to pack the fresh beans that her friend had shelled. He packs them in a transparent polyethylene bag and hands them to my friend, who graciously accepts them as a blessing.

Watching this small, touching example of friendliness, I cannot help wondering how a place can be so contradictory. But Kapchorwa is such a place. Its beauty leaves you breathless, and its seemingly friendly people are generous with their time and resources.

But at the same time, Kapchorwa is still plagued by the mutilation of women. The resulting death and disability do not seem to matter. Although a good number of people have come out strongly against it, there are also those who insist it is a tradition that should be maintained.

Perhaps the most disturbing aspect of this practice is the secrecy surrounding the actual rituals performed. Any woman who has been circumcised, including those who now denounce it, will tell you that she cannot reveal these rituals, these secrets of the tribe.

Beyond the Music and the Dance

LILLIAN TINDYEBWA

I can hardly believe her when she tells me her age. She was born in 1948 in Kisenyi village, in what was then Sebei district, now called Kapchorwa. At sixty, she looks almost ten years younger, with self-confidence and a lively demeanor.

She is of medium height with an oval face and a smooth chocolate-brown complexion. It is my fifth day in Kapchorwa, and I have noticed that the people of this area smile a lot and have very white teeth, which make their smiles magnificent. She is no different, and her smile helps me relax and look forward to our interview.

"Habari?" I greet her in Kiswahili, asking how she is, as we sit together waiting for the interpreter.

"Muzuri," she replies—"fine."

I am happy to make this little opening and to be able to communicate with her directly, and I do not want this chance to pass.

"Pole, umengojea sana," I continue, apologizing for her long wait and praying that her Kiswahili is good enough to allow us to proceed with the

conversation. I know that many Ugandans do not speak it well. But at least people from the eastern part of Uganda know a bit of Kiswahili, as they are close to Kenya.

"Hakuna tabu," *she answers with a smile, telling me it's OK.*

We are doing quite well, I think, but then the interpreter arrives.

It is the month of November, usually a dry season in Kapchorwa, but this particular month is wet and cold. The weather is similar to that of southern Uganda, where the wet November season brings grasshoppers out of their hiding places, only to be caught and turned into a mouthwatering delicacy. The month of November is called Musenene in most of the Bantu languages, meaning the month of grasshoppers. The crispy winged delicacy, once reserved for men only, can now be eaten by women, too.

As I interact more with the Sabiny, especially the women I interview, I realize that the inhabitants of this highland, with all its undisturbed beauty, still have concepts and beliefs as untouched as when their ancestors lived in ancient Egypt under the pharaoh. He thought that his numerous women could get amorous with his servants, so he decided to mutilate their genitals to reduce their sexual desire.

I hear from these friendly people that, during the time a Sabiny girl is growing up, one of the things that she is told, apart from the requirement of circumcision, is that even if she studies to the highest level, she has to come back to her home area to live, get married, and work for life. She grows up knowing these things, learned by heart during the time of innocence when children take in all that they hear from grown-ups as the truth, the whole truth, and nothing but the truth.

The journey to this mountainside had been hot until we started ascending the lush and scenic slopes. As we climbed, I remembered the words of that long-gone colonial master, Winston Churchill, when, on his visit to the British colonies in 1903, he described Uganda as "the pearl of Africa." He talked of climbing up, as in the story of Jack and the beanstalk, to reach Uganda. I had wondered whether he could have had Kapchorwa in mind. Going up those slopes, untouched and mysterious, was indeed breathtaking.

Kapchorwa town sits at the top of a plateau that is shaped like a giant altar cup, held up by a secret rocky hand. You drive up and seem to go up and up without seeing the end of it, past the magnificent Sipi Falls, then leveling off to the plateau upon which the town perches. Nature seems to have left just enough space for the town before commanding the ascent to higher slopes of the mountain.

The organization REACH offers hope to women of this forgotten land, and I meet and talk with these women in their office. I had read anything I could lay my hands on to understand what FGM was all about. Is it as bad and danger-ous as we all believe it to be? If so, what kind of parents would allow their little girls to undergo such a brutal and unnecessary practice? I listen in awe as this woman tells her story.

I grew up surrounded by a loving family. Like any other child, I looked forward to the day when I would have my own loving family. I later discovered, however, that my father loved us, his daughters, particularly because he viewed us as a source of wealth. He looked forward to the time when men would come to marry us and pay him bride-price.

The family consisted of six girls, so that was a good number for him to reap a lot of bride wealth from. We had one brother among this gold mine of girls. The two men in the family must have inwardly been thanking their lucky stars for all these treasures. But at the time, the fact that the girls were viewed as a source of wealth did not bother us. Indeed, even today, many women simply accept it as a fact of life. But my mother silently wanted me, above anything else, to study. So she arranged for me to go to Kenya, where her brother lived. The Sabiny are ethnically related to the Kalenjins of Kenya, and a number of them have relatives across the border. My family was no different.

That was how I was able to stay in Kenya for most of my primary school education. Kenya was a good place, and I liked living with my cousins. But after primary six, I came home, believing that I was coming to visit and would be going back to continue my education.

Up to now, I have never been able to establish whether my uncle intended to send me home at that particular time or if it was a stroke of bad timing that changed my life forever. Later on in life, when I kept thinking back, I suspected that my uncle could have thought I had reached the age for initiation and sent me home during the time of circumcision.

As you know, among the Sabiny, circumcision is done every even year during the month of December, but preparations for it start much earlier. In the months prior to the ceremonies, there is a lot of dancing and singing and drinking of the local brew. The dancing actually starts in August and goes on till December.

When I came home, I found a number of my friends were about to be circumcised. I was not so keen on going through this ritual, and neither was I under any pressure to do so. So I kept my distance, but not for long. My friends persuaded me to join them. They described the dances; they demonstrated all those moves that they could make with their young bodies to the sound of drums and singing. They told me about the gifts they had received, and I made up my mind to join them. But I have lived to regret my decision.

I started taking part in the dances, at first not seriously. I remember it all. At the time I really believed it was all a harmless pastime and I would get out of it at the right time.

But there were things I did not know! One of the things I discovered too late was that when one joins the circumcision candidates, one surrenders her personal free will and becomes part of the crowd. One has to do what everyone else is doing. The young girls dance in groups from house to house in the villages, receiving presents such as *kitenge* wrappers, chickens, or even goats as a way of encouraging them. It deceptively looks like the time of one's life! That is how I missed the right moment to leave. With all the excitement, the temptation to stay a little longer was magnetic. It's funny, but even as the days sped by, I kept thinking that I would leave soon. But soon never came. You see, as they dance, they sing songs of courage and bravery; they sound drums and get lost in it all. It is such infectious fun. For the young, it is totally irresistible.

One thing I remember, though, is that whenever the drumming and the dancing stopped, I would feel different. And, for a long time, I remained uncertain about the whole thing. Deep inside my heart I believed I would not go through with it. Even my parents were not pushing me at all, as maybe was the case with some other families. It was entirely up to me to make up my mind. At various moments there was this tug of war inside me—should I or should I not? Meanwhile, I continued with the nightly dances, getting lost in the beautiful sounds of the tam-tam, accompanied by the voices of the girls singing odes to the glory of becoming a real woman.

Probably I would have withdrawn from it all if some other methods had not been introduced to lure me further, beyond the music and the dance. You see, among the Sabiny, traditional medicines are used for many things, and their use is an especially common practice in the rituals of circumcision. But there is one specific type of local medicine that is meant to raise the level of boldness just before one undergoes this ritual. It is used to kind of uplift one and dispel any doubts. After using the medicine, there is a sudden upsurge of courage and readiness to face the knife. The level of courage is so overwhelming that a former coward will start demanding for the surgeon to come immediately after partaking of it! This medicine is administered easily; it is just sniffed.

I remember the conversation, because I used to think about it a lot. I had this friend called Chelamo, who believed so much in the practice that, together with the mentor, they persuaded me.

"Just sniff a little," the mentor said. But I was hesitant.

"Do not be left out—you don't want to remain a child, do you?" Chelamo asked.

"Chelamo is right," added the mentor. "Everyone will be a woman except you."

They followed me for two days, talking about nothing else but that. Eventually I agreed to sniff it. As I started to take it, I decided I would take just a little, but they were there to cheer me on and ensure that the whole dose was inhaled. I sniffed it and felt dizzy, as if I had taken a strong drug. I told them I wanted to rest. They said it was all right, and I lay outside under a tree. I woke after about an hour, feeling fine and finding all my fears gone. I felt so bold! But I have lived to regret it.

The night before the circumcision, I was one of those girls who danced most and sang loudest. We sang songs of courage that had been sung by our ancestors long before us. The words seemed loaded with new meaning, and I suddenly found great pleasure in sharing them with friends and age-mates in song and dance, lost in the rhythm. I felt contented as I jumped to the frenzied sound of the drums. It felt good to know that these songs were the same as those our great-grandmothers sang. It was inspirational. It made us feel close to these people, and I believed that since it was something they approved and practiced, then it had to be good.

The merrymaking went on throughout the night. My father and mother and many other relatives were there; they had brewed plenty of local alcoholic drinks and slaughtered animals, which made the party big and exciting. I felt happy and proud to be the reason they were all gathered together. We danced the whole night, and those who imbibed the local brew had an unforgettable time.

Since I had not slept, there was no question of waking up. The mentor had done her job of taking us through the "training" the previous night. I had listened with awe to the secrets passed on from generation to generation, secrets that I can never, ever reveal to an uncircumcised person. I will tell you about the circumcision but not about the Sabiny secrets. You see, my sister, I made a vow, and I cannot break it.

On the day we were circumcised, just before dawn, we had to go and bathe in the village river under the supervision of the mentor. It is not just a normal bath at the river; there were rituals too, which I cannot talk about. After the rituals at the river, we eventually went back to my father's compound where we were made to stand in a line. I was among the first ones to be cut. I felt no fear; I was ready to go through it all.

The circumciser worked very fast, and soon it was my turn. I had watched my cousin, who had stood in front of me, and she had not shown any emotion as the knife touched her body. I had to follow her example!

When the knife touched me that cold December morning, I just groaned deep in my throat. Oh, oh, oh! The pain was unimaginable. I had never felt so much pain before. I felt as if I was going to faint, but the mentor had clearly instructed us that there was to be no screaming or twisting of the body. So I bit my lip and tightly closed my eyes. They had told us that if we did not remain still, or if we screamed and tried to run, they would call the muscle men to hold us as we were being cut. I knew it was not a mere threat; they could do it. Nobody wanted men staring at them at such a point of weakness, so I had to go through with the pain.

"Go now," said the circumciser. I heard her voice, but it was as if it was coming from far away, loud and full of echoes. I got up and started walking to the house where the others were. I felt as if my groin was on fire; the pain was unbearable, and I cried silently. Remember, there was no painkiller, not even a local herb. Each one had to get up and walk back to the house! I was dazed, and even now I have never been able to understand how I made it to the house.

Later I heard the voice of the mentor as she came to check the wound. I did not want anybody to make me open my legs, but I had no choice. As she looked at me, she commented that my wound was bleeding a lot, more than the others'. Luckily, all that they wanted cut had been cut out, so there was no question of repeating it! It was a relief to me, because I did not think I could really go through it again. Sometimes the circumciser can leave part of what is meant to be removed, and it is the work of the mentor to check and ensure all was leveled. And when the mentor comes to check on the girls, she brings a knife with her. She actually kind of scrapes the drying part off to see how it is healing.

My sister, we lived up there in the forest. There was no hospital. People there did not believe in rushing others to the hospital. My recovery was slow. The bleeding from the wound lasted for more than a month! I tell you, my sister, it was terrible. I cannot find stronger words to describe my situation. I was in so much pain, and it was no longer just the wound but as if every part of me resonated with the pain. I felt so afraid because I thought I would die. The inconvenience of bleeding endlessly was unbearable! And all the time I remembered that I had not wanted to go through this circumcision. So over and above the physical pain, I blamed myself, and I was consumed with regret.

During this time, the only medicine available to us was our own urine. You see, each circumcised girl is told that there is no other medicine apart from her urine, and that to make it work, she has to press her legs together and urinate. This causes the warm liquid to enter the wound and make it heal. Urine has this stinging effect that the patient must overcome to release the urine onto the wound. So what we used to do, and I know it is still done even today, was to hold on to a tree trunk, wrap our arms around it in a tight embrace, cross our legs, and pass the urine. Holding on to the tree helped us to go through the excruciating pain without screaming. If any of the girls feared to urinate due to the pain, they would beat her.

My bleeding lasted for more than a month. Imagine a whole month of agony and fear that I was going to die. I was so worried that I lost weight. I would cry throughout the night because of pain and fear.

One morning when I woke up, I did not feel the usual wetness. But I dared not even open my legs and just stayed put in my room, waiting for the mentor, who was still coming to check on me daily. When she arrived, she announced that the wound was no longer bleeding.

I was so relieved and happy to see the end of that ordeal, but much later I was to discover that all that bleeding had caused me irreparable damage. My periods did not come regularly as they used to before the circumcision, and they became very painful. But there was nothing I could do. As I told you, there was no hospital nearby, and it was not part of our culture to rush to hospitals.

In this place there was nobody I could tell about my problem and my hope to get assistance. I don't even remember ever visiting any doctor as I was growing up. I just had to bear it all, as I had been taught to be a brave woman. I lived with it all. As soon as all this was over, I enrolled in the local school near home. My dream was to become a teacher. Unfortunately, I never got anywhere near becoming a teacher. One thing you have to understand about our culture is that circumcision is a rite of passage to womanhood. It seems to be a way of declaring to the world that this woman is ready for marriage whether she is in school or not. So, according to my culture, if I was ready for marriage, then that was it. I could not run away or appeal to anybody to protect me.

One day, about six moths after the circumcision, as I was walking from school, I saw a group of young men walking behind me, apparently going in the same direction as I was. I did not feel particularly worried about them, because it was broad daylight and I was not walking alone. There were many other school girls and boys at different points along the road.

Two of the young men passed by my group, then suddenly stopped about ten meters ahead. Then they came back as if they had forgotten something. Meanwhile, two others were coming from behind. Although now I felt a little uneasy, I did not feel that I was the target—until one of them came and stood in front of me, blocking my way. I told him to get out of my way so that I could pass, but that seemed to incense him, and he grabbed my hand. The others joined him, and they forced me to walk in another direction. They started beating me as we moved along the path. I was totally overcome with fear.

After what seemed like an eternity, we reached the home of a certain old man. The young men told me that I was to stay there and become his wife. I was shaking with anger and crying, and they told me harshly to keep quiet. That was how it was in those days. Nobody could do anything, not even my parents. It was one of the accepted methods of marriage! That was Kapchorwa of the 1960s. Once a girl was circumcised, she could be grabbed in that manner. It was an accepted custom. Once married, I had to learn to like my husband. He was an older man with two other wives already. I soon forgot my dream of becoming a teacher.

I began settling down to a new life. That was my home, and I tried to fit in as much as I could. But bedtime was not my favorite time. The scar causes pain when a circumcised woman tries to have sex. You see, the scar is dry and hard, and it causes a lot of difficulty during sex. At first, I wondered if there was something wrong with me, because I had been made to understand that it would be good when one got married. But I had hardly any sexual desire for this man, not because I did not like him—with time we had become quite friendly—but I felt nothing! And as for him, of course he was normal, and he expected normal relations. So we would literally fight before I gave in. Yes, our bedtime was a time for fighting over sex, because I did not have any desire for him, while he found me very desirable. I was his young wife who had no feelings at all that you could remotely describe as sexual urges. I never wanted him near me in that sense, and that caused us several fights.

I believe the men of Kapchorwa understand that female circumcision affects women in that way, so to compensate, they marry many women. I believe too that my husband married me because the others could no longer accept having sex with him every time he wanted to. Unfortunately for him, I turned out to be the same as the others.

Soon there was another hurdle for me. One year passed, two years, three years, four years, five full years, and there was not a sign of pregnancy! What was I to do? I wanted a baby badly! I tried some of our local medicines, but nothing worked. I was given all types, as you can imagine. And every time I got a new one, my hopes would go up, then tumble down with the coming of my period. Like any other man, of course, my husband wanted children from me, and so he shared my frustrations and anguish, but not as desperately, since he had other children from his two other wives.

At first I resented the fact that he was such an old man, but in the long run, it was an advantage for me. He was more understanding and calm, maybe because he knew he had other children already.

When I was desperately trying out medicines, it would hurt me to imagine that he did not mind whether I gave him a child or not. But later I realized that it was better that way. Additionally, in our culture, it is normal for men to marry in old age in order to get someone to take care of them. It was clear that it was my duty, rather than his older wives, to take care of my husband. They, of course, assisted me, but I was assigned the responsibility as the youngest wife.

But, my sister, I have always known, without a shred of doubt, that my barrenness was a result of the circumcision. I did not need a medical person to tell me that. I was not the only one who developed the problem. Among those who were circumcised at the same time as me, a number also failed to conceive. What happened to me was not surprising. The circumciser is not trained; she trains herself or learns on the job. I suspect that the particular circumciser must have cut us in a way that resulted in permanent damage.

Many times I have wished to turn the clock back so that I could reverse the decision I made then. It was a terrible mistake, and I have lived to regret it. I always replay in my mind the dancing and the music that attracted me to join my friends and the day I decided to sniff the medicine. But it was all the folly of youth.

My husband died a few years ago. He was very old. But I still live in his homestead together with the other wives without any problem. Our relationships were always good. I believe when they saw that I could not give birth, I became less of a threat. They saw that there would be no rivalry for property since I didn't have children.

Fortunately, I get along well with the children of my co-wives. In fact, one of them helped me when I wanted to start my crafts business. My regret in life is that the campaign against female genital mutilation started when it was already too late for me, but at the same time I am happy I have lived to see the start of programs intended to eliminate this horrible custom. It seems to be a Sabiny tradition to use force on the body. For example, in the past, they used to remove one's teeth by force, and the purpose of doing that was that if one fell sick and could no longer open one's mouth, they could still administer medicine! There was a disease that used to cause locked jaws, and the sufferer could not open the mouth to take anything.

My prayer now is to see an end to such torture. The new generation should be protected against these practices.

My Mbasuben

BETTY KITUYI

I am enjoying the pleasant ambience of green and hilly Kapchorwa from the backyard of Marsha Hotel with my writer friends. It is hard to believe that we are here. It is hard to believe that the journey—which began simply in a taxi that had been recently unloaded of Irish potatoes and chicken at Nakawa Taxi Park in Kampala—would lead us to a place of such breathtaking beauty.

The hotel sits atop a hill and gives you the feeling that you are eating at the table of a mountain. From where we are seated, we stretch our necks and look down on vehicles snaking along a narrow road, several meters below, that separates two fertile valleys. Small yellow wildflowers, typical of towering heights like Mount Elgon's, add to the magnificent diversity of the place. The people of Kapchorwa greet you with warm but inquisitive smiles. They can tell we are strangers, and they quickly ask where we are from and what we have come to do. But otherwise they seem at peace with themselves in their natural and serene environment.

In the dying glow of the sun and the quickening shadows of the cold evening, we wonder whether the happiness of the Kapchorwa people stems from their good-natured environment or from the secrets that are told to the circumcision candidates on the night before circumcision day. The fresh and clean air in this place is not a force for cultural understanding but rather makes us shiver and wonder why a people with such a sanctified climate would indulge in the ancient but harmful practice of female genital mutilation, which harms the womenfolk.

Nothing had prepared me for the energy, enthusiasm, and fire in the young woman who was a proud circumcision candidate for the upcoming December 2008 season. Brenda Cherop is a beautiful young woman with light, flawless, and apple-smooth skin. Her eyes have a rare brown tint and glimmer with joy. The sparkle in her eyes is that of a woman who has never felt a lot of pain in her life. She easily smiles; I am quickly enchanted by her natural beauty.

She wants to be cut because, in addition to the pressure from her mother-in-law, she wants to have a mbasuben.

"When you are circumcised in a group, you get one strong friend known as a mbasuben," she says. Her father has a mbasuben, the boy candidate who stood before him in the circumcision line, which is arranged according to the candidate's father's age. "When he invites him for a visit to our home, he slaughters a sheep for a feast as a sign of respect. When his mbasuben's children who are circumcision candidates come singing, dancing chest to knee, and swishing an ox-tail fly whisk in the air, my father ensures that they are relaxed in a chair and showers them with gifts. Sometimes he gives them goats, sometimes a cow or a bull!" Brenda says. "Unfortunately for my father, he has not had any of his children circumcised, since I am his firstborn child, and therefore his mbasuben has never paid in kind what my father has given him."

Brenda feels guilty about the fact that she and her siblings have not given their father the opportunity to win his mbasuben's respect. Brenda is obsessed with getting herself a mbasuben. The interviews that I had held earlier with other women had shown that no woman was willing to sacrifice her womanhood in order to form a strong friendship with another woman, but, listening to Brenda, I see that the mbasuben is an important and enduring non-kin friendship and a source of support that is greatly treasured in the Sabiny community. Brenda's desire to be accepted and recognized as a fully committed adult member of her community is quite evident in her talk. But after hours of hearing her resonate with passion for circumcision, one gets the feeling that she is a victim of another cultural attitude and is not aware of the dangers circumcision could inflict on her and other women in her society. Brenda Cherop's thirst for the knife generally represents the views of other young women to the practice of female genital mutilation in Kapchorwa.

*I*f you belonged in the circle of my mother and my grandmother, who have all been cut, you would understand this urge, which is deeply embedded in me, to do it just like they did. In the eyes of the Sabiny, I am a girl and not a woman, even though I am married and the mother of two children. When my neighbor comes to my home to borrow an axe to split her firewood and I am somewhere in the home where she cannot see me, she says, "Have you seen the other girl?" I find that so insulting. For how long will I be called *chepta kai*, the girl of this home? Between me and my five-year-old daughter, there is no difference. Eyes follow me whenever I go to the shops to buy salt, matches, or tea leaves. Often I catch people laughing at me and speaking in whispers whenever they see me, as if they are saying, "That's Martin's wife; she is a *chepta kai*." They would rather give respect to a fly falling in the visiting *mbasuben's* chicken soup than me.

The secrets of the circumcision night are a mystery to everyone who has not undergone circumcision. There are things the mentors tell you. We are told there is an animal that passes by and makes four marks on your right hand. The candidates are escorted to the river by people who have undergone circumcision, and they strip naked to bathe in the cold, biting waters of the gray morning, to gain strength and numb the pain when the time comes for the cutting. No one is supposed to tell those secrets to anyone who is not circumcised. It is believed that the circumcision spirits would hound her forever if she dared to do so. I do not want to be excluded from my tribe's secrets, since I am a Sabiny. Sometimes people say, "What if there are no secrets and those elders just lie to lure you to do it?" But you see, I want to find out for myself.

I am aware that these are changing times and that this is an old custom that some people denounce, but the changes are viewed from outside the community. How are we supposed to deal with the crushing views of those in the family, the immediate people we live with? My mother-in-law will use any small excuse to remind me that I am a senseless girl. When my two young children play with and spoil her banana leaves, her banana plantation being near our house, she says they have no sense because their mother is not circumcised. She introduces my daughter to her friends as "the daughter of the uncircumcised girl," and then the girl asks me tearfully, "Mummy, what is wrong with Kukhu? Why does she call you *chepta kai*?" What I am I supposed to tell my daughter when my mother-in-law jeers at me for my cowardice?

My husband, Martin, also wants me to get cut. He is circumcised and I am not. According to the tribe, I should be a taboo to him. I have been married to him for five years now. I was a circumcision candidate the year that I discovered I was pregnant with his child. We had been dancing for two weeks when I began vomiting every time the girls sang vulgar songs. When we went for group bathing in the river at cockcrow, whenever I poured water from a calabash on my body, a sour-milk taste would hit my mouth, and I would start shivering violently, as if possessed by some spirits. Rumors spread in my circle of aunties that I showed the symptoms of becoming a circumciser in the future. They began treating me with respect, and it was decided that I would be first in the line we would form in my father's courtyard, which also coincided with my father's being the eldest among the candidates' fathers.

As the circumcision day drew closer and we continued dancing from Kaserem to Sipi, Nyenge, Kaptwanya, Tegeres, and other villages, I became dizzier with each dance step. We had to rehearse many times to perfect the dance. Sometimes I would faint. Still, they believed that I had those special powers of the circumcision spirits. I was confused and scared about what was happening to me.

One night when we were dancing outside the home of one of the girls, I noticed the new moon, which looked very delicate, as if it were about to roll off the clouds. Just then, one of the mentors sang and urged all the girls to look up and enter the moon and be cleansed in its clear waters before the circumcision weekend. Normally, my monthly period coincided with the appearance of the new moon. My heart missed a beat when I remembered that exactly one month earlier, Martin and I had been intimate.

During the next moments, instead of feeling the warmth that flows down my back just before my monthly period begins, I felt betrayed by the moon and felt the chill of the cold evening for the first time. I was pregnant! I could not imagine facing the scrutiny of the surgeons and circumcisers. I could not go through with the ceremony when I was like this. It was taboo. Besides, it could also be dangerous to me and my baby. I kept this knowledge to myself that night.

The following day, I sought Martin at his shop and found him weighing maize for a customer. He was surprised to see me, because he knew I was supposed to be dancing with the other village girls.

After his customer had gone, I sat down on a wooden bench where his customers sit to drink soda. When he asked how I was, I told him that I was pregnant. He rolled his tongue over his teeth, ran to me, lifted my face in his hands, and kissed me.

"That is very good news," he shouted.

His kiss did not rub away the realization that my life had taken a new turn, that I had got off the narrow path of education to a wider road of marriage and children. I was nineteen years old and would be a senior four candidate at Kapchorwa Senior Secondary School the following year. I loved to study, and my intention was to become one of the few female doctors in our district. I was very good at sciences. Besides, I felt too young to be a mother.

"What will happen to my education?" I asked him.

"Don't worry, my sweetheart. Education is good, but having a child is better," he answered.

I told him that I wanted to abort the child so that I could continue with my education, since the school would not accept me while I was pregnant.

"If that is what you want, then my auntie who is a midwife in Kenya will help you to terminate the pregnancy," he said.

That possibility comforted me for a while. I thought it would be very easy to end the pregnancy.

Because I feared a confrontation with my family and the law but also the danger the circumciser's knife would put me through, he convinced me to elope with him to Kenya that night, and I agreed. I did not have time to go back home. As the moon hid behind the clouds that night, we fled, leaving the enchanting girls' voices to be swallowed by the roaring Sipi Falls behind us.

My aroused circumcision spirit was quickly hushed by the deafening silence of the sleeping hills on our way out of Kapchorwa. I wished that the Sipi Falls would sweep us downstream more smoothly and faster to our destination, but we had to endure hours of nose-wrecking stench from chicken droppings as we crouched between bunches of bananas on a truck headed for the border town of Malaba. In Malaba, we stayed in a place called Kongoni, where Martin's aunt lived.

Five days after we were married, Martin changed his mind about my having an abortion. He spoke like one of those old men in our village back home when he said, "I cannot use my money to kill my own seed." Then I realized that he had tricked me. I felt betrayed at first, but when I saw how supportive and loving he was, I decided to bring forth our child.

I delivered a healthy and beautiful baby girl with round cheeks. We stayed in Kongoni for two years, and we were happy. Martin was able to open another small grocery shop there. No one cared whether you were circumcised or not. We were mixed with other tribes, like the Bantu, and circumcision was not popular, although there were sister tribes like the Kalenjin, the Nandi, and the Pokot who shared our ancestry.

When we came back to Kapchorwa after two years, the bubble surrounding my globe burst, and I was rudely reminded of my cultural obligations. I was referred to as a disgraceful, cowardly girl who had fled the knife. I was hit with the Sabiny reality that the pain I bit between my lips during the births of my children did not qualify as a rite of passage to a full woman in my tribe. It became clear that I would not be beautiful to my husband until the hidden parts of my girlhood were gripped and cut by the sharp knife under the public scrutiny of courage. Even if he doesn't say so, sometimes I wonder whether Martin finds me unclean or if we shall reach another level of sexual satisfaction when I get cut. But I also know that my getting cut will earn him the respect of his friends and clansmen.

Five years ago, I joined the circumcision group out of sheer excitement and dancing, enticed by the vulgar songs sung by my age-mates, like *"Fungua siliwale fungua haa,"* which means "Open your knickers." Circumcision time is the only time young people get away with speaking obscene words, because in a crowd, one can say anything. But I did not do it because of my escapades with Martin.

This time around, my urge to do it is different. They have abused me to the point where I am now strong. When you have gained courage like I have now, your energy flows into preparing other things that accompany the ceremony. It is a simple ceremony. Two months away from the event, I am preparing the millet and maize to make *komeka teshonik*, the alcoholic brew. My people will drink that. They drink to forget the pain of their daughters when the shadows are long on the day of cutting.

The elders sit on small wooden chairs around a pot and suck up the brew through special long straws. We shall make tea for the teetotalers. I may have the circumcision in my home and not my father's; I am allowed that choice. My home is very near my father's home, so it really doesn't matter much. Besides, this is the first time so many people will be invited to my home. It is such an honor. My sister is also preparing to be circumcised with me. Other candidates can join us if they wish.

I am still waiting for school to close—which will happen after the students have finished their examinations—so that together we can start rehearsing the songs. It is going to be a joyous occasion accompanied by chants, ululations, and vulgar circumcision songs. We shall sing through the night and go from one relative's home to another. I will tie a *lesu* cloth around my neck and let it fly as I dance. The *lesu* covers the ordinary clothes beneath it and signifies a woman of valor. I will tie a belt around my stomach for strength. I will also hold a cow's tail and swing it as one of the pieces of dignifying regalia accompanying my dance steps.

Very early on the morning of circumcision, we shall bathe in the cold water to numb our bodies to the anticipated pain. While holding the whisk firmly in my hands and raising it above my abdomen, at the same time lying flat on a sand-specked sisal sack, I will pop out my eyes and not blink as the circumciser bends to cut me. That will display my courage to the many eyes witnessing; they will know I do not fear the knife. I know that it is going to be painful since it is done without any anaesthetic, but that will be viewed as a test of my courage. Bravery and self-control during the operation are an integral part of the Sabiny personhood, and I am ready to display these.

I am looking forward to seeing the smile on my grandmother's face, exposing the gaps in her lower teeth. Women of her generation drilled holes in their lower teeth. My grandmother has been gently encouraging me to go for it. She will die peacefully, knowing that the custom of her mother and grandmother before her has been passed on to my generation and that of my daughter.

I think that, on that day, my mother-in-law will be contented. I imagine her dancing and carrying a *kiset* full of presents—like a bottle of

honey, ghee, a *lesu*, and other things—while leading the people march-
ing in a line with gifts. They will celebrate and congratulate me on my
courage and welcome my rite of passage into the tribe's much-cherished
womanhood. I think my mother-in-law will be my best friend after that,
because my not being circumcised so far has been the only thing standing between us.

My husband is likely to keep quiet and be contented, now that everything is in place. My father too will feel proud and will regain recognition
in the community. Most important, he will get gifts from his *mbasuben*.

The Intrigue

HILDA TWONGYEIRWE

Yemo says to me, "Most husbands sodomize their circumcised wives because the wives cannot handle normal sexual intercourse. That has become the norm for most of the circumcised women. But no one can talk about it. Each wife is silent—silent so as not to shame her husband, silent so as not to shame her society, silent so as not to shame herself. It is heartbreaking. Every married woman knows that bedroom matters are very personal and very private. As I talk to you now, I feel as if I am making a confession in front of a Catholic priest. I feel as if I am undressing right in front of you. But it is OK. I want to tell you my story."

I encourage Yemo to speak. I tell her that, together, we have to break the silence. I tell her that it is not right that social norms continue to silence women in matters that affect them so seriously.

"I agree with you," she responds. "But these are things I have never talked about to anyone before, not even my fellow circumcised women. We are all silent. When I tried to talk to my mother, she just told me to be patient; she did not give me her ear. I had hoped that maybe she would share with me her own experiences. But she did not. She did not treat it as a matter of any importance. 'Just be patient,' she said to me, and she changed the subject. She sounded as if we were not supposed to talk about it. I pressed on, but she just did not talk.

"After that attempt, I decided I would live with it silently, and that is what I have done for the ten years of my marriage. Silence. I have kept quiet and pretended that all is well. Tell me, what else can I do?"

I do not respond to Yemo because I am not sure what else she could have done. It is difficult to respond to issues about which one does not have firsthand experience. Sometimes we hurt people when we try to tell them what they know as if we knew better. So I keep quiet and just listen.

I have three young sisters. I am the firstborn in our family. Fortunately they are all not circumcised. As I looked at them growing up, I was very inquisitive, especially when we would be in the bathroom or in our bedroom dressing up. That is when I realized that they were not like me. Sometimes my mother would ask me to help her bathe them, and I would jump at the opportunity to discover them in order to discover myself. But when I discovered what I discovered, I fell silent. I did not ask anyone to explain, even though I felt a strong urge to ask. Later I started hearing about circumcision, and I came to realize that I was circumcised. Slowly I started becoming a very withdrawn child.

My early childhood was not exciting at all. As we were growing up, there was a very distinct difference between my sisters and me. While I was very reserved, they were very free-spirited. As a result, my mother started mentioning my circumcision as if to confirm what I already knew. She would shout at my sisters and insult them that they were stubborn and not well behaved because they had not been circumcised. On the other hand, she always commended me for my calm behavior.

According to my mother, and maybe according to custom, I was sensible and well behaved because I was circumcised. Of course she is right, because for the bigger part, my lack of spirit, my silence, was a result of my recognition that I was different, the recognition that something was wrong with my womanhood. I don't hate my mother and I know that I am my mother's favorite daughter, but I feel sad that she looked on as a knife changed my life. I fail to understand how a mother gives birth to a normal child and then offers up the child to be disabled. To tell you the truth, I have a great sadness that sits deep in my heart. I have an anger that makes me calmer than my sisters. An anger that makes me resigned. An anger at what took away what I should have been.

What reason do I have not to be resigned?

I have every reason to be resigned. I will tell you that since I got married ten years ago, I have never enjoyed sex. To date, I still bleed every time my husband and I meet. No matter how many times we have done it, no matter what we do, it never ceases to hurt. Tell me the truth, my sister, what brings a husband and wife together? You and I know that all other reasons that we always give are an apology for the real reason. So tell me, why shouldn't I be resigned?

I was circumcised when I was six months old. And my mother tells me that I was a baby of slight build.

My great-grandfather was a medicine man. He was very influential and was believed to be very knowledgeable about almost every cultural and medicinal issue. That is what I was told about him. Thank God I never met him in my adult life. By the time I grew up, he was long dead.

I was his first great-granddaughter who came among several great-grandsons. When I came, the family celebrated my arrival. My great-grandfather was especially happy. As a special child, therefore, I had to get special and preferential treatment. I was the lucky child, and so I had to be circumcised by the renowned, knowledgeable medicine man. I was cut by my great-grandfather.

What I have always asked myself is how he found and cut the little parts. I look at my little daughter today, and the parts are too small and slippery. How that man gripped and cut me at six months of age is not comprehensible.

My only joy comes from the fact that FGM is now a crime in Ethiopia. But of course it is still going on behind curtains. The target is small girls and babies, who they know will not talk or report them. But at least criminalizing it makes it easier for those who are fighting it. There is a need to educate women so that they can fight for their daughters without waiting for things to go wrong, like it did for my mother and me.

After my great-grandfather cut me, he went back to his home. He was from my mother's lineage. My father, I understand, was not aware of my circumcision. My mother had hoped that she would nurse me quietly and I would heal without involving my father. Unfortunately for me and my mother, my wound festered. My mother gave me antibiotics, and the great medicine man also sent the best of his collection, but the infection dug deeper and wider. My mother has told me several times how she almost lost me to the infection, a tiny baby with massive, massive wounds. How, during countless moments, she sat and held me in her hands and cried over my tiny and formless body. How she saw me slip through her fingers and regretted the act of circumcision. What am I supposed to do? Sympathize with her?

After several weeks of trauma, she took me to the hospital, where we spent several more weeks. The most incredible thing is that my mother's relatives said that I got the infection because I was visited by an evil spirit. They blamed me, the baby. They said that I had a bad omen that attracted the evil spirit. It was disgusting as I listened to my mother explaining to me about the evil spirit. She too believed it. She still believes it.

As if my pain was not enough, my father also denied me. He said that I was not his daughter since my mother and her people were doing whatever they wanted without his involvement. Interestingly, my father has never accepted me to date.

My mother suffered so much with me. When I finally recovered, she swore that if she got more daughters, she would never have any of them circumcised. "You were the sacrificial lamb," my mother always tells me.

◎◎

When I got married at the age of twenty-one, I did not have the slightest idea what lay on my bridal bed. I had kept myself pure and had never had any sexual intercourse. When my boyfriend proposed to me, I was very excited. I wanted to be his wife because I liked him a lot and we had been friends for some time. Shortly after that, he proposed that we inform our parents and seek their blessings so that they could help us to organize our wedding. We, especially him, did not want to have sexual intercourse before we were officially wedded, officially husband and wife. And so, by the time we were wedded, we wanted each other so much. I had looked forward to our wedding night. I had waited for him just as he had waited for me.

It was funny though. On our wedding night, we remembered that we were not supposed to share a bed. So we slept in different rooms. Our religion prohibits sex after the wedding for at least seventy-two hours! That was too long, but we waited patiently. After the seventy-two hours—although I don't remember whether we quite spent all the seventy-two hours apart—we sought each other. I had not at all anticipated any challenge, but as we locked and rocked round and round without success, I sensed danger. It was as if the task was to pull down the moon with our bare hands. By morning, I was tired and he was tired, but we had not gotten anywhere. Our hearts were sore, our eyes were sore, our bodies were sore. We were consumed by a fire of desire and pain. The second night came and went just like the first one.

In the middle of the third night, I offered to divorce and free the man I loved most. But you see, my wedding was very dramatic, which did not offer me many options. When my husband and I agreed to get married, none of our relatives supported us. They thought we were too young for marriage. He was twenty-one years old and I was twenty. But we felt ready. He was already out of school and working, and I was about to complete university. I was in my final year. We were in love, and we knew that we wanted to be husband and wife. When our parents refused, we did not argue with them. We had already made up our minds. His parents did not want to see me near their son, and my parents did not want him anywhere near their daughter.

After one year, my boyfriend and I had gone ahead and secretly organized our wedding. We went to a monastery several kilometers away from home, and we stayed with the monks for two days praying and getting to know each other more. We also used that time for planning our wedding at a church near the monastery. On the third day, we went with our rings and were wedded. We stayed at the monastery still, in two different rooms, to fulfill the seventy-two-hour ritual. When it was all over, we proceeded to his home where my real womanhood journey was yet to start.

The major reason I offered to divorce him was not because we had failed to consummate our marriage but because he insulted me. As he hit against the rock of my womanhood in the middle of the third night, he looked at me with daggers in his eyes and told me that I was a virgin not because I was a good girl but because other men had failed to penetrate me just like he had failed. He was so angry for failing to consummate our marriage. I was so angry and in pain from his continuous rubbing and pressing as he tried to force entry. I was so angry that, after many years of purity on my part, the reward from my dear husband was to taunt me. That is when I offered to divorce. I got up, picked up a jacket, stepped into my shoes, and staggered out of his house into the darkness outside. One part of me told me to slump back on the bed and stay, but I was determined to leave him. It was not easy leaving my marriage behind, but the physical pain I was suffering propelled me out of the house.

I was in a sorry state, walking like a duck, careful not to open myself wide and cause further damage and careful not to rub against myself and cause more pain. Fortunately our homes are less than one kilometer apart.

When I got home, my mother was not amused to see me for two reasons. One, I had eloped against her wish, and so I had no right to leave the marriage I had gone into with eyes wide open. Two, she thought that I had started my marriage with a fighting spirit. She suspected that I was leaving because maybe I had discovered another girl in my husband's life. But that was very unfair. I really needed someone to talk to. Finding my mother at home had been such a relief, because I knew that as a woman she would understand. You can imagine my disappointment when she bashed me instead!

My mother did not even notice that I could hardly walk. But perhaps I shouldn't blame her. I, in my hurry to leave, did not even notice that I had put a different type of shoe on each foot. One was brown and flat while the other was black and low-heeled. I noticed this later as I sat down to talk to my mother. But still, I wouldn't have cared even if I had noticed before. All I wanted was to get away from my husband's house.

As I talked to my mother, I was shocked by her response. "You are not the first woman to be circumcised," she said to me. "Maybe you are a *chincha*," she taunted further.

In my language, a *chincha* refers to a naturally frigid woman who runs away from men. *Chincha*s normally don't get married because they cannot bear the touch of men. But how could my mother call me a *chincha* when she was fully aware of the role of the knife?

When she called me *chincha*, the tears I had held all along the way as I came home tumbled out of my eyes. When my mother saw the pain she had inflicted on my feelings, she started counseling me. She told me that I should be patient and that with time it would be OK. I did not tell my mother that it was not me but my husband who required patience. I was determined not to go back, because I did not see how anything was going to be OK.

The following day, I was in bed when my sister came to call me and said that I had a visitor. I told her to tell whoever it was to come inside the house. When she insisted that the person was in a hurry and could not come in, I guessed it was my husband. You see, in our custom, a husband is not supposed to enter his in-laws' house during such a time. I did not feel ready to see him, and so I refused to come out. He was determined to see me, and so he stayed at the gate and sent for me many more times, each time begging for my understanding. In the end, I went and met him.

When we talked, he apologized for his insults and said that he had said what he had said out of frustration. He begged and promised that he would be very patient with me and that together we would agree on what to do. He told me that if I agreed to go back, everything would be on my terms. I did not believe him, but you will be surprised because I agreed to go back. I felt sympathetic, and I decided I would give it one more try. But I knew what awaited me. Whatever plan we would hatch, whatever strategy, we would have to be husband and wife.

One day after his visit, I went back to his home. You see, being with my mother at home did not make things any easier for me. When I got there, I found my husband drinking *arkie*. There was a lot of *arkie* in our room. *Arkie* is a local brew in Ethiopia. I think his friends brought it to him to console him after I left. From the look of things, my husband had been drinking heavily, perhaps since I left.

When I got back, he offered me *arkie* too. As if possessed, I received it and gulped it down as if I did not taste its bitterness. He was a little surprised when I asked for more. I drank more and more, and he too drank with me. When I got drunk, I allowed him to touch me. He too was drunk. The more we got drunk, the more we loosened up, and eventually I became too drunk to stop him. But when he tore into me, I felt my whole being ripping open! Unfortunately I was too drunk to struggle, and he was drunk enough not to care about my screams that tore into the night silence. I am sure that his mother and his other family members heard me scream, but they did not come to my rescue.

He raped me, and I bled profusely. I think I must have passed out for hours.

For more than ten days, I could not give in to his sexual advances again. I was even careful not to drink anymore *arkie*. When I agreed to drink it the first time, I was doing it for courage, to be a wife to my husband. But now I had to be fully conscious. My husband begged and pleaded, but I could not agree. He even told me that if I did not give in soon enough, I would close again and be even tighter. I cared, yes, but on the other hand, I did not care.

Later, his pleas melted me, and I gave in again. I had hoped that there would be less pain, but that was just wishful thinking—it was still very painful. With time, it became a different pain. It shifted from the pain of tearing flesh to the pain of forcing entry into a very narrow opening, the pain of heavy pressure. Even today, it still hurts. Even today, I still literally fight with my husband before I give in to his sexual demands. I understand that there are some women who ask their husbands for sex, but that is unheard of in my life. On many occasions, I cause differences so that my husband and I are not on speaking terms. When we are in such a situation, he stays away from me, and that is my joy. However, he has discovered my trick, and so he sometimes refuses to stay away from me.

These days, I use a special lubricant to soften me up. But every time we do it, there is always blood, with or without lubricant, with or without force. But God has his own miracles. In all this mess, two children still found their way to us. In both cases, I delivered normally. I have no idea what happened afterward, because when I healed, I went back to my size, the size that created the fights over my marital obligations. I had somehow hoped that normal delivery would do something for me. But I guess it is also about feelings. The knife takes all the feelings away.

After my second child, I was fed up with the institution of marriage, and I wanted out. I was sure that I wanted a divorce this time.

But no. I am not divorced, my sister. You see, my husband and I love each other very much. It is so difficult for me to have sex with him, but I still love him. It's a dilemma the two of us were thrown into by the circumcision ritual, which turned me into rock. When I told him of my intentions to divorce, he begged and pleaded with me, and I ended up staying again. And I have decided to stay to this day.

But I will tell you the truth, my sister: I cry during every single sexual encounter with my husband. But of course it is only the four walls of our bedroom that know what goes on in there. Outside, we are a very happily married couple: handsome husband, cheerful wife, and two gorgeous children. But every single day, I ask God why he does not perform a miracle to return my senses to me and take away the rock that I am. I know it will never happen—but God can do it, can't he?

GLOSSARY

◎◎

afooyo, afooyo ba: A greeting in the Acholi language. The phrase also means "thank you."

African Centre for Treatment and Rehabilitation of Torture Victims (ACTV): A nongovernmental organization that provides medical treatment to torture victims in Uganda and the neighboring countries in the Great Lakes region. The organization also advocates against torture in an effort to prevent its occurrence.

akeyo: A type of vegetable.

amamera: Fermented sorghum.

arkie: An Ethiopian brew.

ARVs: Antiretroviral drugs. These drugs are used in the treatment of HIV/AIDS.

Ayuik: Circumcision spirits.

Bafumbira: A tribe from the Bufumbira region of Uganda.

"Banange, laba enkuba ezze": "Oh no! Look, it's raining!"

Banyarwanda: Rwandese people.

Bashemera: "They are beautiful." A nickname men give to their wives in praise of their beauty.

bazungu: A white person.

Bikira Maria: Mother of Jesus, the Virgin Mary.

biwempe: Papyrus reeds.

biwempe **churches:** Newly established Pentecostal churches in Uganda that are built with papyrus reeds while church members solicit funds to construct permanent structures.

boda boda: A motorcycle that is a form of special hire transport in Uganda.

boo: Green vegetables eaten mainly in eastern and northern Uganda.

Bufumbira: A region in southwestern Uganda that borders Rwanda.

bushera: A locally made sweet drink from sorghum, found especially in southwestern Uganda.

chepta kai: "The girl of this home."

chincha: A naturally frigid woman who runs away from men.

co-wife: A woman with whom another woman shares a husband.

ekigali: A wide, flat basket.

ekishubaaka: "The thing that has returned home." This is said of a woman who returns to her childhood home after a failed marriage.

embasha: A bone disease that attacks the legs and hips.

emihingiro: Gifts that a woman receives from her parents at her wedding.

engyemeko: A special earthenware pot specifically made for married women to use when they warm water for bathing.

enjugano: Bride-price.

enkoni: A walking stick; also a cane used for corporal punishment or beating animals.

ensiima: Appreciation for the acceptance and sealing of the marriage agreement between two families.

FIDA: The International Federation of Women Lawyers. The Uganda branch is called the Uganda Association of Women Lawyers.

FGM: Female genital mutilation.

HSC: Higher school certificate.

indanga muntu: The Kinyarwanda word for "identity card."

KABNETO: Kabale Networking Organisation and Legal Aid Services.

kamunye: Herbs believed to heal wounds very fast.

Kapchorwa: A district in eastern Uganda where female genital mutilation is prevalent.

Karamojong: People from Karamoja; also a district in northeastern Uganda.

kateerarume: A go-between in marriage ceremonies.

kiset: A locally made basket.

kitenge: An African garment often worn by women, wrapped around the chest or waist or around the head as a scarf; also used to make clothes.

komeka baka: A special alcoholic drink made with millet.

komeka teshonik: A special alcoholic drink made with maize.

kongo ting: A local alcoholic brew.

kraal: A wooden structure where cows are kept.

kukhu: Grandmother.

lacoyi **beer:** A locally brewed beer from northern and eastern parts of Uganda.

lakwal **seeds:** Red seeds from a wild plant.

lesu: A piece of cloth that women tie around their waists to keep clean when working or for strength when they are troubled, such as during mourning.

Local Council (LC): Local Council authority.

Lord's Resistance Army (LRA): The rebel group that was at war with the Uganda People's Defence Force in northern Uganda for nearly two decades.

lutetyo: A whetstone made out of cement for sharpening a knife.

mabati: A corrugated iron roof.

majaani: Nonsensical.

malaya: A prostitute.

mandazi: Half cake or fried bread.

matooke: Plantains.

mbasuben: An age-mate whom one is circumcised with. They form a bond for life and support each other's children when their turn for circumcision comes.

mbuzi: A goat.

Mildmay International Client Support Association (MICSA): A support center for HIV/AIDS patients, especially children, in Uganda.

Mirinda: A type of soft drink.

Mufumbira: A person from the Bafumbira tribe in southwestern Uganda.

muhara: Daughter.

mulokole: A born-again Christian.

murram **roads:** Roads that do not have tarmac.

Musenene: November, the month in which grasshoppers come.

musiru: A fool.

musota: Literally, a snake; figuratively, a bad person, a demon.

Mutwarekazi: A respectful form of address for a woman.

muvule: A type of a tree that is quite strong.

muzungu: A white person.

mwana wange omulungi: "My beloved child."

Mwiru: A person that is not of the royal clan.

"my mother's daughter": A way to say "sister" to another woman.

Nnabagereka: The title of the King of Buganda's wife.

nyabo: A lady.

obufumurarugo: The direct translation of this word is "a fee for breaking through the fence." It is a fee levied on a man who elopes with a girl. The assumption is that such a man must have broken into the father-in-law's fence to snatch the girl.

obuga: A type of green vegetable.

okuhingira: A Ugandan give-away ceremony.

OLF (Oromo Liberation Front): A defunct liberation movement in Ethiopia.

omuhingiro: A singular piece of dowry that a girl is given at a give-away ceremony.

omutemu: A murderer.

opobo: Cleasing herbs.

Oromo tribe: One of the smallest tribes in Ethiopia.

otok: A locally made stool, especially used by the Langi people of Lango.

owangye: "Mine." Used especially in reference to a husband or wife.

panga: An implement for chopping wood.

posho: A maize meal.

Radio Maria: A radio station in Kampala.

RDC: Resident district commissioner.

REACH (Reproductive, Educative and Community Health): A non-governmental association in eastern Uganda that implements women empowerment projects, especially anti-FGM campaigns.

Sabiny: An ethnic group in eastern Uganda that practices FGM.

slim: A slang term for HIV/AIDS. It is connotative of what the disease does to people—it reduces their body weight.

stepmother: The term used to refer to the co-wife of one's father as distinct from one's birth mother.

suuka: A piece of cloth for wrapping around the waist or around the shoulders as a shawl.

takamuda: A type of tree.

tam-tam: A drum.

TASO: The AIDS Support Organisation.

"Umugore tiyubaka inzu cyangwa akaba nitaka": "A woman does not build a house or own land."

UNDP: United Nations Development Programme.

UPDF: Uganda People's Defence Force.

UPE (Universal Primary Education): A program in which education is free for all school-age children.

uruho: Liver cancer.

urwagwa: An alcoholic drink made from bananas.

CONTRIBUTORS

◎◎

Maryam Sheikh Abdi is a program officer for the Population Council's Reproductive Health program, where she works to end female genital mutilation. Abdi previously worked for the United Nations High Commissioner for Refugees, the World Food Programme, and CARE. She holds a bachelor's degree in education from Moi University in Kenya and a master's degree in development studies from the University of Nairobi.

Margaret Aduto, a published poet, has a degree in social work and social administration. She is a member of FEMRITE, and her stories of women's experiences in armed conflict were published in audio form on the website for IRIN—the humanitarian news and analysis service of the United Nations Office for the Coordination of Humanitarian Affairs—and in *Today You Will Understand* (IRIN/FEMRITE, 2008).

Apophia Agiresaasi holds a bachelor's degree in social sciences and a master's degree in population and reproductive health, both from Makerere University. She is the author of a children's book, *Victor* (Macmillan Publishers, 2008); her stories have appeared on the IRIN website and in *Today You Will Understand* (IRIN/FEMRITE, 2008); and she has written book reviews and articles for Uganda's leading daily newspapers. Currently the general secretary for FEMRITE, she was a Makerere University School of Public Health–CDC HIV/AIDS fellow at the Parliament of Uganda in 2010. She now works as the executive director of the Action Group for Health, Human Rights and HIV/AIDS (AGHA) in Uganda.

Catherine Anite holds a bachelor's degree in law from Makerere University. Her poems have appeared in FEMRITE's *Painted Voices*, volumes 1 (2008) and 2 (2009).

A graduate of Makerere University in history, **Violet Barungi** is the author of two novels, *The Shadow and the Substance* (Lake Publishers: Kisumu, Kenya, 1998) and *Cassandra* (FEMRITE, 1999), as well as short stories, including the collection *Tit for Tat*, and children's books. Her play *Over My Dead Body* won the British Council New Playwriting Award for Africa and the Middle East in 1997. She is currently working on her third novel.

Bananuka Jocelyn Ekochu's first novel, *Shock Waves Across the Ocean*, was nominated for the International IMPAC Dublin Literary Award in 2006. Born in Mbarara district, western Uganda, Ekochu attended Makerere University, where she received a degree in commerce; she also holds a postgraduate diploma in financial management and a master's degree in management studies from the Uganda Management Institute. She is a member of Women of Purpose, a faith-based association aimed at supporting Uganda's less-advantaged women and girls.

A peace activist and published writer, **Betty Kituyi** currently works with Café Scientifique and is a member of the Uganda Peace Research and Education Association and the International Peace Research Association Foundation. She is passionate about women's and girls' issues and coordinates two grassroots women's groups in her village. She also works to mobilize the community on environmental issues through the Bushunya Environment Group. Kituyi holds a diploma in secondary education, a bachelor's degree in education, and a master's degree in science.

Beatrice Lamwaka's short stories have appeared in *Gowanus Books*, *Word-write-FEMRITE Literary Journal*, and anthologies including *Words from a Granary* (FEMRITE, 2008), *Today You Will Understand* (IRIN/FEMRITE, 2008), *Students Aloud: Illuminating Creative Voices*, and *Michael's Eyes: The War Against the Ugandan Child*. In 2009, she was a finalist for the PEN /Studzinski Literary Award and a fellow for the Harry Frank Guggenheim Foundation/Africa Institute of South Africa Young Scholars Program. She is the author of *Anena's Victory* (Fountain Junior HIV/AIDS series, 2007), which is used as a supplementary reader in primary schools in Uganda. In 2011, she was runner-up for the Caine Prize for African Writing. A member of FEMRITE, she is currently working on her first novel.

Sharon Lamwaka is a freelance journalist who writes on gender and human rights issues. She is a founding director of the Rehabilitation Centre for Victims of Domestic and Sexual Violence (RECESVID). She holds a bachelor's degree in journalism and a master's degree in psychology. Lamwaka previously worked with Akina Mama wa Africa, an international women's organization, and the African Centre for the Treatment of Torture Victims (ACTIV).

A graduate of Makerere University in English and French, **Winnie Munyarugerero** is a freelance journalist. Her fiction was included in *Words from a Granary* (FEMRITE, 2001). She is working on her first novel.

Beverley Nambozo, founder of the Beverly Nambozo Poetry Award, was nominated for the 2009 Arts Press Association Awards for revitalizing poetry in Uganda. Her poetry collection, *Unjumping* (Erbacce, 2010), was short-listed for the Erbacce Press Prize. A former radio host, Nambozo has a degree in education and is currently studying for an MFA in creative writing.

A midwife by profession, **Glaydah Namukasa** is the author of *Voice of a Dream*, a young adult novel that won the 2005/2006 Macmillan Writer's Prize for Africa–Senior Prize; *Deadly Ambition*, a novel (Mallory, 2006); and three children's books. Her short stories have been published in anthologies in Uganda, South Africa, England, and Sweden. In 2008 Namukasa was an honorary fellow at the University of Iowa's International Writing Program.

Born in Neuss, Germany, **Waltraud Ndagijimana** lives in Mutolere, Kisoro district, and teaches literature at St. Gertrude's girls' secondary school. She has published two short stories—"The Key," which was broadcast on the BBC World Service in 1996, and "The End of a Journey," which was published in *Words from a Granary* (FEMRITE, 2001). She is currently working on a collection of short stories.

A business administrator by profession, **Margaret Ntakalimaze** has had poems published in the *Uganda Poetry Anthology* (Fountain Publishers, 2000) and the *Monitor* and broadcast on Radio Uganda.

Philomena Rwabukuku's poetry has been published in *Dhana*, Makerere University's literary journal, and her fiction was included in FEMRITE's *A Woman's Voice* (1998) and *Pumpkin Seeds* (2010). She holds a bachelor's degree in literature and psychology and a master's degree in counseling from Makerere University.

Rose Rwakasisi was born in Buhweju, western Uganda. She is the director of St. Luke Secondary Schools, where she also teaches. She has published short stories in different anthologies and has written several children's books. Rwakasisi was awarded a Certificate of Recognition by the National Book Trust of Uganda for her outstanding contribution to children's literature. She holds a bachelor's degree in botany and zoology and a postgraduate diploma in education.

A member of FEMRITE, **Rosey Sembatya** teaches literature and English at Mukono High School. Her poems have been published in volumes 1 and 2 of *Painted Voices*, and her stories of women's experiences in armed conflict were published on the IRIN website and in *Today You Will Understand* (IRIN/FEMRITE, 2008).

Lillian Tindyebwa's first novel, *Recipe for Disaster* (Fountain Publishers, 2005), became an instant success when it was recommended by the Ministry of Education and Sports as a supplementary reader for all secondary schools in Uganda. Her short stories and poems have been published in various anthologies. She holds bachelor's and master's degrees in literature and is a lecturer at Kabale University.

Passionate about women's issues, **Hilda Twongyeirwe** has initiated writing projects that give voice to marginalized women. She is the author of children's books, short stories, poems, and literary articles; in 2008 her book *Fina the Dancer* was awarded a Certificate of Recognition for its outstanding contribution to children's literature. Twongyeirwe serves on the board of directors of the National Book Trust of Uganda and is a member of the Banyakigezi International Community's Uganda chapter. She holds a master's degree in public administration and management and a degree in social sciences from Makerere University, as well as a diploma in education. Currently she is the coordinator of FEMRITE, the Uganda Women Writers Association, and a judge on the panel for the Sustainable Tourism Media Awards in Uganda.

Ayeta Anne Wangusa holds bachelor's and master's degrees in literature from Makerere University. She is the author of *Memoirs of a Mother* and in 1997 was an honorary fellow at the University of Iowa's International Writing Program. Her short stories and poems have been published in anthologies and literary journals. Wangusa is currently working on two novels, *Restless Souls* and *My Mouth Carries Few Words*, and is employed by SNV Tanzania.

INDEX

⊚⊚